AFTER
SOUTHERN
MODERNISM

AFTER SOUTHERN MODERNISM

Fiction of the Contemporary South

Matthew Guinn

University Press of Mississippi
Jackson

www.upress.state.ms.us

Copyright © 2000 by University Press of Mississippi
All rights reserved
Manufactured in the United States of America

08 07 06 05 04 03 02 01 00   4 3 2 1
∞
Library of Congress Cataloging-in-Publication Data

Guinn, Matthew.
After Southern modernism : fiction of the contemporary South / Matthew Guinn.
p.   cm.
Includes bibliographical references and index.
ISBN 1-57806-272-1 (alk. paper)—ISBN 1-57806-273-x (pbk. : alk. paper)
1. American fiction—Southern States—History and criticism.   2. American fiction—20th
century—History and criticism.   3. Postmodernism (Literature)—Southern States.   4.
Southern States—In literature.   I. Title.
PS261 G84   2000
813′.5409975—dc21   00-036640

British Library Cataloging-in-Publication Data available

To Kristen
for keeping the late watches with me

CONTENTS

INTRODUCTION

Should we plan now for rational slumber?
It is a century of no belief
. . . .
If history is fabulous no longer.
We cannot live by that death.
How could we still draw breath
If ever the fable were lost?

—*Donald Davidson, "Woodlands: 1956–60"*

Postmodernity has come late to southern literature. As recently as the 1970s critics could still expect to encounter new regional fiction that adhered to the established modernist patterns and nuances of the Southern Renascence, could still hope to weather the distant yet disquieting developments of poststructuralism anticipating that the postmodern era might pass by and leave the southern critical industry relatively unscathed. No longer: the generation that followed the Renascence and offered the traditional critic the comfort of at least attenuated modernist techniques for scrutiny (William Styron, Walker Percy, Flannery O'Connor) has given way to a new class of writers who approach literary convention with either indifference or hostility. The region still produces much of the country's best fiction, but the forms and intent of this fiction have evolved significantly, to the confusion of southern criticism in general. How else can one explain Cormac McCarthy's 1992 National Book Award and Richard Ford's 1996 Pulitzer—prizes given to southern writers for works set in the Southwest and the urban Northeast, respectively, and which exhibit the influence of Ernest Hemingway and John Updike more than that of William Faulkner?

One option for the critic is to ignore such extraregional influences and trends and to continue treating contemporary fiction as a seamless extension of past works. This approach is a continuation of the methods established for Renascence literature by what has been termed the "Rubin generation": one looks for the stock motifs of history, place, and community (as established by Louis D. Rubin and others) in new works, finding them sporadically in such contemporary writers as Fred Chappell, Wendell Berry, and Lee Smith. Yet this method can hardly establish a viable theory of contemporary southern writing, for it ignores the large number of authors who do not fit the pattern. Several collective projects have sounded an angry response to this mode of reading. In *Southern Literature and Literary Theory* (1990) and *The Future of Southern Letters* (1996) Jefferson Humphries and others oppose poststructuralist theory to the traditional practice that Humphries describes as "a thinner, watered-down version of the nationalist, ideological organicism of the Old South" (xv). Following a similarly poststructuralist course, Michael Kreyling's *Inventing Southern Literature* (1998) proffers a convincing indictment of the old school critical establishment's hegemony grounded in the anti-essentialism Humphries espouses. Kreyling disputes the existence of a fixed and immutable "South" that critics of the Rubin generation see at the root of southern studies and demonstrates how earlier critics have constructed a canon fraught with—and not exempt from— ideology.[1] The shape of southern criticism in the twenty-first century will be dictated by the manner in which this schism is resolved—by how the critical establishment will incorporate postmodernism into an evolving tradition.

Outside academe the literature itself has (of course) continued apace—quite apart from any programmatic adherence to the theories of either faction in the ongoing critical battle. Thus, in essaying to offer a theory of contemporary southern writing, my goal is to negotiate some kind of middle road between these two camps. My intent is to break from the anachronistic technique of seeking threads of continuity between Renascence literature and contemporary fiction—a technique that threatens to return the evolving canon of southern fiction to the days of local color by reducing an expanding southern vision to a checklist of regionalisms. This hermetic focus on literary lineage demonstrates the extent to which the collective definition of "twentieth-century southern fiction" is bound up with modernist tropes; it implicitly argues that a contemporary writer from the region can be either southern or postmodern but not both.

Yet in the following pages I try to construct a literary history, not to engage strictly in an exercise in contemporary theory. While acknowledging that the postmodern period seems to thwart any unified critical vision, I nonetheless attempt to sketch several of the predominant tendencies in the region's fiction since the mid 1960s using the various poststructuralist approaches appropriate to each author while maintaining a continuous dialogue with the region's literary history. My aim is to update the historical approaches of first-generation southern critics while avoiding the marsupial's response with which some of their successors have greeted postmodernity.

My contention is that the best way to read today's most innovative southern fiction is by seeking not continuity but discontinuity—by examining the ways that younger writers reject what Noel Polk has called "the southern literary pieties" of Renascence criticism as they carry southern fiction into the twenty-first century ("Southern" 29). This disruption is most evident in the representative works of nine authors: Dorothy Allison, Larry Brown, Harry Crews, Richard Ford, Kaye Gibbons, Barry Hannah, Randall Kenan, Bobbie Ann Mason, and Cormac McCarthy. These authors differ greatly from their predecessors in southern fiction and among themselves, yet they share a decisive break from the themes, patterns, and concerns of earlier twentieth-century southern fiction. In their own ways they write against the Southern Renascence mode, declining to carry on the tradition maintained, however tenuously, by such post-Renascence authors as Percy and Styron. This break from tradition likely accounts for the relative dearth of criticism on authors such as Allison, Brown, Ford, and Kenan and the hostile responses that others (such as McCarthy) have received from the old guard of the southern critical establishment. What is also common to this group of authors is an inimical approach to the cultural mythology established by southern authors of the 1920s through the 1950s. For disparate reasons, these contemporary writers treat the sacrosanct elements of the cultural mythology engendered by southern modernism with disregard or disdain; they do not behave as aspirants to the southern pantheon should. They defy the traditional approaches to history, place, and community. One finds Hannah engaged in parodic postmodern treatments of venerated Civil War heroes on the one hand, and Ford treating the southern heritage with complete indifference on the other. In a similar manner, McCarthy's career illustrates a drift from the traditional modernist prose style to a postmodern poetics that explodes conventional southern cultural fixtures and finally moves westward from a region his artistry seems to have exhausted. Gibbons and Mason interpolate feminist concerns into traditional prose, while Kenan uses the South as a vehicle for constructing his own version of what Toni Morrison has called an "American Africanism." Finally, Allison, Brown, and Crews write from a perspective seldom incorporated into the literary tradition as they deconstruct the southern pastoral and dismantle Agrarian fantasies of the southern yeoman.

What seems to be evolving is a new disposition in southern letters, an attitude toward the South's past and cultural mythology as the tarnished icons of a bygone era. Either through the new perspective of poor-white and blue-collar writers or through postmodern suspicion of cultural memory, the mythology erected by Renascence literature is being questioned and challenged with a new rigor. These writers demonstrate the constructedness of the "South" in modernist belles lettres—they show that the South as it has been conceived by earlier generations of writers and critics is in many respects the product of nostalgia and elitism, of an ideology that excludes the dissident. This iconoclastic movement is perhaps the most important development in southern letters since the African American rebellion that began with Richard Wright. In a manner similar to Wright's, these writers seek to puncture the ideology that construes the region as a cultural Eden, a sort of literary Solid South, without admitting the voices of those excluded from literary participation by the accidents of race or social class.

The new skepticism in contemporary literature coheres around two approaches in the writing considered here: a resurgence in literary naturalism and an iconoclastic spirit that manifests itself in what I call the literature of "mythoclasm." The former constitutes another renaissance of a sort. It is a revival of American naturalism through which newly educated poor southerners use naturalistic techniques to express their experience of the South—appropriately enough, by using the traditional naturalist focus on the lower classes to expose the fallacies and injustices of a culture that W. J. Cash and others have described as obsessed with the notion of aristocracy. Mythoclasm provides a similarly innovative view of southern culture but is more aggressive in its approach; its authors use postmodern techniques to undermine, attack, and parody the traditional themes, motifs, and cultural fixtures of southern writing. Both modes are taking southern literature in new directions, presenting new views and interpretations of the culture that engendered them and, however alarming they may seem to the traditionalist, ensuring that the literary culture of the South remains an active one.

Not since the days of Wright and Erskine Caldwell has naturalism been so prominent in southern fiction: the novels of Allison, Brown, and Crews depict a culture nearly as replete with deterministic poverty and social indifference as it was in the 1930s. Writing from the almost unprecedented perspective of southern poor whites speaking for themselves, these authors expose the dark underside of an ostensibly genteel culture. These new naturalists all hail from backgrounds of poverty and occupy a contemporary space analogous to Allen Tate's shopworn but still serviceable metaphor of the crossing of the ways. Situated between the poverty of their origins and the middle-class Zeitgeist of the Sun Belt South, their upwardly mobile progression exemplifies Tate's notion of the interstice between two cultures. Their naturalistic vision stems from the uncertainty of this condition. Like the first American naturalists, they reflect the ominous social tensions of an evolving culture.

These neonaturalist writers belie the conventional notion of modernism displacing literary naturalism. What becomes clear in reading them is that people of their class had no participation in the movement called southern modernism. Lewis Lawson stresses that one of the basic components of modern southern fiction was a belief in the individual's status as a "free moral agent" whose "actions were not determined by force, either exterior or interior, of which he was unaware and over which he had no control" (15). Allison, Brown, and Crews demonstrate that such free will is a product of class status beyond their own, that to espouse an autonomous existence is to ignore the quality of southern life at its lower socioeconomic levels. Consequently, they bring the sensibility of an earlier literary movement to bear on the contemporary South. They abjure the traditional southern patterns of romantic fiction, as well as the mythopoeia of the southern modernists, and instead opt for a realistic prose style that reflects the pessimism of their backgrounds as accurately as the romance fit chivalric notions of the region. In the process they dismantle the aristocratic-agrarian ideal that critics such as Mary Ann Wimsatt find throughout Renascence fiction. Their late arrival to the southern literary consciousness represents a latter-day renaissance, another outpouring of art from another nexus between cultures.

The poor-white writers of the postmodern South demonstrate powerfully the extensive influence of Zora Neale Hurston and Richard Wright on southern fiction: beyond the context of race, Hurston and Wright cleared a space for marginalized voices in a regional literature almost entirely defined by writers occupying the culture's ideological center. One discerns the influence of Hurston in Allison and Gibbons, in the recurrence of tightly bound communities of outsiders who celebrate the group's liminal qualities while refusing the marginal role dictated by the dominant ideology. Wright's particular brand of naturalism likewise allows Crews and Brown to fashion a perspective shaped by protest and outsider status into a literature that validates the cultural materials and voices of a group long despised by the organic "community" constructed by those of higher social standing. The revisionist impulse inaugurated by Hurston and Wright now seems self-perpetuating, a mode of expression by which fiction after the Renascence finds its catalyst not in the senescence of the old order but in the struggle of the disenfranchised for cultural agency and autonomy.[2]

Harry Crews's unlikely literary career may be viewed in hindsight as the beginning of a new era in southern literature. Crews was born into a stratum of society that did not speak for itself in the region's literature but was instead depicted by outside observers, from the Southwestern Humorists in the nineteenth century to Faulkner and Caldwell in the twentieth. When Crews completed college and began his career as a writer, southern literature gained a new perspective: that of the poor rural southerner speaking for himself, describing southern agricultural life from the neglected bottom end of the arcadian myth, using naturalism—not pastoral—as the dominant mode.[3] Crews's memoir of a southern agricultural boyhood, *A Childhood: The Biography of a Place*, powerfully refutes *I'll Take My Stand*. Crews provides a Georgia sharecropper's version of the agrarian life, and the meanness and squalor of his childhood stand in sharp contrast to the pastoral evocations of the Agrarians' manifesto. The personae of Crews's fiction come from backgrounds similar to their author's. Through a character type I term the grit émigré, Crews charts first the deprivation of the agricultural life for its poorest practitioners and then their migrations to the city in an attempt to escape it. This character type is at the core of Crews's post-Renascence vision in *The Hawk Is Dying*, *The Knockout Artist*, and *Body*. Together with *A Childhood*, these novels demonstrate the importance of Crews to the region's literature; if Crews's works do not entirely deconstruct the aristocratic-agrarian motif, they certainly augment it with a necessary appraisal of its costs.

The same may be said of Dorothy Allison's devastating *Bastard Out of Carolina*. Like Crews, Allison speaks authoritatively of the "white trash" experience in southern culture. She also gives voice to portions of the southern community muted in *I'll Take My Stand*. It is not too great an exaggeration to say that Allison's work reacts against the Agrarians' in much the same way that Charles

Chesnutt's stories refute those of Thomas Nelson Page. In her widely acclaimed first novel, Allison created a bildungsroman of the lower classes that depicts the South not as Arcady, but as a repressive environment of rigid class distinctions and deterministic poverty. As a novel of development, *Bastard Out of Carolina* is ironic, for Allison's protagonist endures an initiation into the prescribed social roles of "white trash" adulthood that makes no room for individual development but instead demands compliance or impotent defiance. The novel is a deconstructive depiction of southern culture from a poor-white perspective; it also constitutes another voice from the margins that deserves full consideration in order to achieve any comprehensive understanding of the region.

Larry Brown, the last naturalistic writer considered here, most fully exhibits an authoritative inheritance of the American naturalist tradition. Fusing the conventions of literary naturalism with those of southern fiction, in *Dirty Work* and *Joe* Brown uses naturalism as his dominant mode for depicting the common people of the South, exploring the lower strata of southern society seldom incorporated into earlier conceptions of the region. What emerges from an engagement with Brown's South is the conviction that too many of his predecessors excluded too much from their social novels—that the problem facing the contemporary southerner is not the rejuvenation of history, but what to make of a diminished thing.

A similar sense of marginalization pervades the works of Kaye Gibbons and Bobbie Ann Mason, who, like many of the female southern writers preceding them, make accommodations to the predominantly male paradigms of narrative form while maintaining a view of the South as a restrictive environment. Such a subversive message has been obscured in readings of Mason's work that evince an overwhelming tendency to link the author to Renascence conventions despite the female perspective of her fiction: by interpreting Mason as the quintessentially postmodern practitioner of "the past in the present," critics have effectively silenced her critique of the southern past and its effect on the region's women. The local-color elements of Gibbons's fiction have facilitated the same kind of ameliorative criticism. Read as a traditionalist, Gibbons appears to be linked solidly to earlier writers like Eudora Welty on the issue of community. However, the networks of female community throughout Gibbons's novels— what may be termed her "matriarchal ideal"—are not products of the organic, regenerative community that southern critics so often seek. Rather, they exist in a subversive and antagonistic relation to what Gibbons sees as a constrictive patriarchy. Such a view has radical ramifications on the artist's conception of southern culture and history: in *Charms for the Easy Life*, a beneficial culture is achieved only in opposition to the dominant one, and *On the Occasion of My Last Afternoon* suggests that the South's tragic history of Civil War defeat may be attributed more to male ineptitude and belligerence than to vanquished high ideals. In the work of both authors, the foundations of southern culture are queried through prose forms that conceal the subversive content beneath the surface.

This tension between dominant and muted cultures abounds in Randall Kenan's work. Where contemporary white authors demonstrate how the house of southern cultural mythology, constructed by white southerners, is being dismantled from the inside, Kenan offers a perspective succinctly stated in his 1993 interview with Dorothy Allison as "a spy in an enemy camp." Kenan's fiction combines the approaches of Hurston and Wright into a prose that is at once southern and critical, creating in works like *A Visitation of Spirits* a vision of the South that makes room for its black inhabitants by forging a balance between the insular communities of Hurston and the disillusioned emigration of Wright. Kenan's use of literary inheritance follows Henry Louis Gates Jr.'s theory of Signification and consequently offers insight from an African American perspective on the general pattern of revision that characterizes contemporary southern fiction. In adapting established literary and cultural materials for a postmodern African American fiction, Kenan's Signifyin(g) fiction remains regional even as it challenges and expands the ideological foundations of southern culture.

Cormac McCarthy and Barry Hannah are among the most important postmodern writers in southern fiction and also the most inimical to southern mythology. As mythoclastic authors, they evince a tendency to confront social narcissism with either hostility or the playfulness of postmodern irreverence. Both writers are pivotal in southern literary history because they quite consciously bring a postmodern sensibility to landmarks of southern history that were largely sacrosanct to their predecessors. They follow a pattern of artistic development described by Brian McHale in his *Postmodernist Fiction*. Like other postmodernists such as Vladimir Nabokov and Robert Coover, McCarthy and Hannah began their literary careers with novels in the modernist tradition: *The Orchard Keeper* and *Geronimo Rex*, respectively. But following the pattern McHale sees in other postmodernists, these writers have moved into an increasingly postmodern style with each successive novel. Concomitant with this stylistic development was an increasingly rigorous questioning of southern culture. (Indeed, it is difficult to imagine a Hannah novel lacking this antagonistic stance.) As Walter Sullivan's scathing attack on McCarthy in *A Requiem for the Renascence* demonstrates, this movement threatens the very foundations of the modernist reclamation project. Yet the result is two tour de force novels—*Suttree* and *Ray*— that belatedly bring southern fiction into the postmodern era.

Richard Ford's career has followed a similar pattern. His first novel, *A Piece of My Heart*, is firmly rooted in the Faulknerian and modernist traditions; it is also his weakest effort. As Ford has moved away from southern settings and concerns and into representations of the postmodern world, the quality of his work has improved. In his most recent fiction he has abandoned the South altogether and replaced the ornate prose style of southern tradition with a pared-down language that has produced two of the most significant works of American realism in the twentieth century, *The Sportswriter* and its sequel, *Independence Day*. In these novels, Ford chronicles the life of an expatriate southerner who not only has abdicated his regional connections but seems indifferent to them. As Ford has left the South behind, the traditional concerns of stability, loyalty to place, and tradition have been left behind as well. Because of these issues, I characterize Ford as a postmodern realist, for while his work adheres strictly to the code of verisimilitude, it does attempt to capture a world in which reality seems increasingly problematic. In style Ford may seem to be a traditional realist, but his world is postmodern in its themes and concerns: it is pervaded by rootlessness, fragmentation of the individual psyche, and the delegitimization of metanarratives. Ford's sportswriter novels demonstrate the immense distance southern literature has covered in the last fifty years; the gulf between Ford's sportswriter and traditional southern expatriates such as Quentin Compson is immense. Ford may be seen as indicative of an end to the regional project of the Renascence: he constitutes the southern writer's willing acquiescence to a national literature. But in depicting the death of the autochthonous ideal and the abdication of history, the sportswriter novels hold forth the promise of a viable if iconoclastic southern fiction for the postmodern era.

Perhaps the central pursuit of the Southern Renascence was the quest for cultural identity. As a widespread reaction to modernism, the Renascence was remarkably coherent in this regard. This quest helped to define southern modernism, from angry reactions to H. L. Mencken's tirade against the "Sahara of the Bozart" to the late high-modernist novels of Faulkner. As the twentieth century unfolded, the quaintness of the local-color movement, exploded by the skepticism of the modern period, gave way to an increasingly desperate search for a redemptive myth of southern history and identity, a usable past. The framework of a specifically "southern" literary consciousness began to emerge as literary southerners between the 1920s and 1950s reached into their past for material. Following the example of T. S. Eliot and others, these reluctant modernists turned to the past for guidance and found that the most salient elements of that past were the Civil War and the agrarian tradition. In some instances this past was not portrayed as entirely glorious. Works of high modernist poetics (like Faulkner's novels) used the Civil War as a historical backdrop or counterpoint for the concerns of the early twentieth century, and historical events were accordingly imbued with twentieth-century uncertainty. Southerners such as the Nashville Agrarians used the past in a more didactic fashion, turning to southern history as something close to a panacea for contemporary problems, an antidote to modern disorder. Regardless of which use the writers of the period made of history and culture, the recovery of cultural identity figured prominently in their fiction. A cultural mythology began to emerge.

Ironically, even as modernists such as the Fugitives fled the oversimplified plantation mythology of "high-caste Brahmins of the old South" they began to construct a mythology of their own. Southern fiction of the twentieth century began to show a pattern. More and more its subject was the past. While brilliant stylistic advances were incorporated into the literature, some residue of premodern local color remained: writers tended to pay a great deal of attention to dialect and local customs even as their themes sought to attain the universal. A sense of humanity's incompleteness, typical of modernism, was in the South tempered by the Calvinistic tradition, such that southern fiction of the era strained more toward an essentialist conception of an organically whole past. Analysis of these elements came to be one of the staples of southern literary criticism, to such an extent that the "southernness" of a novel was to some extent determined by their presence or absence.

But the cultural reclamation project was also pervaded by a sense of fatalism, by seldom-acknowledged doubts of its plausibility. Despite the formidable achievement of southerners in the first half of the century, the era was plagued by anxiety. The conservative artists of the early twentieth century were compelled to seek a precarious balance between their native culture and the intellectual currents of the era. As Mark Royden Winchell has observed, the region's modernists existed on a fragile blend of cynicism and tentative faith. As Winchell notes, "southern modernists such as the Fugitives and Agrarians tended to be skeptical of the philosophy of progress, to be antiliberal and antihumanistic, and to stay one step short of despair by maintaining an essentially spiritual (although usually nonsectarian) view of man and his place in the cosmos" (4). These writers were caught between the established Calvinistic temper of their region (which viewed human beings as fallen creatures redeemable through Christian faith) and the new cynicism of the modern era. The southern view of humanity was fundamentally pessimistic, achieving an ameliorative conception of human beings only through myth. For many southern modernists, the means of staving off despair in a changing intellectual climate became the dual myth of Christianity and the South's heroic, tragic past—what Lewis P. Simpson has called "an effort to achieve a vision . . . of the South in terms of the classical-Christian historical order" (*Dispossessed* 75). Thus projects such as the Agrarians' manifesto clung to the mythology of the past even while being aware of the waning of tradition. Whatever efforts they made to the contrary, southern thinkers such as the Agrarians were, in Daniel Joseph Singal's words, "intellectuals of transition" (112).

Because of the uncertainty of the era, the Southern Renascence always contained a thread of "melancholy" in even its most powerful artistic moments (Winchell 1). As the artistic effluence of a waning culture, it flourished within a cultural shift well exemplified by the "millennial glow" Cleanth Brooks discerns in Faulkner's *The Unvanquished* (*Yoknapatawpha Country* 93). Like the Old South society of Faulkner's novel, the southern modernist movement was acutely aware of the transience of its efforts to preserve the old order. Lewis Simpson terms this awareness "an ironic consciousness of the futility of the effort" to resist the encroachment of modernity (*Dispossessed* 65). With the progression of modernity, the old myths that had been fodder for the Renascence were adulterated, their power diluted for the southern literary imagination. Novels centering on southern history (one thinks of Faulkner's Sartoris novels and *Absalom, Absalom!*, Andrew Lytle's *The Velvet Horn*, and Allen Tate's *The Fathers*) became increasingly rare and were replaced by those of a younger generation, such as Percy's, which did not offer a transcendent southern mythology. Dissident strains in even canonical figures such as Faulkner and Welty began to attract the interest of younger scholars. Although conventional criticism has preferred to ignore the iconoclasm in their work in favor of explicating the traditional-culture-giving-way-to-modernity theme, new readings of Faulkner and Welty began to explore a subversiveness present beneath the surface, an underlying animus to the dominant culture.[4] Prominent writers older than those considered here have also participated in this developing skepticism: Doris Betts, William Hoffman, and particularly Will D. Campbell and Ellen Douglas have increasingly interrogated the prevailing assumptions of the South's bourgeoisie and upper class. Hoffman's *Tidewater Blood* (1998) deconstructs the supposed superiority of the tidewater aristocracy and reveals the price extracted by southern feudalism on its underclass, following a narrative structure indebted to Toni Morrison's *Song of Solomon*. For decades Campbell has offered a yeoman's perspective on southern culture and race relations; his nonfiction work *And Also with You* (1997) eloquently juxtaposes Mississippi's involvement in the "chattel dispute" of the Civil War with its role in the Civil Rights movement a century later. Douglas has made a career of exploring the minefield of social relations between blacks and whites in the South, especially in *Can't Quit You, Baby* (1988) and her book of creative nonfiction, *Truth: Four Stories I Am Finally Old Enough to Tell* (1998). *Truth* is an almost explicitly mythoclastic exploration of racial history in the Deep South—from a writer born into Mississippi's aristocracy.

In the most recent southern fiction, this evolution has resulted in a full flourishing of naturalism and mythoclasm, as contemporary writers question the validity of all metanarrative systems and "record the breakdown" of their predecessors' "endeavor in reconstruction" (Simpson, *Dispossessed* 71). As the myths that sustained the southern modernists have waned, a new generation of southern writers has turned to the breakdown of these myths as material for artistic exploration. Just as American naturalism introduced "a new strain of critical realism" to the Victorian climate of the late nineteenth century (Singal 4), southern naturalism is now probing and interrogating the cultural adhesives of the contemporary South. The fears of Renascence authors have come to be realized in the present era: the tantalizing promise of an organic wholeness for humanity has been eroded, the validity of history denied. Whether or not these changes are cause for melancholy is debatable, but they certainly signal an end to the methods of the Renascence.

L ouis D. Rubin once remarked, "I find that almost anything you ever talk about in Southern literature has somewhere been discussed by Allen Tate" (Core 81). Indeed, Tate's poem "Ode to the Confederate Dead" and its companion essay, "Narcissus as Narcissus," aptly demonstrate the emergence of naturalism and mythoclasm in southern letters. Although my focus is on fiction—preferring to chart the emergence of southern postmodernism in prose forms—Tate's work offers a rich introduction to the concerns that would shape southern fiction of the latter half of the twentieth century. In "Narcissus as Narcissus," Tate describes his poem as a record of the conflict between naturalism and the mythic imagination; the poem is, by his own description, a meditation on the waning efficacy of myth in the modern era. In "Ode," naturalism and mythoclasm are entwined. As the protagonist struggles with his naturalistic perceptions of the cemetery, the validity of the past and historical mythology come under scrutiny. While the poem is cautionary in tone, it also displays the prescience that Rubin discerns in Tate's understanding of southern literature. A reading of the poem with attention to its naturalistic elements reveals it as an omen of the mythoclastic temperament, in spite of its origins in the high period of the Renascence. With the tone of a lament, it predicts the developments that would follow the cultural reclamation project of the Renascence.

"Ode to the Confederate Dead" is an exemplary work of the southern modernist imagination: it posits a dissociated southerner in a Confederate graveyard, where he seeks escape from his solipsistic existence through a connection with the ostensible unity of the past. Like Tate's famous essays "A Southern Mode of the Imagination" and "The Profession of Letters in the South," "Ode" uncovers an archetypal portion of the southern experience, and it does so with an acute understanding of the twentieth-century southerner's ambivalent relation to the past. Yet in contrast to the Civil War biographies of the Agrarians (including Tate's), "Ode" depicts an anguished and failed attempt to connect with history, intimating that this type of connection is no longer tenable. Tate's image of a modern individual, adrift in the graveyard of his ancestors, perfectly captures the themes of a slipping historical consciousness and an incipient naturalistic sensibility.

The tension of the poem is evident in its opening lines. The first images of the cemetery and the poem are marked by deterioration and disorder, not unity or the well-tended memory of heroic sacrifice. The headstones erected to the memory of the Confederate heroes "yield their names to the element" while the wind "whirrs without recollection"—a compound image of indifferent nature vanquishing human endeavor. The fallen leaves, which recur throughout as emblems of time and mortality, pile up like reminders of "the seasonal eternity of death" until the impassive wind pushes them through the tombstones, "sough-[ing] the rumour of mortality." The heroes' deaths appear to be not a kind of transcendent, heroic salvation but a means of satiating a hungry nature, of feeding the grass "row after rich row" (Tate, *Poems* 20). The indifferent wind that presides over the entire poem—occurring in each of the refrains as well as in several of the verse paragraphs—presents nature's alternative to human remembrance. The speaker begins to doubt the possibility of human transcendence over nature, which harbors no recollection or acquiescence to humanity. Thus this twentieth-century ode deviates from the traditional themes of the genre; instead of a tribute to immortal human action, it becomes a meditation on death. The new ode, through the point of view of the speaker, is tainted by a naturalistic sensibility in which the memory of past heroics is threatened with oblivion.

The speaker's perception of the graveyard statuary illustrates an estrangement from the romantic past. The statues no longer represent an abstract higher world. Instead, they are perceived as "uncomfortable angels" perched rotting on the slabs, "a wing chipped here, an arm there":

> The brute curiosity of an angel's stare
> Turns you, like them, to stone,
> Transforms the heaving air
> Till plunged to a heavier world below
> You shift your sea-space blindly
> Heaving, turning like the blind crab. (20)

The speaker's description of the angels lacks a sentimental or romantic register. The angels no longer represent heavenly, ethereal abstraction; rather than cherubic symbols of innocence, they are dumb matter endowed with "brute curiosity." Their unfeeling stares mortify the speaker, who, as Tate notes in "Narcissus as Narcissus," "cannot bring to bear the force of sustained imagination" on his environment. Lacking this imagination, the speaker sees the angels in literal and reductive terms, and they induce him to compare himself to the crab, or "something lower than he ought to be" (*Essays* 604). Like Eliot's Prufrock, the speaker identifies with the crab because he cannot effect a clear direction—like the crab he moves sporadically, laterally—but Tate's juxtaposition of the angels and the crab contains a naturalistic thread absent in Eliot's poem. The angels should be signifiers of a higher world, but they are not; the speaker's focus on their physical properties spurs him into a comparison from the natural world (the crab). The singing mermaids of Eliot's poem have no place in Tate's work, because all mythology is in question for the speaker. The angels merely partake of the same insurmountable physical world as the crab. Mythology, while enticing, is ultimately intangible. This connection leads the speaker to the first of the poem's refrains, which incrementally build the naturalistic theme: "Dazed by the wind, only the wind / The leaves flying, plunge" (20). The speaker cannot muster the imagination necessary to give the wind any significance; the stress placed on his repetition of the word "only" indicates that he is limited to the concrete. Unable to forge an imaginative connection with the past, he is stranded in the present moment.

The dead Confederates, in contrast, purportedly knew enough of transcendent significance to be "hurried beyond decision" (21). These heroes were not plagued by the indecision that forces the speaker to move without direction, like the blind crab. But even while he praises the "vision" that fostered disdain for "the unimportant shrift of death," the speaker notes that inevitable mortality has vanquished the soldiers, who lie dead, "stopped by the wall." The image of the wall is a provocative one; it carries overtones of military battlements, and possibly martial glory, but its reference is ultimately reduced to the cemetery's boundary. Again, irrevocably, the speaker returns to his refrain: "Seeing, seeing only the leaves / Flying, plunge and expire" (21). He returns to the present moment and its untranscendent emptiness, a moment lacking the unity of meaningful resolution.

The stanza in which the speaker most completely gives himself over to praise of the Confederate past culminates in the ode's bleakest refrain. Evoking historical valor, he turns his eyes to "the immoderate past" and utters a totemic, incantatory list of the Confederacy's greatest battles: "Stonewall, Stonewall, and the sunken fields of hemp, / Shiloh, Antietam, Malvern Hill, Bull Run." This list of victorious immolation leads to the image of the "setting sun," a symbol of the speaker's own fading era. These past glories are irretrievable, and this knowledge brings him to a devastating simile: "Cursing only the leaves crying / Like an old man in a storm" (21). This pathetic image contrasts violently with the military glory of the past; the old man is helpless, lacking the transcendent mastery over nature that the speaker believes the Confederates possessed. Instead, he is vulnerable, completely dominated by a menacing nature. It is one of the poem's most powerful naturalist images: an alternative to Confederate power, an image of humanity utterly subjected to the forces of the natural world.

The speaker realizes that the contemporary individual, however powerless, must make a decision about his or her relation to the past. The crux of this problem surfaces in one of the poem's many tortured questions: "What shall we say of the bones, unclean, / Whose verdurous anonymity will grow?" (22). Set among a series of oxymorons that underscore the indecision and paradoxes of the speaker ("Malignant purity"; "grim felicity"), the question vexes. The last refrain provides an answer that settles for a naturalistic response to the past. The speaker says, "We shall say only the leaves / Flying plunge and expire" (22). The speaker's struggle with the pathetic fallacy, which has strained the entire poem and created its tension, is resolved—the leaves are not the voices of the dead but *only* leaves, nothing more. His aversion to the pathetic fallacy, how-ever realistic an impulse, leaves him with a greater sense of solipsism than be-fore—he is isolated and subjected to nature, unable to summon the imagination necessary to surmount the natural world. Yet the other possible responses to his dilemma—suicide or the worship of the Lost Cause—seem equally futile:

> What shall we say who have knowledge
> Carried to the heart? Shall we take the act
> To the grave? Shall we, more hopeful, set up the grave
> In the house? The ravenous grave? (22)

The speaker seems to think that the ancestor worship of the Lost Cause (setting the grave up in the house) is little more than morbid romanticism. Yet ironically, because he cannot identify with the valor and sacrifice of the Confederate dead, he is left not with valiant and heroic death but merely death alone. The poem's final image is the serpent, what Tate calls the symbol of time, the "Sentinel of the grave that counts us all!"—mortality retains its supremacy (23). By refusing to impose subjectivity on his environment, the speaker is left with only natural absolutes, paramount among them death. The dissociated southerner's medita-tion on the heroic past devolves into nihilism. Without an ameliorative para-digm, he settles for something beyond morbid romanticism—morbidity itself. The speaker's experience in the cemetery conveys Tate's fears that in the histori-cally truncated and perplexing twentieth century, death is not a vehicle for transcendent action but only the inevitable passage into verdurous anonym-ity—the silent final phase of a naturalistic existence.

Tate's poem occupies a significant space in southern literary history, an important interval between the historical consciousness of the Renascence and the artistic temperament that would follow it. The poem focuses on the decline of one of the catalysts of the Renascence—what Simpson calls "the

recovery of memory and history" (*Dispossessed* 99). It depicts a modern southerner who "has lost the faculty of explaining mystery through myth" (Young,
"Fugitives" 328). In sharp contrast to Tate's earlier Agrarian and Civil War efforts, "Ode" expresses the ultimate futility of turning to the past. The poem is
pervaded by a confirmed sense of the melancholy that Winchell discerns in
southern modernism and displays an awareness of the waning power of historical mythology for the southern literary imagination—simultaneously a lament
for the fading Renascence and a prediction of the mythoclastic mode in the
southern fiction to come.

As he explains in "Narcissus as Narcissus," Tate sees naturalism as a central
component of this decline. A naturalistic sensibility, he indicates, necessarily
precedes the death of myth—history must be emptied of its transcendent significance for the old myths to lose their power. This process explains the death
of romantic paradigms in the poem. As Tate notes in his essay, the bodies of
the dead soldiers are not privileged with a romantic conceit but with a "naturalistic figure derived from modern biological speculation. These 'buried Caesars'
will not bloom in the hyacinth but only make saltier the sea" (*Essays* 601). No
longer the paragons of valor, the dead soldiers have become, like the leaves,
nothing more than vegetable matter. Consequently, the traditional tropes of
the ode are abolished and replaced with reductive ones. In contrast to the conventional, salutatory metaphors of the genre, this naturalistic ode abounds with
atavistic images: the blind crab, the hound bitch, the mummy. The pathetic
fallacy becomes obsolete as the speaker acknowledges the finality of the natural
world; with humanity's sovereignty in question, nature cannot be represented
as compliant to his emotions. As Tate points out, "the pathetic fallacy of the
leaves as charging soldiers and the conventional 'buried Caesar' theme have
become rotted leaves and dead bodies wasting in the earth, to return after long
erosion to the sea" (606).

In this is a new and iconoclastic perspective on cultural mythology, the naturalistic sensibility systematically deconstructs the tropes of transcendence and
immortality. Tate notes that while the Confederate dead's "heroism in the grand
style" succeeded in "elevating death from a mere physical dissolution into a
formal ritual," the speaker is bereft of such transcendent power (599). The twentieth-century southerner cannot achieve a vision to supersede the limits of the
physical world; in Tate's words, he "cannot 'see' the heroic virtues; there is [only]
wind, rain, leaves" (604). The speaker is limited to the tangible and the concrete, as the refrain emphasizes: "The refrain has been fused with the main

stream of the man's reflections, dominating them; and he cannot return even to an ironic vision of the heroes. There is nothing but death, the mere naturalism of death at that—spiritual extinction and the decay of the body. Autumn and the leaves are death; the men who exemplified in a grand style an 'active faith' are dead; there are only the leaves" (600). A polarity, then, emerges between the historical saga of the Confederacy and contemporary perception. Any dialectic between the present and the past is thwarted by the modern southerner's naturalistic focus on the tangibility of the present moment. The speaker's status intimates an end to the modernist epistemology that would make a narrative of the procession of history. The contemporary individual is stranded in the present moment—severed from a past that ostensibly possessed a coherent unity derived from formal rituals and heroic virtues that can no longer be perceived.

Such a condition has consequences not just for the individual but for the culture as well—it signals an end to the use of myth as a vehicle to achieving meaning. As Tate would have it, this condition is the product of an age that has eroded the foundations by which a mythic order can be constructed. The "fragmentary cosmos" of the twentieth century prohibits the "active faith" that sustained the modern southerner's ancestors (599). Because of the new naturalistic sensibility, the potential of myth can no longer be entertained: "In contemplating the heroic theme, the man at the gate never quite commits himself to the illusion of its availability to him. The most that he can allow himself is the fancy that the blowing leaves are charging soldiers, but he rigorously returns to the refrain: 'Only the wind'—or the 'leaves flying.' I suppose it is a commentary on our age that the man at the gate never quite achieves the illusion that the leaves are heroic men" (599). Tate's poem is indeed more than a "commentary" on an age in which active faith has subsided—it is an astute analysis of such an age. "Ode" is not just a reflection of its time, it is also a harbinger of developments in southern literature, for its depiction of the lone southerner adrift from history forecasts the status of the contemporary southern writer. Today, Tate's decision to create an "ironic" ode that centers not on a "public celebration, but a lone man by a gate" seems prophetic (602). Like Tate's poetic persona, the contemporary writer often cannot commit to the illusions of a mythic past— and must remain, as the speaker does, outside the domain of mythology and literary tradition.

By the late 1960s Tate had begun to see his predictions come to pass. His struggle to conceive a southern myth as an anodyne to disillusionment—what Singal calls a phase of "plunging into southernism in a determined effort to break through his ambivalence once and for all"—had failed (239). Perhaps as a consequence, in "Faulkner's *Sanctuary* and the Southern Myth" (1968), Tate stressed, in prose tinted by nostalgia, the role Renascence writing played in capturing an accurate depiction of the South. By combining the realism of Longstreet and Twain with a large historical scale, Faulkner and his contemporaries redeemed the region's literature from its historical tendency toward a "sentimental literature of Narcissism" (*Memoirs* 146). Yet while Tate is accurate in his assessment of antebellum mythology, he fails to see how his own generation was vulnerable to narcissism as well. The modernists rejected the sentimentality of their forebears but participated in cultural narcissism by embracing what Tate calls the "tragic failure of heroic action" at the heart of the Lost Cause myth (151). Realism made headway in their time, but not enough—evidenced by Tate's claim that the Confederate legend "was every Southerner's myth from 1865 to about 1940, or up to World War II" (151). The writers who were beginning to publish at the time of Tate's later essay challenge the hegemonic assumptions of a myth for "every Southerner" and have subjected the brash modernists to a scrutiny that takes the skepticism of Tate's "Ode" a step farther than he perhaps would have advocated. Tate observes in "Narcissus" that his ode, instead of extolling the transcendence of southern history, culminates in a far different and much bleaker question: "In the midst of this naturalism, what shall the man say? What shall all humanity say in the presence of decay?" (*Essays* 606). With the old myths dead and naturalism on the rise, the problem of cultural decay has become paramount—it has become the issue to be addressed by the present generation of southern writers.

M y debts are many, but I should begin by thanking David Cowart, whose encouragement and direction have shaped every stage of this project. He is a mentor in the fullest sense of the word. I am also grateful to Keen Butterworth, Donald Greiner, Ronald Baughman, and Dan Williams, who offered guidance and support at various important junctures. Noel Polk's help with the manuscript has been instrumental, and I sincerely appreciate the enthusiastic encouragement he has provided toward its completion. I thank Stephen Flinn Young as well for his kind permission to reprint a section of the Harry Crews chapter that appeared in the *Southern Quarterly* 38.1 (fall 1999).

Michael Kreyling offered a very careful reading of the manuscript in an earlier form, with gracious, generous, and thorough suggestions for its improvement. I owe to his critical acuity such emphasis as I have achieved on the larger cultural issues addressed by this body of literature, and he has delivered me from a few perilously close encounters with consensus ideology. Likewise, Seetha Srinivasan and the University Press of Mississippi have been generous with time, advice, and patience.

I owe a tremendous debt to my friends and family in both Georgia and Mississippi. Their unflagging faith has been invaluable. To Wendell and Jane Guinn I am particularly grateful for life-long belief and encouragement. My deepest indebtedness, however, is to Kristen Guinn, my perennial first reader and soundest critic, who has displayed characteristic keenness and forbearance while suffering cheerfully through several years' iteration and development of the thesis presented here. Hagiography would not be inappropriate. I hope that she might see this book as a token of my regard for her, the tangible expression of something more essential and enduring.

AFTER
SOUTHERN
MODERNISM

ARCADY REVISITED

The Poor South of Harry Crews and Dorothy Allison

Beneath [the upper classes] was a vague race lumped together indiscriminately as the poor whites—very often, in fact, as the "white trash." . . . And so, of course, the gulf between them and the master races was impassable, and their ideas and feelings did not enter into the makeup of the prevailing Southern civilization.

—*W. J. Cash,* The Mind of the South

The poor whites of the South: a nice study in heredity and environment. Who can trace their origin, estimate their qualities, do them justice? Not I.

—*William Alexander Percy,* Lanterns on the Levee

The pastoral mode traditionally has been one of the predominant motifs of southern literature. From the early days of colonial writing, the American South has been characterized as a rural region, one in which the pace of the agricultural life largely dictated the mores of civilization and its literature. During the internecine conflict of the nineteenth century, these bucolic depictions of the South intensified as ideology took an increasingly predominant role in

1

American letters: the pastoral became a literary motif by which southerners could rebuke a rising industrial culture and declare their dissent from American society at large. The pastoral and its attendant stereotypes—of a leisurely and ordered culture, aristocratic, organic, and existing almost outside of time—became one of the staple representations of the region.

The Nashville Agrarians ensured the survival of the southern pastoral in the twentieth century. In their angry response to the northern ridicule surrounding the Scopes Trial, they set forth on a regional mission that flourished long after 1930, not only through the prolific literary careers that followed *I'll Take My Stand* but also through the work of the many younger writers who had come under their influence, from Katherine Anne Porter to Peter Taylor. As Lewis Lawson has observed, the Agrarians "were completely successful in articulating a myth that was to support southern fiction for a generation" (12). Whereas William Faulkner often expressed doubt about the supremacy of rural culture, the Agrarians did not; they perceived the southern farm as an oasis of order and stability in an otherwise decadent culture. Their mythic conception of agriculture revolved around the contrast between the ostensibly chaotic existence of life in the metropolis and "a conception of rural or semi-rural life enriched by tradition, religion, stable and predictable social behavior, and feelings of individual worth" (Lawson 12). The Agrarian brand of pastoral became one of the defining characteristics of southern modernism, as its conservative philosophy was adopted and modified by scores of southern writers confronting the encroachment of modernity. Whatever fluctuations occurred in the business of southern agriculture, the agrarian mode remained a vital literary force in the region for decades after the manifesto was published. The declension of the "Proud Lady" provided fodder for scores of southern novels long after John Crowe Ransom first expressed it, and the Agrarian ethos very nearly defined the shape of southern literary modernism as a whole.

But by midcentury one of the nemeses of Agrarianism, the federal Leviathan, began to change the profession of letters in the South. In 1956, after a three-year stint in the Marine Corps, Harry Crews entered the University of Florida on the GI Bill, becoming the first in a family of sharecroppers to harbor aspirations of a college degree—let alone a literary career. A decade later Dorothy Allison, a beneficiary of the social programs of Lyndon Johnson's era, entered college and witnessed a world beyond the poverty of her childhood. Both hailed from strata of southern society almost entirely unrepresented in the Agrarians' conception of the region, and when both began to record their experiences in fiction and memoirs, southern letters entered a new era. Because of their backgrounds among the lower classes of southern society, neither Crews nor Allison could write within the Agrarian philosophy or the aristocratic-agrarian motifs that had characterized southern fiction for nearly a hundred years. The fiction they created from personal experience has in fact worked to deconstruct such conceptions of southern culture, supplanting the traditional myths of a leisurely, aristocratic, and pastoral civilization with unflinching depictions of the brutal poverty at the bottom levels of the culture. Not since the era of Charles Chesnutt and Richard Wright has southern literature witnessed such an iconoclastic treatment of the culture it ostensibly describes.

Perhaps the force of this social iconoclasm derives from its long delay. As Fred Hobson has noted, class "has always mattered in the world of southern letters," although the literary hegemony of the upper classes has often been obscured in recent years by the region's race problems (22). Nonetheless, the white southern writer has long been tied to a tradition of gentility, as Hobson points out: "The idea that the imaginative writer was a product of a 'good family' had broken down in the rest of the United States about the time of Dreiser, but the assumption in the South, through the Renascence, was that the man and particularly the woman of letters, with few exceptions, came either from the gentry or from that educated class of public servants, teachers, and ministers— and the assumption was also the reality in most cases" (21). Thus what is described as southern literature has been for decades a near-monolithic record of southern experience viewed through the lens of the upper classes. While black authors have augmented middle- and upper-class perceptions of the region, until recently poor whites have had little input into the region's representation in literature—and thus the aristocratic-agrarian mode has prevailed.

I do not mean to oversimplify the Agrarians or to cast them as strawmen. In their defense, one can point to the quiet dignity of Willie Proudfit in Robert Penn Warren's *Night Rider* (1939) or to the Ashby Windham sequences of *At Heaven's Gate* (1943) as sympathetic depictions of poor southerners, and at least one excellent younger writer influenced by the Agrarians, Madison Jones, has managed to modify Agrarian perspectives to avoid class condescension. Jones sets *To the Winds* (1996) in a waning agricultural community replete with the mass-culture commercial enticements Andrew Lytle decried in his essay for *I'll Take My Stand*, "The Hind Tit," but centers his novel on a poor family driven to murder by a series of events as deterministic as those in *Native Son*—events propelled not by any outside force but by a corrupt member of the rural community. But these are the exceptions to an Agrarian consensus that has tended, despite occasional moments of egalitarian clarity, to reduce lower-class southerners to a supporting role. Too often the dignity accorded to poor characters retains some measure of the simplistic characterization that is fundamental to the pastoral mode. W. J. Cash's assertion that the Agrarians were "primarily occupied with the aristocratic" element of the South and "refused to observe the faults of the Old South and the operation of its system upon the people who lived under it" has more than borne up under the scrutiny of history (382–83). As Agrarian protégé Richard Weaver put it in the title of his best-known book, ideas have consequences; it is the cost of the Agrarian ideal for poor whites that I intend to address here.

Beyond the strictly literary sphere, Agrarianism has shaped the ideology of southern critical discourse to such an extent that dissenting voices like those of Crews and Allison have been muted in the service of consensus. Ideology and aesthetics are perennially conflated in canon formation, but within southern letters their commingling has resulted in a flawed yet resilient pastoral that persists in ignoring or minimizing critics of southern culture. John Fekete stresses that "the Agrarians elaborated their idyllic versions [of the South] with such confidence that it seems almost crude to raise the ugly blemish of the slave system, the profit fixation, or the ruthless exploitation of natural resources" (69). Southern criticism has tended to fall under the spell of this idyll, tacitly complying with the Agrarians' social philosophy. As Fekete and others have observed of the New Critical elements of Agrarian thought, a conservative ideology of form and culture abdicates social critique, resulting in a kind of political quietism tied to aesthetic theory (82, 90). Thus Agrarianism "cannot offer solutions on the level of social transformation" *within* the South, and its critique never challenges the region's own social structures (67–68). The nemesis (be it Leviathan or industrialism) is always external to the South and its culture. Consequently, social realism, from T. S. Stribling and Erskine Caldwell to Crews, Allison, and Brown, has never occupied a significant place in the southern canon, and the lack of an Agrarian critique of the South itself has been mollified by the southern critical establishment's reading of their manifesto as a humanist metaphor. This cultural stance has serious implications for the writer of impoverished or blue-collar origins. Fekete notes that "for all their outrage at the ignominies of work in a machine economy, at the brutalization and lack of dignity of factory labor, the Agrarians were no friends to the workers" (72).

Consciously or not, their successors in southern criticism have been little more sympathetic.

In pursuing an education and entering the stories of their people into the record, Crews and Allison have expanded the purview of southern letters to correct this historically limited perspective. Like the African American writers who have preceded them, these lower-class southerners demonstrate that the South as it has been construed in previous literature is a constructed entity limited by the ideology of the dominant social classes that created it. And like their African American predecessors, Crews and Allison reveal the fallacies of southern cultural mythology and expose its limitations by writing from outside the dominant ideology that has presented a narrow slice of southern culture as representative. Their fiction and essays have contributed to an increasingly democratic culture of letters in the South. Allison's comment to Carolyn Megan in 1994 is resonant: "When I couldn't find my story, I wrote it" ("Moving" 71).

Crews and Allison are by no means the sole representatives of the rising proletarian chorus in southern literature. Dennis Covington, Tim McLaurin, and Chris Offutt also depict a segment of the South seldom—in literature—seen from the inside, and the nonfiction commentaries of these authors display the friction of emergent social classes too long denied a voice. These writers, in Covington's words, are acutely sensitive to "the scorn and ridicule the nation has heaped on poor Southern whites, the only ethnic group in America not permitted to have a history" (xviii). Pat Conroy's remarks in a recent interview are indicative of this growing perspective: "I think why Mother wanted so badly for me to be a writer . . . was simply because of this: She wanted me to be the voice of her family, especially her voice. And families like Mom's and mine are voiceless for centuries. And suddenly we go to college, and we read the great books of the world. And we look around and we realize our family has stories also" (Powell 52). So, too, is Rick Bragg's declaration that his experience as a poor southerner "is not something I can go look up in a book. Poor people in the South do not make the historical registers unless we knock some rich man off his horse" (xvi). Thus the intrusion of progress, anathema to the Agrarians, has unleashed another sort of attack on the Agrarian ideal—one that criticizes, from inside the region, the iconic rural South of the Nashville group. Rather than being attacked from foreign quarters, the Agrarian ideal is today being assailed by the sons and daughters of southern culture orphaned by its elitist character. In speaking from the perspectives of a group muted by the Agrarian enterprise, the white proletarian movement in southern literature is rapidly exposing the type of fallacy expressed by Stark Young in his contribution to *I'll Take My Stand*, that "education of the university sort, not professional or technical, is suited to a small number only" (Twelve Southerners 339). Poor-white authors of the contemporary era, educated and outspoken for the first time, are modifying the cultural mythology colored by attitudes such as Young's, contributing their own stories from a unique perspective that originates within the region but outside its established cultural mythology.

Crews's *A Childhood: The Biography of a Place* and Allison's *Bastard Out of Carolina* exemplify this movement. As works specifically concerned with the issue of social class, they constitute salient refutations of the aristocratic-agrarian ideal. Together they chart the course of industrialization that the Agrarians feared, from the vanished agricultural world of Crews's memoir to the city setting of Allison's autobiographical novel. They demonstrate, too, the serious deficiencies of the Agrarian formulation of southern society. The South of Crews and Allison is a doppelgänger to the Agrarians' Arcady; it is impoverished, benighted, and repressive—a sort of Third World antithesis to the pastoral plenty of Agrarian conceptions. In venturing to tell their own stories unflinchingly, Crews and Allison have (to paraphrase Conroy) made room in southern literature for other stories, other perspectives, in a literature that had previously taken no notice of them.

HARRY CREWS'S GRIT AGRARIANISM

As a young writer, Crews faced a struggle to discover his own literary voice that was more arduous than most. As he revealed in a 1976 article for his "Grits" column in *Esquire* magazine, Crews found that his literary aspirations clashed with his humble origins. Writing of a period in the 1960s when he was still unpublished, he relates staring in desperation at boxes of rejected manuscripts—five novels and hundreds of short stories—and realizing that he was, in his own words, "a twenty-four karat fake" ("Television's" 128). Ashamed of his background as a tenant farmer's son in "the worst hookworm-and-rickets part of Georgia," Crews had been working at a body of fiction written, he says, "out of a fear and loathing for what I was and who I was. It was all out of an effort to pretend otherwise" (128). Crews termed the insight that followed "the only revelation of my life," the "dead-solid conviction" that "all I had going for me in the world or would ever have was that swamp, all those goddamn mules, all those screwworms that I'd dug out of pigs and all the other beautiful and dreadful and sorry circumstances that had made me the grit I am and will always be. Once I realized that the way I saw the world and man's condition in it would always be exactly and inevitably shaped by everything which had up to that moment only shamed me, once I realized that, I was home free" (128). Crews's revelation was a fortunate one; in the years since his epiphany he has produced thirteen novels and four works of nonfiction that authoritatively explore the demesne of the lower-class southern white, pioneering an artistic viewpoint that until recently could appropriately be termed "absolutely unique among Southern writers" (Shelton, "Poor Whites" 47).

Indeed, Crews's success as an author has hinged upon his relationship to the term "grit"; rather than viewing the word as an epithet, he has accepted it with pride. By drawing on his origins as the catalyst for his writing, he has given voice to a people represented in previous southern literature solely by outside observers as varied as George Washington Harris and Caldwell. As Shelton has noted, Crews writes "from *within* the class, not by observing it from without, the traditional perspective of white Southern writers" (47). And Crews's firsthand experience entails an immediate sympathy for his subjects. Consider his comment in a recent *Georgia Review* interview: "what the rest of the country call 'rednecks' I call 'Grits.' . . . And in my lexicon anyway, they have a great respect for values, for family, and for whatever virtues you wish to name" ("Some of Us" 540). Crews's struggle from the beginning, then, has centered on forging a literary career without the benefit of precedent, a process that necessitated coming to terms with the people he knew best while avoiding the same condescension, pity, or hostility that colored their representation in previous literature.

In this perspective lies Crews's importance to southern literature and the significance of his memoir *A Childhood: The Biography of a Place* (1978), for in recording his experiences in agricultural life from the standpoint of a tenant farmer, Crews has forever altered the southern conception of Arcady. Because of his perspective, Crews's memoir is situated uneasily in the pastoral mode that Lucinda MacKethan describes as a vital component of southern literature. On the one hand, *A Childhood* displays some of the nostalgia that MacKethan discerns in the mode; Crews describes the book as a requiem for "a way of life gone forever out of the world" (4). Crews also, like other pastoral memoirists such as William Alexander Percy and Andrew Lytle, depicts the modern city as a daunting environment. But Crews emphatically departs from the conventions of pastoral in his description of agricultural life itself. For people of his class, the agricultural life was so brutal and bleak as to defy its conventional meta-

phorical use as a rebuke to modernity. It helps to consider MacKethan's description of the metaphorical value of the pastoral motif: "To the extent that many
southern writers have developed their image of the South as a dream of Arcady,
they seem most often to have retained the trappings of that golden land primarily as a device by which they might expose or rebuke, escape or confront, the
complexity of the times in which they have lived" (3). Such an intent certainly
defines the Agrarian enterprise, as well as the motivation for pastoral works
such as Percy's, which comprise an author's reaction to *"the world I know . . .
crashing to bits"* (xx). But the rural environment was hardly a "golden land" for
people such as Crews. His memoir consists not of the "recollections of a planter's son" but of the memories of one of the poor whites Percy described as
"probably the most unprepossessing on the broad face of the ill-populated
earth" (20).

Crews's description of farm life illustrates his lower-class perspective on the
rural experience:

Everybody likes to rhapsodize about how beautiful the rural life is. The rural life, as I
knew it and experienced it in childhood, is, without exception, dreadful. It makes a man
brutal to animals, to himself. It makes him callous and unfeeling. It's not that he hates
the animals. It's not even that he hates himself. This is just the way the world is: I cut
the nuts off hogs. I dig screw worms out of a cow. And the cow is lowing and screaming
and frothing at the mouth, but that's all right you just dig 'em out and put the tar in, and
hope she lives. It's the same way with yourself. You get back to that brutal one-to-one
view of how the world is. There's no way to talk about it. Those rural people don't sit
around and talk about the way the world is. The world is as close to them as their own
skins. ("Arguments" 68)

Here the metaphorical value of the pastoral is eradicated at its very foundations.
In contrast to its conventional use in southern literature, the rural is, for Crews,
antihumanistic. In Crews's experience, an intimate relationship with the earth
engenders brutality as much as enlightenment; it is not progress or industrialism
that strip humanity of its dignity but rural life itself. Rather than an Arcadian or
bucolic journey to self-fulfillment, the pastoral of grit experience is a struggle
for survival. The wasteland is not to be found in the metropolis but on the farm
itself.[1]

Crews brings to the southern pastoral a naturalistic presentation of rural life
that derives from the poverty of his youth. In this sense his memoir of life in a
southern farming community is distinctly at odds with the traditional pastoral
and particularly with the twentieth century's most forceful expression of it, *I'll*

Take My Stand. At the core of this difference in perspective is the issue of social class. As Louis Rubin has observed, the Agrarians came from social and economic backgrounds that "made it possible for them to believe that human beings could *choose* their course of action" (Twelve Southerners xxi). Such a belief in free will is central to humanism, of course, and the Agrarians were fortunate enough in their circumstances to be able to espouse it. Crews was not. From the Agrarians' humanistic faith in choice come such assertions as "[l]abor is one of the largest items in the human career; it is a modest demand to ask that it may partake of happiness" (xl). But as Crews's statement indicates, the labor of those closest to the earth—not the landowners but those who tend daily to the land and the livestock—is brutal and hardly partakes of self-determination. This labor is necessitated, in fact, by a lack of choice and, instead of contented swains, it creates the type of dehumanized proles the Agrarians ascribed only to industrial labor. The relation to the land validates W. T. Couch's criticism of the "Agrarian romance" as lacking "the hard stuff of reality" (429). For Couch, the Agrarian myth was deflated by the question, "Who receives the much prized virtue of farming? The one who owns the soil or the one who actually digs in it, or both?" (426). Crews's answer is emphatically negative for the people of his class. The "virtue" of the agricultural life is a perquisite solely of the landowner, who avoids the meanest farm labor and thus has the privilege of interacting with the soil "by proxy"—a distance more conducive to the conception of a humanistic agrarianism (425).

If the Agrarians misinterpreted the rural experience, they did so because of the very abstraction they loathed. Writing from middle- and upper-class perspectives, they generalized the entire rural experience from the upper portions of its society, neglecting those individuals unable to partake of the "leisure" they associated with rural life. As Rubin has noted, they did not speak for those members of the community who existed "on highly disadvantageous terms" in the culture, and their manifesto "says little or nothing about sharecropping, crop liens, or farm tenantry" (*Wary Fugitives* 191, 235). Thus their depictions of southern agriculture range from the benignly panegyrical (John Crowe Ransom, Allen Tate, Donald Davidson) to the elitist, as in Young's comment that "our traditional Southern characteristics derive from the landed class" (337). Young's statement is trenchant, for it largely explains the Agrarians' limited perspective on southern farm culture. From the aerie of the "landed class" the Agrarians could ignore or downplay the brutal poverty engendered by the system. Unlike their contemporary Couch, who also had roots in the planter class, they had no experience with hard labor or factory work—making their perspective far more limited than they acknowledged (Singal 269–70). Agrarians such as Ransom could claim "there is possible no deep sense of beauty, no heroism of conduct, and no sublimity of religion, which is not informed by the humble sense of man's precarious position in the universe" yet never quite express that humility with such reductive cogency as digging screwworms out of a cow (10). Crews's description of that process certainly includes a large measure of humility and precariousness but no beauty, heroism, or sublimity. The Agrarians could stress that the farmer "would till [the earth] not too hurriedly and not too mechanically to observe in it the contingency and the infinitude of nature; and so his life acquires its philosophical and even cosmic consciousness" (19–20). Crews presents the same process as a backbreaking labor by which a farmer and a mule plow fifteen acres one fourteen-inch row at a time, walking thirty miles or more in a day (118–19). The farmer of Crews's class tills the earth slowly because there is no other choice but to acquiesce to the mule's pace; the farmer works cautiously and deliberately not in pursuit of a higher consciousness but because survival depends on it. The people of Crews's world exist "in their own skins" because they are too exhausted by their labor to move beyond that sphere. In contrast to the Agrarians, their close bond with the earth renders them incapable of the abstractions of rhetoric—and thus the written record of southern agriculture comes under the purlieu of southerners such as Young and Ransom.

Crews has modified these "rhapsodic" versions of agricultural life by approaching the farm from the discomfortingly realistic perspective of firsthand experience. The Bacon County, Georgia, of his childhood recollections is hardly an idyllic setting. He describes the region as a rural wasteland: "The timber in the county was of no consequence, and there was very little rich bottomland. Most of the soil was poor and leached out, and commercial fertilizer was dear as blood" (*Childhood* 13). The people who work such land are not close to nature in a regenerative sense but are "tired," "savaged by long years of scratching in soil already worn out before they were born" (127). In contrast to the Agrarians' depictions, the rural community of *A Childhood* is marked by mobility, for as Crews relates, "subsistence farmers—tenants out on the fringe of things—moved a lot, much more than most people would imagine, moved from one piece of farmed-out land to another, from one failed crop to a place where they thought there was hope of making a good one" (36). The only stable element of Crews's rural South was the ongoing struggle for survival, both economic and physical, which shapes his authoritative understanding of humanity's "precarious position in the universe." The philosophy Crews has derived from the formative rural experience propels him away from the romantic, Agrarian pastoral. Instead, he takes an unsentimental view of the farm as an example of naturalist philosophy in microcosm. The extent to which the rural world is more real and vital than life in the city is, for Crews, directly proportional to the stark drama of survival it displays every day. He therefore departs from the Agrarian practice of viewing the "very vicissitudes" of agricultural life as "contributions" to "bucolic fulfillment" (Sullivan, *Blood Sports* 39). Such an interpretation of nature's vicissitudes as romantic and pastoral is unrealistic as well: for people of Crews's class, the caprices of the natural world translate into matters of life and death, not into fulfillment.

The semantic difference between Crews's and the Agrarians' interpretation of humanity's "precarious position in the universe" is significant. If a sense of the contingency of nature was important to Agrarianism, it was important as a humanistic ordering principle by which humanity could retain a classical sense of its vulnerability; the concept of "human frailty" was a metaphor for the Agrarians. For Crews, it is an indisputable fact and a fearsome one; it reinforces the power that environment exerts over the individual and continually threatens an atavistic return to animal survival. In *A Childhood* he demonstrates that the vicissitudes of agricultural life are fodder for a naturalistic—not pastoral—artistic viewpoint.

The naturalistic strains in Crews's memoir derive from the deterministic poverty of a people caught in the tenant system, prone to the workings of forces beyond their control and lacking the economic means to be self-sufficient. Consider Crews's description of the world of poor-white agriculture: "The world that circumscribed the people I come from had so little margin for error, for bad luck, that when something went wrong, it almost always brought something else down with it. It was a world in which survival depended on raw courage, a courage born out of desperation and sustained by a lack of alternatives" (*Childhood* 40). Here is a different sort of heroism than that which Ransom extols. Whatever courage the poor-white farmer displays may be attributed to a lack of alternatives—courage is of necessity a daily component of the struggle to survive. The notion of choice that Rubin discerns at the heart of Agrarianism is entirely absent here. In its place is a routinely hostile cosmos much like that of Frank Norris or John Steinbeck, in which humanity is buffeted by external forces that continually threaten disaster. Accordingly, Crews's people are unable to determine their fates within this environment. Their courage, then, is not a virtue deriving from bucolic fulfillment but a survival skill, a product of something close to evolutionary adaptation to the rural milieu.

The effect of the rural environment on its inhabitants is antithetical to Agrarian dogma. Aware of their tenuous status, the poor farmers of Crews's class are more dehumanized than self-actualized. They are acutely aware of the forces that shape their lives, as their conversations imply: "They spoke for a while about the weather, mostly rain, and about other things that men who live off the land speak of when they meet, seriously, but with that resigned tone of voice that makes you know they're only speaking to pass the time because they have utterly no control over what they're talking about: weevils in cotton, screwworms in stock, the government allotment of tobacco average, the fierce price of commercial fertilizer" (16–17). The resignation of such talk is hardly what the Agrarians had in mind when stressing consciousness of humanity's slight position in the cosmos. Rather than exhibiting an enlightened humility, the farmers' conversations seem to validate the pessimistic determinism that Stephen Crane expressed in his famous comment that environment "is a tremendous thing in the world and frequently shapes lives regardless" (1).

The predicament of Crews's people is in part attributable to the condition of market farming that Agrarians such as Lytle warned against. As Lytle points out in "The Hind Tit," external factors such as government allotments and retail fertilizer are elements of commercial agriculture that subsistence farming avoids. Crews does include accounts of farmers at market participating in agribusiness, as they listen to cotton buyers tell them "what a year of their sweat and worry is worth" (91). But even the subsistence farmers of Crews's benighted region are driven to dependency by the leanness of nature—in contrast to the self-sufficiency the Agrarians claimed to be possible. As Crews relates, all of the children in Bacon County received government commodities at school, a fact that "may seem strange to those who have a singularly distorted understanding of the rural Southerner's attitude toward charity" and who do not know "what it meant to be forever on the edge of starvation" (133). Crews's language in these sentences reveals the ideology behind stereotypical conceptions of the "rural Southerner." The "singularly distorted" idea of rural southerners and charity derives from the stereotypes produced by the limited perspective of the pastoral mode. Uninformed of the plight of poor southerners, the pastoral mode (and Agrarianism in particular) clings to notions of the rugged, self-reliant farmer. Such a southerner would be loath to accept handouts from the federal government. But this perspective derives from an ignorance of the pangs of starvation, an ignorance of the poor South from which Crews hails.

Crews's memoir derives its importance in southern letters as a record of those rural southerners left out of the pastoral tradition. He writes without rancor of their plight, yet his references to their lack of representation in accounts of agriculture demonstrate that *A Childhood* is an antipastoral work. As Shelton has noted, the memoir depicts a rural culture too impoverished to be conversant with "the generous and beneficent Nature of the writers in the agrarian tradition" (99). Reading Crews's account of farm life, one begins to see the class issues at the foundations of the pastoral; it becomes obvious that the gentility and beneficence of nature in the traditional pastoral have their origins in the perceptions of a social class unaware of the depths of poverty the southern soil can engender. Injunctions such as Lytle's to "[t]hrow out the radio and take down the fiddle from the wall" hearken back to traditions that people of Crews's class have seldom had the means to embrace (244). The entire reactionary rhetoric of Agrarianism, in fact, begins to seem like a hollow metaphor propounded by those with little cognizance of the hardships that accompany an existence close to the soil. The rhetoric of tradition has little resonance for the denizens of the poor South, as Crews indicates in *A Childhood*: "They loved *things* the way only the very poor can. They would have thrown away their kerosene lamps for light bulbs in a second. They would have abandoned their wood stoves for stoves that burned anything you did not have to chop. For a refrigerator they would have broken their safes and burned them in the fireplace, which fireplace they would have sealed forever if they could have stayed warm any other way" (128). Crews's people are not, as the Agrarians might have it, enamored of the accoutrements of progress or the industrial ideal. The problem goes deeper than that, deeper than the superficial issue of preserving tradition in the face of industrial convenience. What has exhausted these poor southerners is the rural life itself, a life which on the lower levels of agricultural society is debilitating in its continuous struggle for even the most essential components of daily living. The grit agrarian experience is one the southern pastoral has never addressed nor included in its configuration of Arcady.

THE GRIT ÉMIGRÉ IN HARRY CREWS'S FICTION

Crews's fiction constitutes the most sustained exploration of the poor-white experience in southern fiction. Indelibly marked by his background as a sharecropper's son, his novels explore the concerns of poor southerners as they attempt to adapt to the modern world. Central to Crews's artistic vision is the interstitial space that poor whites of agricultural background occupy in contemporary society. This condition is most cogently expressed throughout Crews's fiction in a character type I call the grit émigré. Like their author, these characters are dislocated agrarian figures who migrate from various fictional locales in south Georgia to the Sun Belt industrial centers of north Florida. These grit émigrés perhaps best represent the tensions that characterize Crews's work in general. Strangers to the urban setting, the rural emigrants embody the outsider perspective that colors his fiction as they attempt to situate themselves in a changing cultural landscape. Like the "freak" characters for which Crews is notorious, the grit émigrés struggle with the anxiety of separation and dislocation. Disconnected from the familiar rural landscape, they find themselves in alien urban situations and struggle to adapt themselves effectively. This struggle is often abortive, for in the absence of cultural antecedents as guides to behavior, the émigrés lack the order of a familiar community. Consequently, their attempts to adapt to new environments often devolve into violence. As members of the dramatis personae of Crews's grotesque southern landscape, the grit émigrés form a trenchant example of the author's fixation on the convergence of the pre- and postindustrial South.[2]

Crews's fascination with the interstice between the rural and the urban was apparent in his first published novel, *The Gospel Singer* (1968). The novel centers upon the nearly universal desire of its characters to escape the rural poverty of Enigma, Georgia. The Gospel Singer himself has been driven to success by "the prospect of getting out of Enigma"—a dream that has "sweetened his life and cheered his soul" (94). From the pinnacle of his successful career, the Gospel Singer realizes that the people of Enigma "were not his kind, and had not been since he had found the gospel singing voice and probably were not even before that" (51). One character phrases the problem in larger philosophical terms: "There are Enigmas all over this country, all over the world, and men everywhere are struggling to get out of them" (207–8).

The ambivalence the Gospel Singer feels on his return to Enigma would become one of the central dramatic tensions of the grit émigré novels to follow. As Crews has developed and refined his treatment of this ambivalence, his characters have become more sophisticated and his treatment of them more uniquely his own. The emergence of the grit émigré character, building on the model of Crews's first protagonist, seems now to have been concurrent with

Crews's own relinquishment of artistic influence: the grit émigré began to appear at the same time that Crews began to move out from the shadow of Caldwell and others.[3] And as Crews's fiction has improved from early, flawed novels such as *This Thing Don't Lead to Heaven* (1970) to the later works, the grit émigré has been central to its development. The evolution of this character type has been as important to Crews's work as was his early discovery of the importance of his grit heritage. It has been the means by which Crews has harnessed an artistic talent that, like the Gospel Singer's voice, threatened to separate him from his origins. It is Crews's adherence to these origins and his continuous exploration of them that have been the source of his unique perspective in southern letters. Crews's unlikely literary career has been a model for a second, younger generation of lower-class white authors such as Larry Brown and Dorothy Allison; it is difficult to imagine this career enduring without the grit émigré.

George Gattling, the protagonist of Crews's 1973 novel *The Hawk Is Dying*, is the prototype grit émigré character; his trials in the city lay the groundwork of urban anomie that has shaped three decades of the author's fiction. An emigrant from the "hookworm-and-rickets" town of Bainbridge, Georgia, George's life in Gainesville, Florida, is far removed from his dirt-poor origins in south Georgia—he owns a large home and a thriving automobile upholstery business and appears to have made a successful transition to urban life.

Yet George finds his existence in the city to be pervaded by abstraction, and he views his material success as little more than "the incomprehensible paraphernalia of his life" (21). George feels no sense of connection or purpose in Gainesville; removed from the farming culture of his youth, he senses that urban life is a pointless series of unessential motion. Unlike the concrete existence of the farm, life here is complex and alienating. He sees his upholstery business as ludicrously unimportant, and he feels himself "pushed here and there willy-nilly, without purpose" in an environment he cannot understand (106). When his nephew drowns in a freak accident, the anxiety that has been growing in George "slowly like a secret cancer for years" erupts into despair (20). George thinks: *"I'm at the end of my road. I was warned about everything except what I should have been warned about. I was warned about tobacco and I don't smoke. I was warned about whiskey and I don't drink except when I can't stand it. I was warned about women and I never married. But I was never warned about work. Work hard, they say, and you'll be happy. Get a car, get a house, get a business, get money. Get get get get get get. Well, I got. And now it's led me here where everything is a dead-end"* (70–71). As a newcomer to the city, George has adopted the urban ethic of acquisition. But faced with a family tragedy—and consequently the reemergence of his former connections—he relinquishes the urban.

George throws himself into his hobby of capturing and training hawks with a new passion born out of desperation, aware now that "manning" a hawk—training it to fly on command—is his only hope of rekindling a link with his agricultural past. Like farming, the ancient art of hawking, with its equal measures of brutality and precision, counteracts his anxiety by reducing experience to absolutes. Driven to desperation by the apparent mendacity of urban life, he believes the tangible pain and controlled violence of manning a hawk to be "the only thing . . . that could be reckoned as meaningful" because the pain of it "was real. It was not something you could call by another name" (21, 103). George notes that the brutality of the manning process is anti-abstraction itself: "This pain was directed toward an end he could understand, and therefore it was bearable" (88). Further, the manning process exists outside of any economic or commercial sphere. As George observes, "It was not reasonable. It was not sensible. It made no money. . . . It did not get you ahead in the world" (199).

The immediacy of hawking echoes the rhythm of the agricultural labor of George's youth and a return to a personal interaction with nature. When he turns to making leather hoods for the hawk, he finds himself "focused on the hawk in a way that he had never been focused on anything before" (217). An employee suggests that George sew the hawk's hoods on the industrial machines of the upholstery shop, but George will not have his labor abstracted from him and performed on machines. Instead of crafting Naugahyde into seat covers, he works leather with his own hands into a necessary product, returning to the tempo of craftsmanship. If the purpose of his work is no longer for physical survival (as with farming), it is a necessary means of avoiding spiritual extinction in the city. As an austringer, George effects a symbolic return to the cadences and meaning of agricultural labor; he comes to understand his place in a natural relationship as regenerative and transformative. After weeks of training, he finally flies the hawk over his nephew's grave, forging for himself a return to blood and nature, to vitality and freedom.

To an extent George's experience in the city corroborates the Agrarians' theories about industrial life. The manner in which the ethic of acquisition fails him is reminiscent of the "infinite series" of industrial desire that Ransom describes in the prefatory "Statement of Principles" to *I'll Take My Stand* (xlv).

Moreover, George's anomie closely parallels the "satiety and aimlessness" that Ransom discerned as the scant reward of industrial labor—a restlessness that can only be countered by the craft work of sewing hoods by hand (xlii). But George harbors no illusions about his agricultural past and is glad to have escaped it. There is no nostalgia in his memories of his childhood home, with its "fireplace in the winter where your shins cooked and your back froze there in the dim unpainted living room in the unpainted house on the unpaved road under the black limbs of chinaberry trees" (*Hawk* 117). Clearly the past provides no refuge from the bewildering present. It is in Gainesville—not Bainbridge—that George finds "some immutable continuity" for "the first time in his life" (221). George's route to self-fulfillment lies in salvaging materials from his bleak past into a workable existence in the city. Like the Crews of *A Childhood*, he feels an attraction to the agricultural past not because it promises any bucolic escape but because it reduced experience to its absolute elements. His memories of struggle and survival puncture the abstraction of city life and allow him to approach the present with a clear vision. If George resembles an Agrarian in his diagnosis of the urban malaise, he hardly reacts to it in an Agrarian manner. Rather than returning to the land, he makes a stand in the city, in the interstice between two cultures. The hawk is an emblem of his freedom from the constraints of committing himself entirely to either the rural or the urban.

The Knockout Artist (1988) continues Crews's exploration of the city as an alienating environment, yet it also presents a scathing depiction of agricultural life. Like Crews himself, Eugene Biggs left the family farm and did "what the people in South Georgia had been doing since the Great Depression. . . . He got on the Greyhound bus and went to Jacksonville, Florida" (18). The prize-fighting career that Eugene begins in Jacksonville culminates in a crushing defeat in New Orleans, where Eugene, deserted by his trainer, remains. Capitalizing on his own glass jaw, he learns to knock himself out and begins to exploit the last vestige of his former prowess for economic survival. His bizarre act is popular with the New Orleans underworld; he commands high prices performing for the subculture he calls "the stinking, hairy underbelly of New Orleans" (78). In an inversion of the boxer's performance role, Eugene becomes the object of voyeuristic perversity—the once-transcendent athlete as sideshow freak.

Eugene's perception of New Orleans is typical of the grit émigré's response to the metropolis. The city is as alien to him as a foreign country, and in his letters home he relays anecdotes to his father as if writing from an exotic culture. He experiences the city as an outsider, marveling at its international tourists and commercial excess, the seedy subculture of Bourbon Street, and the effects of industry on the Louisiana landscape. He observes smoldering chemical plants on the Mississippi River and muses that "the fish must think they've died and gone to hell" (199). The pollution in "the calm, lovely cobalt water" of Lake Pontchartrain provokes Eugene to think of fish "cancerous with chemicals, their scaly backs spotted with open, spongy ulcers" (237). Like so much of what he has encountered since leaving Georgia, the lake contains a repulsive underside pregnant with possibilities for grotesque meditation.

The corruption Eugene perceives in his surroundings elicits in him a sharp nostalgia for his agrarian childhood, and he frequently seeks out connections to home. He enjoys New Orleans beignets because they evoke poignant memories of his mother's kitchen and the Sunday afternoons of his childhood, and he writes home habitually. He is drawn to the New Orleans farmers' market because the familiar produce and tempo of the place console him, even as he contemplates its close proximity to the seediness of the French Quarter. His slow walks through the market remind him of the crops he harvested in the past, producing lyrical internal monologues in which Eugene longs to be "back on the land . . . back where the people talked straight and where things were what they seemed, where he could see unfolding plants break ground in spring and grow green and lush until harvest" (92). The pastoral language of Eugene's reverie is powerful.

But Crews's hardened realism prohibits a romanticized notion of farm life, and Eugene is snapped back into reality by his father's letters. The marginally literate letters the elder Biggs writes denigrate the Arcadian image and remind Eugene and the reader of the hardscrabble reality of agricultural life:

Dear Eugene
Your brother broke his arm an is off work til it is heeled up if it ever does and its been no rain here for so long I bout forgot what it looks like. the crops is burning up on the feeled an you ma has been sick in bed near bout 2 weeks with the female trouble. 4 of the calfs has got the scours an two of them have shit there selfs to death. eugene we are all of us fine an hope you are the same. . . .

mebbe it will rain soon an you brothers arm will heel up if it ever does and your ma will git over the female trouble but I guess them two calfs that shit theirselfs to death is gone forever.

love daddy (54)

Hardly the correspondence of a gentleman farmer, the letter awakens Eugene from his nostalgia. He concludes that his fantasy of returning to Bacon County and buying a good farm is "just so much bullshit"; he has "become someone else" in the city, a process he sees as "irreversible" (92).

As a transformed grit émigré, Eugene chooses to leave New Orleans and repudiate his knockout act. He settles on the single word "No" as the perfect reaction to the city as he has found it in New Orleans. "No" is a "huge, warm cocoon of a word, wrapping and holding, serving to affirm and deny in the same instant" (262). The simple negative expression undercuts the entire abstraction of city life and the knockout performance, and it connects him to a realism that can accept his concrete, flawed humanity. Finally Eugene has discovered something legitimate that is solid and self-determining: "He only meant No. It was one of the few utterly clear moments in his life when he was able to say exactly what he meant, exactly" (261–62).

"No" is significant to the evolution of the grit émigré theme because it directly addresses the industrial ideology that confronts the rural emigrants in the city. It stands in sharp contrast to the rhetoric that George Gattling had largely internalized, and Eugene's rapturous discovery of the word differs sharply from the anxiety George feels pervasively. "No" is free of external influences—it belongs solely to Eugene—and it represents a decision made by the individual acting outside of urban ideological influences. While George's philosophy of the work ethic is imposed on him by external forces, Eugene's simple word hearkens back to the absolutes of rural existence and pure survival. Stripped of empty rhetoric, it is the necessary step toward autonomous action, toward leaving the city behind. Even though Eugene's departure from the city lacks the specific objectives and promise of George's work with the hawk, his exodus is tentatively hopeful. By putting him in uncharted territory, it suggests possibilities not limited strictly to the rural or the urban, an existence in the irresolute present with a consciousness of the past. The redemptive quality of "No" lies in its search for alternatives; "No" confirms the existence of other options.

The urban carnival of *Body* (1990) posits a rural emigrant at the center of a struggle for identity as Shereel Dupont, a grit émigré from Waycross, Georgia, joins other bodybuilders at the Ms. Cosmos contest in Miami. Here she finds herself at the pinnacle of her athletic career, for in the years since leaving Georgia she has shaped her body in anticipation of taking home a world title at the event. Her goals resemble those of Crews as a frustrated young writer: she hopes to join an international culture, but her ambivalent attitude toward her rural background confuses her. Without the benefit of precedent, she is working toward the unknown. Her family's arrival at the event threatens an intrusion of her grit past into the glamorous world of bodybuilding, however, and she feels herself at the center of a tense convergence between two disparate cultures. Her struggle for a reconciled identity becomes the novel's central conflict.

Shereel's bodybuilding career has been marked by the cultivation of a new postgrit identity, the eradication of her background and the creation of an ideal-ized self worthy of the abstract title "Ms. Cosmos." Her trainer, Russell Morgan, has forced her to lose her Georgia accent and has changed her given name from Dorothy Turnipseed to Shereel Dupont. As Russell says, "Nobody named Dorothy Turnipseed could ever be Ms. Cosmos" (20). Indeed, the strong clash between the names Dupont and Turnipseed emphasizes the difference between Shereel's old and new identities. "Turnipseed" evokes agricultural images of the less bucolic variety, but "Shereel Dupont" connotes a parallel to the archetypal industrial company, the epitome of big business and thus to commodity. "Sher-eel Dupont" is less a name than a title or brand name, and Russell and Shereel craft an appropriate model bodybuilder without a past or any other connections except to bodybuilding. The ahistorical, commercial aspect of Shereel's stage persona approaches the abstract to such a degree that one character asks in disbelief, "How can Ms. Dupont be related to something called a Turnipseed?" (50).

Shereel's organic origins—flawed and humble despite her athletic achieve-ments—resurface with the arrival of the anachronistic Turnipseed clan. The Turnipseeds' appearance at the contest signals an irruption of the past into Sher-eel's carefully ordered competitive world, a threat to her new identity. By re-minding Shereel that her bodybuilding persona is an artificial construct, the Turnipseeds illuminate the disparity between urban and rural cultures, the fan-tastical and the actual. They are confounded by Shereel's new name, and in true grit fashion they view it as a betrayal of blood relations and historical connec-tion. Her fiancé, Nail, is particularly disturbed by the stage name; he remains unconvinced that the new personality is harmless. He maintains the importance of tradition and says, "We talkin' blood. Your mama and daddy ain't named you no Shereel Dupont" (65). Shereel tries to placate him about the change:

"Names don't mean a thing. I'm the same girl."

"Names mean everything and you ain't the same girl," he said. "But I guess that's just something else you'll have to learn the hard way." (125)

Shereel will find that names—and titles—do mean everything. The spaces be-tween Turnipseed and Dupont, and between Shereel Dupont and Ms. Cosmos, are chasms to her, dangerous intervals without sure footing.

The bodybuilding competition brings her identity crisis to its crescendo. Shereel's "whole future, the rest of her life," rests solely upon the outcome of the competition (228). As she competes onstage with her main rival, Shereel considers the magnitude of her devotion to the contest. Her thoughts cohere around the mental image of a ledger: "On one side of the ledger was winning and its consequences. . . . Shereel Dupont, Ms. Cosmos, was somebody, somebody to reckon with. As Ms. Cosmos, she saw her name on gyms, on food supplements, on sportswear. . . . On the other side of the ledger was the alternative to winning. And she did not know, could not imagine, the consequences of not winning. That side of the ledger was not only blank, it was dark" (228–29). Shereel perceives that her commitment to an idealized, manufactured identity as Ms. Cosmos has been monolithic; as the novel's title implies, the singular pursuit of "body" has left no room for the cultivation of the soul. Unlike George Gattling and Eugene Biggs, she has no alternatives. The binary construction of the ledger symbolizes a complete break from the past, an utter lack of options. Her defeat in the Ms. Cosmos contest, her failure to attain the abstract self by which she has defined herself, leads her to suicide. Nail's observation about Shereel and the contest proves to be prophetic: "It's some hereabouts thinks she's a Dupont, whatever the hell that is" (65). With her historical connections severed, Shereel's inability to establish an identity ("whatever the hell a Dupont is") is devastating. Her self-destruction stems from the challenge that Crews surmounted as a young writer: the struggle for postagrarian identity.

Body is the first of the grit émigré novels to end in defeat. It is also the first of these novels in which Crews's tone (barring the comedy of Mr. Biggs's letter) approaches condescension toward his rural personae. Crews makes much of the Turnipseeds' Snopes-like mannerisms, at times rendering them in the same appalled tone that his city-dwelling character Russell Morgan uses. The novel's conclusion seems to confirm the sense of mocking desperation in Crews's prose. Nail's final act of murder-suicide is a gesture of retribution against the city that has ruined Shereel, but it also results in his own destruction. It would seem that by 1990 Crews had given up on the project of integrating the country and the city in his work, that his new technical approaches to the grit émigré in tone and denouement indicated the end of this phase of his career—that Crews's own postagrarian identity entailed the immolation of his persistent character type. While *Scarlover* (1992) signals a more positive resolution of the grit émigré's struggle through the formation of a community of émigrés *within* the city, its ambivalence is telling. The tentative union between displaced compatriots in the novel emphasizes yet again the precarious existence of the grit south-erner, of a people, finally, without a place of their own.

Crews's artistic journey with these uprooted characters has been the most effective channel of his own brand of social commentary, the vehicle by which he has best expressed his keen perceptions of social change in the contemporary South. The grit émigré character has allowed Crews to go beyond the vision of his predecessors in southern letters—to bring Tobacco Road into the city. Through their migrations, the grit émigrés dramatize the dynamic interval be-tween a waning southern culture and a new one. Thus the rural emigrants oc-cupy a space similar to the "crossing of the ways" Tate observed but with economic hindrances that prohibit them (unlike the Nashville Agrarians) from proposing a nostalgic return to the land. They therefore allow for a completely new perspective in southern fiction. The interval they occupy, rife with com-bustibility, carries the potential for horrific violence—a rejection of the new culture—or a refined regional consciousness. For Crews and his grit émigré characters, the necessity of cultural transformation is irrefutable, yet the change is tempered by a sense of loss, the transition a poignant exodus from a world that "would always exist, if nowhere but in memory" (*Childhood* 14).

DOROTHY ALLISON AND THE POOR-WHITE BILDUNGSROMAN

Dorothy Allison's *Bastard Out of Carolina* (1992) explores the poor-white ex-perience at a stage beyond Crews's grit émigrés. Instead of living on farms, Allison's characters inhabit a more urban sphere as their parents have, and their livelihoods are earned in the cafés, factories, and textile mills in and around Greenville, South Carolina. Despite this different environment, the characters of *Bastard Out of Carolina* are, like Crews's characters, misfits—"white trash" who are as repressed by the class system of a small southern city as any of Crews's urban newcomers.

The role of geography is altered in Allison's chronicle of poor whites. Instead of the migrations Crews charts, Allison explores the inner spaces of poor-white experience through the narration of the novel's protagonist, Ruth Anne "Bone" Boatwright. As the bildungsroman of an impoverished young woman coming of age in the South, *Bastard Out of Carolina* carries Crews's innovations to a new level. Drawing on Allison's own childhood experiences (the author has widely acknowledged that the novel is autobiographical), *Bastard* achieves a psycholog-ical complexity that has always eluded Crews in his use of the fictive first person—for example, in such a flawed novel as *The Gypsy's Curse*. By combining the immediacy of Crews's perspective in *A Childhood* with fictional form, Allison has crafted a novel of development related from the decidedly unusual viewpoint of the southern lower class. As she modifies the perspective of the bildungsroman, Allison also alters its conventional themes. The class ramifications of Bone's development are stressed throughout the narrative; she is not so much expected to develop as she is to conform to societal expectations of her class. Bone's education—her passage to maturity—is not an exercise in free will at all but an initiation into a social hierarchy that allows her no autonomy or self-determination. A successor to Crews's grit émigré novels, *Bastard* answers the promise of geographical mobility with a bleak depiction of social stasis, yet it also signals a new hostility to the southern class system—the beginnings of a deconstructive approach to Arcady.

The social status of Allison's characters is foregrounded through Bone's perception. Bone is acutely aware of her family's position in the social hierarchy. She says, "We knew what the neighbors called us. . . . We knew who we were" (82). Her family, as she describes them, fit the stereotypes of "white trash." Bone's description of her grandmother is an appropriate example: "My granny wore sleeveless print dresses that showed the sides of her loose white breasts and hitched up on her hips. She kept her thin gray hair curled tight in a permanent wave, tying it back with string when it went limp in the heat. She wore dark red lipstick that invariably smeared down onto her knobby chin, and she was always spitting snuff and cursing" (55). The men in the family are little better; they "think that a working man just naturally turns up in jail now and then, just like they believe they got a right to stay drunk from sunset on Friday to dawn on Monday morning" (127). Their only appearance in any kind of social register is through crime stories in the local newspaper, where their photographs look "worse than crazy," showing men who appear "moon-eyed, rigid, openmouthed, and stupid" (293). If there is any constancy to the family's appearance, it lies in the bewildered and tragic aspect that the family calls "the Boatwright look"—the prematurely aged, bitter visage with which the family confronts the world (8). If members of the family are not resigned to defeat, they are resigned to the immutability of the class system that labels them "trash."

The result of this environment is a pervasive sense of determinism. Bone feels like an "exile" from society because of her class, and she doubts the possibility of ever escaping her family's sphere of violence and poverty (134). She describes the passage to adulthood as a grim prospect: "Growing up was like falling into a hole. The boys would quit school and sooner or later go to jail for something silly. I might not quit school, not while Mama had any say in the matter, but what difference would that make? What was I going to do in five years? Work in the textile mill? Join Mama at the diner? It all looked bleak to me. No wonder people got crazy as they grew up" (178). Bone has little reason to adopt a more hopeful view of her future. She has witnessed her mother's perpetual fatigue, sadness, and fear throughout her short life and sees a similar fate as ineluctable. All of her efforts to escape poverty and ignominy seem to be inconsequential in the face of an omnipotent and inflexible class system.

Bone's illegitimate status symbolizes these concerns. Her birth certificate is an emblem of the state's power over people of her class, of the rigid social distinctions that seem to work only to the detriment of the poor. To be branded a bastard is to confirm the expectations society has of Bone's people; it reinforces the ideology behind the term "white trash," comfortably separating those in higher positions from the masses below. Bone's mother, Annie, is aware of the significance of the birth certificate: "Mama hated to be called trash, hated the memory of every day she'd ever spent bent over other people's peanuts and strawberry plants while they stood tall and looked at her like she was a rock on the ground. The stamp they put on that birth certificate burned her like the stamp she knew they'd tried to put on her. *No-good, lazy, shiftless*" (3). Annie knows well the intransigence of labels such as "trash" and "bastard." In the society in which she lives these labels are very nearly as palpable as physical obstructions to progress. They are the means by which the poor are kept in place; they support a social order intent on maintaining a separation between classes. As the county clerk tells her, the declaration on the birth certificate "is how it's got to be. The facts have been established" (4). A lawyer tells her that the illegitimacy statute is an archaic ordinance that is "[m]ostly . . . not enforced anymore anyway." Her response is trenchant: "Then why . . . do they insist on enforcing it on me?" (9). A comment made by one of Bone's uncles resonates with understanding of the function of social institutions: "The law never done us no good. Might as well get on without it" (5).

The effect of such labels is to configure the poor whites of Bone's sphere as the Other, as things observed. Bone's people are constantly subjected to scrutiny through the lens of social class. They are objectified in the process of being labeled "trash," and nearly every episode of the novel conveys a sense of its characters being monitored by individuals of higher social standing—thus the relentless focus on the visual in the novel. Beyond being looked at "like a rock on the ground," Annie Boatwright experiences this type of observation in her yearly pilgrimage to the county courthouse. Each time she attempts to expunge the scarlet letters of the birth certificate, Annie must endure the bright-eyed scrutiny of the courthouse secretaries who witness the drama of the county clerk giving her a "look" of "pure righteous justification" as he refuses her request (5). Even her lawyer smiles "at her much like the clerk" (9). Bone experiences the same condescension. She discerns a look of "tired patience" in the eyes of her teacher, as well as "a little shine of pity, and a contempt as old as the red dust hills I could see through the windows of her classroom" (67). When Bone is caught shoplifting from the store of the aptly named Tyler Highgarden, he "swallows an urge to laugh" at her as he delivers a stinging homily on the vices of thievery (96–97). Throughout the scene, Bone's small stature emphasizes the plight of her people in society. Highgarden looms over her in a symbolic fashion, looking down on her as she is initiated into a rite of class distinction that will be played out time and again throughout her life. The look with which he appraises Bone is the visage of oppositional definition that her mother has known for years. It separates people like the Boatwrights from the mainstream of society, consigning them to a low position that consequently elevates the beholder's status. The only reaction to such scrutiny that Bone has been taught is the "Boatwright look."

The shoplifting incident is a turning point in Bone's development. Instead of capitulating to the social hierarchy—and adopting the "Boatwright look"—Bone feels the seed of defiance taking root: "I knew I was supposed to feel ashamed, but I didn't anymore. I felt outraged" (97). She bides her time, then breaks into the store. Armed with the grappling hook she found in the river, she enters the building from its roof—from a plane above even Tyler Highgarden—and uses the bottom-dredging tool to destroy the glass cases full of merchandise beyond her means. Her act is one of defiance, not theft; she steals nothing from the store but instead destroys the emblems of Highgarden's superiority with the tools of the subterranean. The hostility of the act displays Bone's nascent antagonism toward the class system. If it is adolescent in its intensity and objectives, it nonetheless exhibits a sense of righteous anger that will indeed be formidable when channeled into more productive outlets.

Bone's act has transformative consequences for her. She begins to see behind the cultural mythology that casts her as subaltern to a superior middle class that Highgarden and the teacher represent. For the first time she begins not only to question her community's class assumptions but to take a stand against them. This progression from naïveté to hostility is exemplified in two passages of her narrative. The first is a pastoral description of her environment that takes no polemic stance on her social position.

Greenville, South Carolina, in 1955, was the most beautiful place in the world. Black walnut trees dropped their green-black fuzzy bulbs on Aunt Ruth's matted lawn, past where their knotty roots rose up out of the ground like the elbows and knees of dirty children suntanned dark and covered with scars. Weeping willows marched across the yard, following every wandering stream and ditch, their long whiplike fronds making tents that sheltered sweet-smelling beds of clover. . . . But over at Aunt Alma's, over near the Eustis Highway, the landlord had locked down the spigots so that the kids wouldn't cost him a fortune in water bills. Without the relief of a sprinkler or a hose the heat had burned up the grass, and the combined efforts of dogs and boys had reduced the narrow yard to a smoldering expanse of baked dirt and scattered rocks. (17–18)

At the early stages of her self-consciousness, Bone describes Greenville objectively, save only the romantic elements she employs to endow the scene with its pastoral tone: the verdant trees and grass, the sweet-smelling clover. But the reader is aware that this is no typical pastoral scene, even if Bone is not. Although she makes no judgment of his actions, the landlord's parsimony is evident through Bone's scant pastoral in the locking-down of the spigots that has reduced an Arcadian setting to a "smoldering expanse." Bone's Arcady is atypical, for despite its bucolic traits, it is marked by the distinctly unpastoral presence of property and economics that complicate the conventional "rural peace and simplicity" associated with the genre (MacKethan 3). It is not a retreat from the concerns of quotidian existence, because these concerns are ubiquitous for Bone and her family. For the poor white, rural beauty is problematized by the workings of commerce beyond the control of the ostensibly contented swains. Yet at this point Bone is not yet aware enough—or angry enough—to comment on this condition.

After the dime-store vandalism Bone becomes cognizant of the gaps in the Arcadian myth. Her intellectual development, which has previously been conducted with little self-awareness, leads her to the stark realization that there have always been people like the Boatwrights. Reading—her previous means of escape from her sordid environment—begins to confirm her suspicions of an iniquitous social hierarchy. No longer an escape, reading becomes an act of defiance for Bone, a route to intellectual armament. Bone experiences an epiphany as she reads the most salient incarnation of the Arcadian myth, *Gone with the Wind*. She realizes that

> this body, like my aunts' bodies, was born to be worked to death, used up, and thrown away. I had read these things in books and passed right over it. The ones who died like that, worked to death or carried off by senseless accidents, they were almost never the heroines. Aunt Alma had given me a big paperback edition of *Gone with the Wind*, with tinted pictures from the movie, and told me I'd love it. I had at first, but one evening I looked up from Vivien Leigh's pink cheeks to see Mama coming in from work with her hair darkened from sweat and her uniform stained. A sharp flash went through me. Emma Slattery, I thought. That's who I'd be, that's who we were. Not Scarlett with her baking-powder cheeks. I was part of the trash down in the mud-stained cabins, fighting with the darkies and stealing ungratefully from our betters, stupid, coarse, born to shame and death. I shook with indignation. (206)

These sentences illustrate a key passage in Bone's development, for they represent both an epiphanic moment of self-awareness and the beginnings of her awareness of the cultural myths of which she is a part. Here Bone sees the narrative of her own life within the larger cultural narrative that has scripted her into an assigned role; she becomes conscious of the stock characters and themes by which the South has traditionally defined itself in mythic terms. Bone's indignation stems from the limited participation allowed her by this system. Her people are never the heroines of the Arcadian saga because they are relegated to the "mud-stained cabins" at the bottom of the plantation hierarchy, where they enact brutish and coarse lives as they are "used up" for manual labor before being discarded. If they serve any purpose beyond menial labor, the "trash" are useful in illustrating the nobility of their betters by contrast.

The differences Bone sees between the mythos of *Gone with the Wind* and her own life allow her to puncture the ideology of the southern class system. She becomes conscious that her life, like the fiction of the southern Arcady, is marred by two-dimensional conceptions of the poor imposed from above—that she is a flat character in the drama of southern culture. Like Emma Slattery, Bone and the other Boatwrights are denied a significant voice in a society that clings to aristocratic notions of itself. If Bone needs confirmation that such conventional ideas are pervasive in her era, she need look no farther than Tyler Highgarden, who perceives her as "stealing ungratefully from [her] betters," or to the teacher who assumes that she is "stupid" and "coarse." The "mud-stained cabins" of the plantation South persist into the 1950s as well, in the ramshackle rental homes the Boatwrights occupy among scorched lawns created by the landowners' concerns over exorbitant water bills.

Bone reacts to the injustices of Arcady with anger. She claims that anger "was like a steady drip of poison into my soul, teaching me to hate the ones who hated me. Who do they think they are?" (262). Yet instead of settling for the impotent rage of the "Boatwright look," Bone begins to consider incorporating the narrative of her people into the cultural myth. Her intellect becomes a means of channeling her anger. She thinks: "We're smarter than you think we are" and feels "mean and powerful and proud of all of us, all the Boatwrights who had ever gone to jail, fought back when they hadn't a chance, and still held on to their pride" (217). Even at a young age, Bone perceives the power that lies in the righteous anger of the unvanquished poor. Her anger allows her to survive her childhood and tell her story, using her voice as a weapon against the social order that has kept her family muted for generations. She is in fact a bastard to southern culture, a member of the social class that is illegitimate in the eyes of those who would perpetuate the aristocratic and Arcadian myth of the South. But in speaking from outside the myth, Bone determines her own position, dismantling the myth from below. She provides the voice of the poor white as Emma Slattery and others did not; her unprecedented story is the bildungsroman of a poor-white female. Her journey to development becomes an initiation into class-consciousness and anger—for a young woman of Bone's class, the passage into maturity and intellectual awareness could be nothing else.

The most potent of Allison's salvos against Arcadian conceptions of the South lies in the novel's scenes of incest. As a fundamental taboo, incest is a sexual transgression that destabilizes "normative" relations in the culture, posing a visceral challenge to the defined roles and interaction of society. Further, Allison makes use of a female survivor's perspective to cast the South in an uncompromising light more damning than any of Crews's depictions. The father-daughter incest Daddy Glen practices on Bone makes the male dominance of southern patriarchy painfully salient and irrefutable, emphatically asserting another facet of repression in the culture that commodifies and discards individuals such as Bone. Certainly Allison is not alone in presenting the domestic sphere as the site of incestuous predation; Maya Angelou and Alice Walker also have used sexual abuse in their work to expose what Minrose Gwin calls "the ideology of dominance" in the culture (417). Gwin observes that "these southern women's stories trace the workings of patriarchal power within the father's house" and "explore the ideological construction of 'home' (both as the material space of the house and the cultural space of the patriarchal family) as a space of female entrapment" (419). The larger culture, too, is implicated in these narratives of "patriarchal power carried to its most egregious form" (417). Such is evident in Sheriff Cole's appearance in the novel. Despite his words of assurance and consolation, Bone thinks: "He was Daddy Glen in a uniform. The world was full of Daddy Glens, and I didn't want to be in the world anymore" (295–96). The gender that defines this world is patently clear; Bone's experience of physical as well as psychological exploitation has allowed her to puncture its subtle ideology. The home of Daddy Glen and the larger cultural sphere of Sheriff Cole are finally conflated. In such a context the conventional southern dynamic of defining the self through connections to place and local custom becomes grotesque; the materials of self-definition provided by a patriarchal culture are reduced to patent exploitation and brutal male dominance.

Allison connects these issues to social class in an unprecedented manner. Consider a comparison between *Bastard* and a contemporaneous incest narrative by a male writer, Jim Grimsley. Grimsley's *Dream Boy* (1995) is also the bildungs-roman of a poor white in which development and self-consciousness are tied to homosexuality and wherein "home" is a nightmare space haunted by a menacing father. For Grimsley's protagonist, sexual awakening after incest must take place "on the borders of the farm, at the edge of wild country"—marginal settings where "the shadow of Dad vanishes" (106, 111). Although Grimsley's characters enjoy moments of pastoral freedom in these settings, the rape of the protagonist by a schoolmate in an abandoned plantation house reasserts the male brutality endemic to the southern Arcady. Consequently, ultimate freedom is to be found outside the influence of the southern father—in flight, "up north somewhere" beyond the patriarchal shadow of the region's culture (195). Such escape vali-dates Gwin's observation that many incest survivors' narratives suggest that " 'home' may not be grounded in place but in the *r*eplacement of the self else-where," where "the daughter can begin to write her own cultural story, create her own felicity" (437). This pattern is enacted from a male perspective in Grim-sley's novel: following Gwin's formulation, "home" is constructed elsewhere, beyond the reach of the regional patriarchy. Yet for Allison, the constraints of poverty and, to some extent, gender prevent the kind of relocation that con-cludes *Dream Boy*. Given the determinism of her environment, Bone has no such option of mobility. Rather than lighting out for a better existence, her saga concludes with geographical stasis—waiting and watching "the night close in around" her (309). It is a final irony in Allison's reworking of the bildungsroman. Self-development is again thwarted, this time by a reversal of the conventional quest motif of the genre. The protagonist's agency is reduced and with it her authorship of "her own cultural story." Gwin rightly notes the centrality of narrative to the southern sense of self and place: "Southerners have always maintained that place makes us who we are and that the stories we tell ourselves about 'home' . . . are the means through which we negotiate identity" (437). Allison's novel problematizes that dynamic profoundly. The result is a new conception of a tragic South, illumined from beneath by the story of a southerner expendable to the region's established cultural narrative, a young woman whose native means of negotiating identity call the validity of the entire culture into question.

Dorothy Allison's "Shit-kicking Anger and Grief"

Allison's achievement in *Bastard Out of Carolina* is significant. Like Crews before her, she manages to produce a well-crafted novel dealing with experiences outside the traditional sphere of the educated classes. If Susan Donaldson is correct in arguing that the profession of letters in the South has "always had a peculiarly haunted air, an aura of repressed ghosts besieging the white male writer and destabilizing his writing," then *Bastard* may be read as a return of the repressed—the rebuke of one pushed to the margins of southern literary consciousness ("Gender" 493). The novel intelligently and eloquently voices the concerns of poor whites, drawing on Allison's own childhood experiences while avoiding the temptation to devolve into either hagiography or tirade. As such, it is an important contribution to southern literature that, like Crews's novels, augments the aristocratic-agrarian vein of southern fiction with a vital lower-class perspective on the region's culture.

Yet Allison is not merely a chronological successor to Crews; she is also a more vocal critic of southern culture. In her essays she demonstrates that the anger central to Bone's development derives from her own conviction that the culture of the South—even more than most cultures—is seriously flawed in its configurations of social class and gender. At the core of Allison's artistic motivation are the emotions she describes as "the shit-kicking anger and grief" of her life (*Trash* 12). This sense of anger and grief is directed at the culture that labeled her "trash" and hindered her education and development. If Crews was a forerunner of the poor-white's literary expression, Allison is a genuine inheritor of his innovation—a poor-white author not only intent on forging a literary career for herself but also on dismantling the southern class system through her writing.

Allison's journey toward a literary career carries significant echoes of Crews's struggle to become a writer. She, too, had first to come to terms with the daunting facts of her childhood poverty, despite her unwillingness to expose her origins. In her essay "A Question of Class," Allison describes a process of repression much like the one Crews experienced several years earlier: "But what may be the central fact of my life is that I was born in 1949 in Greenville, South Carolina, the bastard daughter of a white woman from a desperately poor family, a girl who had left the seventh grade the year before, worked as a waitress, and was just a month past fifteen when she had me. That fact, the inescapable impact of being born in a condition of poverty that this society finds shameful, contemptible, and somehow deserved, has had dominion over me to such an extent that I have spent my life trying to overcome or deny it" (*Skin* 15). Like Crews's artistic epiphany, this passage illustrates the seemingly immutable nature of growing up poor in the South: Crews described himself as "inevitably shaped" by the "dreadful and sorry circumstances" of his childhood ("Television's" 128); Allison cites the "inescapable impact" of the origins that have "dominion" over her (*Skin* 15). Yet Allison differs from Crews in that she expresses a full awareness of the cultural mythology of the poor. She notes that the "myth of the poor in this country" has never encompassed her family, which were neither the hard-working "good" poor nor entirely the "bad" poor who deserved their low status (17–18). As "a child who believed in books," she could not find herself accurately portrayed in literature; the poor she encountered in her reading were either "made over into caricatures or flattened into saintlike stock creatures" (*Trash* 9). The goal of her literary career became the creation of realistic depictions of the poor, to reclaim, in Jillian Sandell's formulation, "the label 'white trash' as a political strategy to expose class-based discrimination in the United States" (215).

At this point Allison found herself at odds with her native culture. Southern culture, in her estimation, places an undue emphasis on the upper classes and retains a narcissistic fascination for aristocracy. As she relates in *Two or Three Things I Know for Sure* (1996), Allison was excluded from such a society: "I was born trash in a land where the people all believe themselves natural aristocrats. Ask any white Southerner. They'll take you back two generations, say, 'Yeah, we had a plantation.' The hell we did. I have no memories that can be bent so easily. I know where I come from, and it is not that part of the world" (32).

These sentences aptly demonstrate Allison's importance to southern letters. Building on the success of poor-white authors such as Crews in forging an unlikely literary career, she has introduced a new militancy to the expression of poor-white experience, cutting to the heart of the myth of Arcady. In much the same way that Richard Wright built upon predecessors such as Charles Chesnutt and Zora Neale Hurston, Allison has used the accomplishment of her forebears as an inroad to an increasingly critical appraisal of the South. Like Wright, she evinces an understanding of the ideological foundations of the culture she writes against—and a similar hostility to them. Sandell notes that "the fact that stories about impoverished whites have been virtually *un*tellable suggests a profound collective anxiety about what such narratives might reveal" (213). Much as Wright did with his Jim Crow South, Allison quite consciously mines this collective anxiety to tell the stories of a subculture muted by the region's dominant narrative. Using critical intelligence and "shit-kicking anger," she undermines the existing mythology of the poor and elevates the literature of the poor white to the level of ideological criticism.

Perhaps it is the relative absence of this anger—or the lapse of incisive cultural critique that accompanies it—that explains Allison's disappointing second novel, *Cavedweller*, which appeared in 1998. Lacking these, place and community become a handicap, the conduit of a clichéd depiction of southern society. Despite passages of lucent prose, the successor to *Bastard* is a cumbersome novel that overall lacks the visceral power of Allison's debut. Allison seems content here to replace with stereotypes the sharply etched characters, defined by their place and time, of the prior fiction. The memorable Boatwrights and their Greenville environs are succeeded by a large cast of characters who bear a greater resemblance to mass media portrayals of southerners than to actual people of the contemporary South—as if Allison has capitulated to the definition of a "southern novel" that a national readership might expect. As Shannon Ravenel has noted, southern regionalism is "a two-way street" that, taken in "the wrong direction," can result in a hackneyed vision of the South akin to that of *Hee Haw* (viii). *Cavedweller* surrenders to cliché, and thus its cumulative effect is hardly one of outrage or injustice. Rather, it is the uneasy sense that the South of *Cavedweller* is one that we have seen before—too many times—on television and in films.

The novel succeeds in the manner of *Bastard* only when Allison transcends these clichés, or rather goes beneath them, in the descriptions of Cissy's cave exploration. Like Bone, Cissy (the cavedweller of the title) finds herself through the subterranean, in mapping the caves that lie just beneath and outside Cayro. Here she discovers the "dirt cradle," the "hillbilly hiding place," where she feels she belongs (307). Among the portions of the earth that are like her—"dirt pressed hard, unvalued and ignored"—she begins the process of self-discovery and sexual awareness that cannot take place above ground in Cayro (324). Her experiences in the caves provide the novel with its most powerful prose and imagery, as when Allison writes: "Every time she crawled up into the light again, she knew herself different. It was as if her passage through the dark offered Cissy what she had always wanted, confrontation with God in the imagined body of a woman, the mama-core, the bludgeoned heart of the earth" (308). Here is subversion of the patriarchal order that defines existence on the surface—the type of subversion that makes *Bastard* an important contribution to southern literature. Its belated appearance in the novel is welcome but ultimately too delayed to redeem the preceding three hundred pages.

The central weakness of *Cavedweller* lies in Allison's late deployment of such subversion. While Sandell is certainly incorrect in asserting that *Bastard* does not "alleviate class oppression, or even necessarily challenge the status quo," her criticism applies with unfortunate accuracy to Allison's second novel (214). Allison's capitulation to southern stereotypes dilutes the cultural critique so powerfully evident in the earlier novel, compromising the legitimacy of an iconoclastic stance. Sandell argues that the literary "marketplace frequently offers a limited, but contained, space within which to articulate some measure of resistance to the dominant social order" (214). Allison's debut capitalized on this moment of dialogue, but *Cavedweller* seems to acknowledge its transience, abdicating the kind of anger and protest crucial to politically charged depictions of poor-white experience. Sandell's criticism of *Bastard* is more appropriate to the later novel: "The commercial and critical success of *Bastard Out of Carolina* suggests . . . a profound collective desire to engage with the issue of impoverished whites in the United States, while at the same time it suggests a form of disavowal that keeps such issues at arm's length—class issues become safely located in books and popular culture to be consumed as a leisure activity" (216). The hackneyed South of *Cavedweller* makes the novel a culturally passive text, safe to be consumed as a product outside politics and ideology in a momentary suspension of class hierarchies. The protest of social realism is lost. The novel that Valerie Sayers describes as an "amalgam, a Victorian novel of the late-20th-century South," is consequently too conflicted to function as an effective vehicle of Allison's vision. It is only in the concluding pages of what Sayers calls Cissy's "psychological unfolding" that the author operates at her full powers. This psychological development of young southern women excluded from the majority not only by poverty but also by sexual orientation is Allison's forte, and one hopes that her future work will return to the exploration of such seldom acknowledged facets of southern experience.

Despite her limited and uneven fictional output, Allison occupies a preeminent place in the poor-white literary movement that may be the last great "crossing of the ways" in southern literature. Her interrogations of the region's precarious class ideology have laid the groundwork for subsequent literary engagements with the region's social structure, as more white writers of humble means continue to contribute to the region's letters. Over half a century ago W. J. Cash expressed skepticism about the inherent aristocracy of the southern character; Allison and Crews have confirmed his conviction that the genius of southern culture does not lie solely in its upper classes. In the same year that Cash published his analysis of southern cultural mythology, the planter-poet William Alexander Percy posed the question of who might speak for the poor whites of the South. As if speaking for all those at the lower reaches of the social hierarchy, Allison offers an answer: "If I can write a story that so draws the reader in that she imagines herself like my characters, feels their sense of fear and uncertainty, their hopes and terrors, then I have come closer to knowing myself as real, important as the very people I have always watched with awe" (*Skin* 14).

THE NEW NATURALISM
OF LARRY BROWN

Terrible things must happen to the characters of the naturalistic tale.

—*Frank Norris, "Zola as a Romantic Writer"*

One of the questions about human nature that interests me most is how people bear up under monstrous calamity, all the terrible things that can befall them, war, poverty, desperation.

—*Larry Brown, "A Late Start"*

In the early 1980s authorship in the South took a quiet but auspicious turn: an Oxford, Mississippi, firefighter named Larry Brown sat down at a portable typewriter and began to teach himself how to write literary fiction. Like his predecessor Harry Crews—one of the many writers who had influenced him— Brown's background was very different from those of the canonized southern literati who preceded him. Brown had grown up in relative poverty, and consequently he brought the perspective of poor-white southerners into his fiction from the vantage point of firsthand experience. Despite his lack of a formal education, Brown's determination to become a writer reaped considerable dividends: in the next twenty years he would publish four novels, two collections of short stories, and a memoir to wide acclaim, winning numerous awards and becoming the first writer to win the Southern Book Critics' Circle award twice, for *Joe* (1991) and *Father and Son* (1996). The enthusiasm of book reviewers seemed matched only by their astonishment that a self-taught writer, the son of a sharecropper with no college education, could have attained such literary prowess on his own. But most important to southern literary history is that Brown confirms the existence of a rising tide of poor-white southern literary voices. Brown's fiction, along with the work of younger writers such as Dorothy Allison, indicates that Crews's unlikely literary career was not a fluke but merely the harbinger of many such new voices, the prologue to a new chapter in southern literature in which lower-class and blue-collar whites, aided by Sun Belt prosperity, have belatedly joined the southern literary consciousness.

Perhaps because of this unconventional perspective, southern literary criticism has been slow to recognize Brown. Fewer than half a dozen articles dealing with his work have appeared in the twelve years since he began to publish. Even a critic as eminent as Cleanth Brooks experiences difficulty in situating Brown in the context of tradition. In an essay commissioned by Algonquin Books for the publication of *Joe*, Brooks rightly notes that the novel "is not imitation Faulkner," but his comparison of Brown's work to Bertram Wyatt-Brown's *Southern Honor* never moves beyond the level of tentative connections ("Affair" 1). Brooks concludes that *Joe* is a "significant" story and a "very fine novel," but he appears unwilling or unable to proffer a meaningful context for its significance (4). Brooks's ambivalence is revealing. Brown offers the traditional critic a setting that is superficially familiar, but his particular attention to the oppressive hierarchies of that community is something new that cannot readily be assimilated into orthodox reading strategies. As Thomas McHaney notes in his 1979 review of Brooks's second Yoknapatawpha study, Brooks's Agrarian affinities caused him to resist such iconoclasm in Faulkner's work as well, even to the point of simply ignoring it. McHaney observes that Brooks "never relents in his insistence upon community as a citadel of value, a preserve of tradition, and a mark against which modern alienation is quickly measured . . . he upholds the uniqueness of the stable, wholesome rural southern community" (34). Brown is more systematic than Faulkner in debunking such nearly pastoral notions of regenerative stability; his familiarity with lower-class experience allows him to reveal the human cost of traditional southern ideology.

The plight of Brown's poor characters demonstrates to whom the intrusions of modernity posed a threat and how the traditions of a stable community can operate to the detriment of its disenfranchised members.

Brown's work—and the influence of his background on it—thwarts traditional readings in the mode established for southern criticism in the great critical response to the Southern Renascence. And no wonder: as the example of Brooks demonstrates, Brown does not fit the old paradigms by which critics have defined Southern Renascence literature. One may indeed find in Brown's work the conventional motifs of loyalty to place, attention to dialect and local color, elaborate codes of honor, and the dominance of tradition, but these are all altered or inverted by the author's familiarity with the poor southerner's experience—a perspective not incorporated into the codified, modernist checklist of a work's "southernness." Such a critical method, which reads backward from contemporary writers like Brown to the constellation of southern modernist giants like William Faulkner and Flannery O'Connor, is outdated in Brown's case. Brown's break from the past is best exemplified by his reaction to an article in *Studies in Short Fiction* that attempted to establish a line of influence between *The Sound and the Fury* and his story "Waiting for the Ladies." Brown has tersely rejected the article as "totally off base" (letter to the author, 2 May 1995).

Brown's autobiographical essay "A Late Start" explains his discomfort with criticism focusing on what he calls "the handing down of some sort of symbolic literary torch" (1). While he is aware that comparisons between himself and Oxford's preeminent writer are inevitable, Brown points out that his background is much different from Faulkner's. His childhood was "a series of rented houses" in north Mississippi and Memphis, Tennessee, following a sharecropper father "looking for a better existence" (1, 3). As Brown puts it, "It was like trouble followed us from place to place" (3). Out of this background of poverty and mobility came the artistic vision that, Brown notes, has troubled many critics: "more than a few [reviewers] seem to register a certain uneasy feeling, and I wonder if this is because I make them look a little too deeply into my characters' lives. Maybe I make them know a little more than they want to about the poor, or the unfortunate, or the alcoholic. But a sensible writer writes what he or she knows best, and draws on the material that's closest, and the lives that are observed" (2). Brown's persistent exploration of his background separates him from traditional twentieth-century interpreters of the South. If his familiarity with "the poor, or the unfortunate, or the alcoholic" has given him a fresh interpretation of southern culture, it has also endowed him with a sensibility at odds with southern literary tradition.

It seems, then, that the crucial flaw in misreadings of Brown's work lies not in the effort to situate him within literary tradition but in the choice of traditions by which to evaluate his work. Despite the stylistic flair that Brown has gleaned from earlier southern writers like Faulkner and O'Connor, his social sensibility has at best a tenuous connection to Southern Renascence literature. On the contrary, he is philosophically most allied to an older movement in American literature: naturalism. Instead of evaluating Brown in the Faulknerian and Southern Renascence tradition, one should view him as a new naturalist, the most thoroughly naturalistic writer of contemporary southern fiction.

It is not surprising that critics have misconstrued Brown's work; such misinterpretation has long been characteristic of critical responses to naturalism. As J. C. Levenson observes of the reaction to the first American naturalists, criticism "simply had no terms by which to grasp the new kind of narrative" (155). In the case of Brown's contemporary revival of the naturalist style, history seems to be repeating itself. While even the most cursory examination of Brown's work reveals all the criteria of naturalist fiction, no one seems to have noticed. In *Dirty Work* (1989), a multiple-amputee Vietnam veteran lies in a hospital bed for twenty years, so maimed by forces beyond his control that he lacks even the means to end his own suffering. In "The Rich" (from 1988's *Facing the Music*) a travel agent meditates on his wealthy and enigmatic clients, whom he hates for living "so high above the everyday human struggles of the race" even as he knows that "the rich can never be poor, and the poor can never be rich" (39–40). Brown's novel *Joe*—which was originally called "Nomads"—deals with a homeless family on the extreme margins of society, scions of the brutish and alcoholic Wade Ransom. The novel is a meditation on the primitive in humanity, the threat of heredity, and the myriad forces of social determinism. The panoramic social fabric of *Father and Son* demonstrates Brown's commitment to the sweeping verisimilitude practiced by such naturalists as Frank Norris and Theodore Dreiser, to the web of interconnectedness in society that, through the naturalist's eyes, seems to reduce chance to inevitability.

Consider what Brown sees as the basis and impetus of his fiction, the manner in which he conceives his characters. He has told Susan Ketchin that his work "is about people surviving, about people proceeding out from calamity"—about common people with "some major problem that's disrupting their life. . . . It's got to be a major struggle. More than one, nothing simple" (129, 137). Brown describes this method of creating dramatic tension with the military metaphor of "sandbagging": "I think you should sandbag your characters—load 'em up with as much as you can, then see what they do" (137). Norris prescribed much the same technique as the basis of his writing: "The naturalist takes no note of common people, common in so far as their interests, their lives, and the things that occur in them are common, ordinary. Terrible things must happen to the characters of the naturalistic tale. They must be twisted from the ordinary, wrenched out from the quiet, uneventful round of every-day life, and flung into the throes of some vast and terrible drama that works itself out in unleashed passions, in blood, and in sudden death" (1107). The parallel is central to Brown's status as a contemporary practitioner of the genre. Like Norris, his artistic modus operandi is to begin with ordinary characters (such as Braiden Chaney and Walter James of *Dirty Work*) and fling them into a "vast and terrible drama" (the Vietnam War) with only their innate capabilities to assist them. The result, typical of most naturalist fiction, is the conflict between common human beings and uncommon circumstances.

Further evidence of Brown's strain of naturalism lies in the distinction he perceives between his own work and that of the contemporary "dirty realists" and minimalists. Again like Norris, Brown writes fiction on a scale larger than that of realism, as his comment about "major struggles" indicates. The result is a consciousness of the distinction between his style and conventional realism, a distinction Norris frequently emphasized. Brown's philosophy is true to what Donald Pizer has observed in the difference between realism and naturalism: "A naturalistic novel is . . . an extension of realism only in the sense that both modes deal with the local and the contemporary. The naturalist, however, discovers in this material the extraordinary and excessive in human nature" (11). Brown echoes Norris's famous comment that realism is "the drama of a broken teacup" (1166) when he says that "the main thing wrong with all this minimalist crap" is that "the worst crime a story can commit is to be dull, to be not about anything, for nothing to happen" (letter to the author, 8 May 1996). Brown's concept of sandbagging his characters, with its close parallels to Norris's credo, is a pure expression of the naturalistic sensibility. If naturalism is truly, as Norris said, the exploration of "the black, unsearched penetralia of the soul of man" (1169), then Brown is its preeminent contemporary practitioner. Rather than an epigonic southerner caught in the shadow of the Renascence or a "dirty realist" using the South as his setting, Brown is an inheritor of the naturalist tradition—in Peter Applebome's words, an astute chronicler of "ordinary people coping with extraordinary pain."[1]

One may rightly question the value of situating Brown in the naturalist tradition. If indeed his work is noteworthy for its innovative qualities, an effort to link him to literary history may seem misguided. Yet in Brown's case the aesthetic and textual merge with his cultural context, making a partial deference to traditional critical practices necessary. Because the historical absence of naturalism in southern critical discourse is inextricably tied to misreadings of Brown's work, a reappraisal of the naturalist aesthetic is mandatory to understanding his challenge to Renascence conventions. Brooks's inconclusive essay on *Joe* makes this clear. As John T. Matthews has observed of Brooks, his "new critical methods of close reading contain embedded attachments to the social and aesthetic vision of his teachers and predecessors in the Agrarian movement" (216). These attachments are apparent in Brooks's reading of *Joe*, from which one senses that he deems the novel an important work but is uncertain precisely how or why it is important. Brooks's uncertainty lies in the fact that the naturalistic perspective has never been incorporated into the social and aesthetic vision of the Agrarians, a view of the South and its literature that has shaped not only Brooks's interpretation but also the bulk of twentieth-century southern criticism. The perpetuation of this imperfect paradigm is evident in Jan Nordby Gretlund's reading of *Joe*, which rightly notes Brown's almost Agrarian love of the land (familiar territory for the New Critic) while simultaneously demonstrating a profound misunderstanding of the manual labor of the timber industry so crucial to Joe Ransom's social environment. When Gretlund observes that "Brown's knowledge of . . . 'no-counts,' boozers, bar-room brawlers, and wife-beaters is singular in American literature" but concludes that it is "difficult for readers to go in search of answers to existential questions with people they hardly know," the textual and cultural connections of Brown's naturalism become clear (234, 235). Gretlund's distinction between readers and characters reveals the class hegemony of a critical practice that omits the poor people of Brown's naturalism from its lexicon. If these characters are indeed people the reader "hardly knows," the disjunction between the two demonstrates the insufficiency of the South's established criticism. Without naturalism in the critical vocabulary, a reading such as Gretlund's can hope at best to elide the issue of social class. At worst, elitism is vindicated through the limited aesthetic.

For a writer of Brown's social standing, naturalism is more than an aesthetic dalliance with pessimistic philosophy. Accordingly, it should be read in his work as more than a simply textual strategy for presenting the South in fiction. As with Crews and Allison, the realist-naturalist style is for Brown implicitly political; the cultural and the aesthetic are linked. Like the autodidactic discoveries Richard Wright chronicles through his early reading in *Black Boy*, these authors have turned to a narrative practice largely ignored by other writers of their region because its protest qualities suit the tenor of their experience. Wright was drawn to "men like Dreiser, Masters, Mencken, Anderson, and Lewis" because their work "seemed defensively critical of the straightened American environment," and claimed that "all my life had shaped me for the realism, the naturalism of the modern novel" (*Later Works* 413, 250). The same holds true for the southern neonaturalists, whose life experience dictates the form of their art in a manner far more emphatic than that of their white contemporaries. Wright's original conclusion to *Black Boy* is resonant with parallels to poor-white experience: "The pressure of southern living kept me from being the kind of person that I might have been. I had been what my surroundings had demanded, what my family—conforming to the dictates of the whites above them—had exacted of me, and what the whites had said that I must be. Never being fully able to be myself, I had slowly learned that the South could recognize but part of a man, could accept but a fragment of his personality, and all the rest—the best and deepest things of heart and mind—were tossed away in blind ignorance and hate" (414). The determinism of this passage is pervasive in Brown's fiction, as it is in Crews's and Allison's, and it derives its authority from the authors' own lives. The challenge facing critical appraisal of Brown lies in accepting the whole vision of a writer self-educated in dissent just as Wright was—and resisting the tendency to discount depictions of a South that the consensus would prefer not to acknowledge.

DIRTY WORK IN A DETERMINISTIC COSMOS

Brown's first novel, *Dirty Work*, is set in a Veterans Administration hospital in Memphis, Tennessee, and deals with the aftermath of Vietnam for two southerners, Braiden Chaney and Walter James. Although Braiden is black and Walter white, both men were born into the margins of southern society, marked by race and the stigma of poverty; both come from "cottonpicking cottonchopper" families (16). The men are further bound by their war wounds: Walter's face was disfigured by a Claymore mine, which damaged him badly enough to cause seizures twenty years later, and Braiden has been lying in a hospital bed for twenty-two years, his arms and legs amputated after extensive machine-gun injuries. Each man finds himself placed in the naturalistic conundrum of being forced to live in what each considers to be a state worse than death. Walter's reluctance to rejoin society is compounded by the seizures that render him unconscious without warning, dooming any attempt at social connection. Braiden finds himself unwilling to live without limbs yet paradoxically unable to take his own life. When Walter is committed to the hospital after his worst seizure, the ensuing day and night reveal that the sole route to deliverance lies within and between two outcasts in a fallen world.

While Vietnam has served as a rite of passage into a deterministic philosophy for Walter and Braiden, the war was not a singularly protean event in the men's lives; rather, it was the decisive experience that confirmed each man's nascent sense of determinism. In this sense *Dirty Work* is a revolutionary depiction of warfare in southern literature. The novel contains none of the chivalry of Civil War works such as Allen Tate's *The Fathers*, for Brown takes pains to undermine efforts to read *Dirty Work* as a tragedy in the traditional sense—his characters begin their odyssey too low in the social stratum to effect much of a conventional tragic fall. In addition, the inchoate objectives of the United States in the Vietnam War are as perfectly suited to the aims of a naturalistic novel as they are different from the warfare depicted in novels of the Renascence. The lack of concrete goals in Vietnam forms a stark contrast to the valorous convictions of fictive accounts of the Civil War. Unlike Tate's veterans, the characters in *Dirty Work* are "hurried beyond decision" because they are prey to social forces beyond their comprehension, not because they have willfully joined a great cause (*Poems* 21). Patriotic sacrifice is replaced with senseless slaughter. If the conclusion of the novel derives its force, as Owen Gilman has noted, from "the power of kinship as it transcends social norms" (113), this is only because the entirety of *Dirty Work* effectively establishes a cosmos in which social norms are perverse enough to create a conflict like Vietnam—in which love and violence, mercy and death, become indistinguishable.

Dirty Work begins with a meditation on the importance of history as a determining force. On one of the many mental "trips" he takes to escape the "junk pile" of the hospital, Braiden visualizes himself in Africa under different circumstances, envisioning "what things would of been like if it hadn't been for slave traders about three hundred years ago. If history had been different. If I'd of lived in Africa and had me a son and been a king in my own country" (1). But Braiden finds himself without such self-determination. He is far from his native country in a backwater of America, the veteran of a war forced upon him by the government that enslaved his forebears. His vernacular speech eloquently describes the machinations of history: "We wasted about two hundred years picking fucking cotton" (20).

Walter also has been shaped by circumstances beyond his control, and if the presence of these forces has been more subtle than chattel slavery, their effect has been no less powerful. The poverty of his rural childhood has given him a sense of separation from society, the conviction that "people don't know what it's like to be poor" (33). He describes a life of deterministic poverty, of "people who looked down their noses at us because we were on welfare," and an experience with the world that closely parallels that of Braiden (33). He, too, knows life to be a series of responses to forces beyond the individual's sphere of power, a rudimentary struggle in an indifferent world. His sense of determinism has been enhanced by the decline of his family: "Daddy started drinking a lot worse after I came back in the shape I'm in. We lost our place. He'd got us to where we had over two hundred acres. Now we've got two. He got deeper and deeper in debt. They finally foreclosed on him. It's just a bunch of shit" (78). Like Braiden, Walter is a quintessentially naturalistic character, an individual shaped by his environment and caught in a daily struggle to establish a small measure of personal dignity.

The brutality and indifference of Braiden's and Walter's backgrounds groomed them perfectly for the Vietnam War. Within the context of the novel, the war seems to be a crucible of naturalism, an example of the naturalistic cosmos at its most salient. The advice given to Walter by his father, a World War II veteran, presents survival in cold-blooded, simple terms. Walter's father has informed him that "in war you've got to kill all the people you can to try and keep yourself alive. The less of them, he said, the better the chances for you. He said to keep my eyes open, look and listen and learn all I could. Trust nobody. Depend on nobody" (61). After the war, talking with Braiden, Walter indicates that he learned the mentality of warfare thoroughly: "Your values are not the same then. You want to live, right? Sometimes for you to live, somebody else has got to die. But his life's not the same as yours then, is it? His life is less than yours, isn't it?" (165). Braiden confirms the instinct for survival. He describes the day he was injured in poignant terms of suffering, yet he concludes the story with a declaration that only emphasizes the primal drive to survive at any cost: "I started crawling to that little knoll and that's when he cut loose. I felt them bullets run up my legs, man, just punching holes in me. Couldn't move. Then he just raked me. Just all over. Lord he shot me all to pieces. Lord he hurt me. But I would have done it to him if he'd give me the opportunity" (161).

The result of the baptism by fire for both men is a confirmed sense of a naturalistic cosmos. Brown breaks from the conventional intrusive narration of earlier naturalistic novels by allowing the characters to explain this philosophy themselves, yet even through the idioms and dialect of two sharecroppers, a cogent philosophical vision is expressed. For Walter, the world is defined by the vicissitudes of chance, by the fact that "one little thing could mess up your whole life. Just being in the wrong place at the wrong time" (156). Braiden, the older of the two men, most eloquently expresses a veteran's perspective on a brutally indifferent world. He commingles a naturalistic sensibility with an embattled faith in Christianity, and his exegeses on the problem of suffering go straight to the heart of faith in a fallen world. Braiden thinks, "Whole world's a puzzle to me, though. Why it's got to be the way it is. I don't think the Lord meant for it to be this way originally. I think things just got out of hand" (12). The theology that he has adopted is a sort of Christianity of determinism in which God exists but does not interfere in the workings of the world.

Such is an appropriate faith for a veteran who has suffered the trials of Job. For Braiden, however, faith is complicated by the nagging suspicion that God may be indifferent or, worse still, impotent to intervene in human suffering. What emerges from his theological musings is something very close to a pure expression of naturalism:

There is things you ain't got no control over. And everybody want to blame it on God. Or say God done it. Say Oh God made that happen. It's for the best. He got a plan in the scheme of everything. I've heard preachers get up and tell it. Stand up in church and say it. Listen, Walter. God don't cause no shit like that to happen. You think he'd let some kid burn up in a house? . . .

But He cain't protect everybody. And bad things happen every day. Hundreds of times a day. Thousands of times a day. The thing that happened to me that day was just one thing that happened in the middle of a lot of bad things that happened that day. Shit, Walter. It was over three hundred killed some weeks. He ain't responsible for all that. It ain't no way. Man does all this stuff to himself. (177–78)

The skeptic might query Braiden about the need for a God who never intervenes, who remains distant enough to be inscrutable. For even as Braiden claims that "God got a plan for everything," he sounds a distinctly nihilistic note:

"World don't change for no man. World gone keep going on. Don't make no difference what you do, what I do. World keep turning" (226).

Braiden's visits with Jesus reinforce the notions of a deity passive to events in the physical world. Braiden's Jesus is distinctly humanistic, perhaps because while Braiden claims really to see him at times, he also admits to "making up" some of his visions (91). His Jesus is compassionate and earthy but world-weary; he seems very much like a tired blue-collar worker as he sits on Braiden's bed smoking Marlboros and talking in idiomatic English. He describes the cosmos in the same mechanistic terms as Braiden, sounding regretful that heaven's policy admits murderers and delineating the challenge of dealing with disobedient humanity: "Look, Braiden. I been around a long time. You know God made man in His image. Made him out of dust and blowed the breath of life into him. Give him Eden, and give him Eve. And they had two sons. And look what happened there. It ain't been any different since" (93). He insists that Braiden cannot take his own life but indicates that Braiden's salvation may lie in Walter. In Braiden's theology the focus is always returned to the tangible and the imminent, to a person's actions in the perceptible world under the obscure shadow of eternity.

The novel's final action confirms the demarcation between heaven and the physical world. In a naturalistic inversion of the passion story, it is Walter—the nominal murderer—who sacrifices himself. Braiden is happy to escape his suffering, but it is Walter who is condemned to life; the believer goes on to the next world while the nihilist remains trapped in this one. In this context we may see Walter's action as ultimately moral, a true sacrifice. It is only through violence that mercy may be dispensed, although Walter has yet to adopt Braiden's scarified faith in transcendence: "I stood over him for a long moment. He opened his eyes and looked at me when I closed my hands around his throat. He said Jesus loves you. I shut my eyes because I knew better than that shit. I knew that somewhere Jesus wept" (236).

While the conclusion seems to be devastatingly bleak, Walter's actions belie his words. Even if he claims to have no faith, his act displays compassion, mercy, and personal sacrifice—the antitheses to animalistic self-preservation. The brutality of the world may in fact be the product of (as Braiden says) what people do to themselves, but in the act of euthanasia Walter demonstrates that humanity's penchant for violence may also contain the seeds of transcendence, the means of surmounting its animal nature. In helping Braiden escape his suffering, Walter kills as he has done in the past but this time with an entirely different motivation. As Gilman notes, Walter has been compelled to act for duty and honor before, but now he acts for love (113). If the wholesale carnage of Vietnam has made a grotesquerie of humanity's godlike power, Walter's act in a forgotten ward of an obscure hospital confirms that, within the small sphere of personal action, humanity can achieve dignity on a reduced scale. Walter's life has been a series of reactive gestures to a daunting cosmos; now he enacts a proactive deed, accepting the bitter cup of responsibility for a fellow sufferer.

Such a denouement is not anathema to the philosophy of the naturalistic novel, as Pizer has observed. Pizer stresses that beneath the apparent pessimistic determinism of naturalism lies the conviction that humanity holds the key to its own redemption. He notes that "the naturalist often describes his characters as though they are conditioned or controlled by environment, heredity, instinct, or chance. But he also suggests a compensating humanistic value in his characters or their fates which affirms the significance of the individual and of his life. . . . The naturalist appears to say that although the individual may be a cipher in a world made amoral by man's lack of responsibility for his fate, the imagination refuses to accept this formula as the total meaning of life and so seeks a new basis for man's sense of his own dignity and importance" (11). This generalization is true of *Dirty Work*. The novel moves through hellish Vietnam flashbacks, grim and inescapable poverty, and the workings of chance—staples of deterministic naturalism—to a decisive, self-willed action that makes the most of the diminished thing that is the world and humanity's place in it. This is the philosophical underpinning to Brown's concept of sandbagging. Like many of Brown's characters, Walter is faced with monstrous calamity in an amoral world, but his response to his predicament introduces morality to that world. Within the moral triage of *Dirty Work*, he acts with dignity and compassion and, even if he does not realize it, affirms the value of the individual.

The novel's most impressionistic sequence illustrates Brown's beleaguered optimism. As Walter moves toward his terrible duty, he joins Braiden in his imagination, taking a "trip" with him through the black smoke and flames and chattering guns of Vietnam to the "sleep of silence" in a Mississippi cotton field, to the peace and serenity in "the long rows of white"—and even farther back, to the vast plains of Africa, to a sun "miles wide" with a lone human figure moving across its horizon (236). He moves back to origins and new beginnings, to a pristine nature unsullied by humanity. His visions hold forth the tenacious promise of Brown's particular brand of naturalism. They depict a beautiful natural world that is the domain of humankind, if only humanity can find its proper place in it.

ATAVISM AND MORALITY: JOE

Brown's second novel, *Joe*, puts him even more firmly into naturalist territory. As its title implies, the novel deals with common people, yet its expansive scope moves beyond the life of its protagonist into a meditation on the shaping forces of environment, heredity, and community. Joe Ransom is an authentic naturalist character; he comes from the lower classes of society and has suffered jail time and a divorce as consequences of his predilection for alcohol. His life at the time of the action has a precarious sort of stability, however, because of his lucrative job as the leader of a crew that deadens timber for the lumber industry. Whatever stability he maintains, however, is threatened by the appearance of Gary Jones—the son of a cruel itinerant farm worker, Wade Jones—who provokes Joe's calloused sense of morality into action and forces him to commit an act of moral violence. Like Walter James, Joe is an ordinary individual caught in extraordinary circumstances, a common man who feels himself propelled toward an act of uncommon sacrifice.

The naturalistic focus on the lower classes is evident in the first pages of the novel. *Joe* opens on a deserted road in the rural South, in "regions of Johnson-grass and bitterweed," with the Jones family slowly making its way through daunting heat toward an unknown destination (5). The Joneses are homeless, so destitute that they can hardly be considered members of society at large. Gary has been so deprived that he is illiterate, does not know what a church is, and brushes his teeth for the first time in a whorehouse. The only possessions that he and his family own—moldy blankets, sundry pots and pans, and shape-less clothes—are carried on their backs until they begin to occupy an abandoned cabin several miles from the town in which Joe lives.

The Joneses also bring a sordid family history with them. Gary can remember *"other states, other days, mild ones, mountains in the distance, the little tarpaper shacks where they had once lived. Miles and miles of blacktop highway, the bundled clothes, the mildewed quilts after a night on the side of the road. All his life he'd been hungry"* (331). In their peregrinations around the country they have lost two of their children, one to a farming accident and another ("brother Calvin") who has been bartered away to a wealthy childless couple in exchange for a Lincoln automobile. The family's entire history has been shaped by the poles of Wade's bitter life: the monomaniacal pursuit of alcohol and his loathing of physical labor. The family's meager existence is best defined in a typically short exchange between Gary and his father. "I'm ready to go home," Gary tells his father. Wade replies, "Well, I ain't. They ain't a goddamn thing at home" (91).

Joe occupies a slightly higher position in society. But despite his job and house, he also exists on the margins of his culture. He has spent twenty-nine months in the penitentiary for shooting a police officer and still courts legal troubles as if they are the only way to give his life a sense of definition. The people of his class have their own problems, even if these are defined in less violent terms than the Joneses'. Joe has been shot by Willie Russell (a man he insulted in a gambling house), and Joe's girlfriend, Connie, comes to stay with him because her stepfather has been pursuing her sexually. Brown's description of Connie finding Joe asleep is a classic example of social determinism: "And the next morning she found him there, naked, sprawled beneath the faded bedspread like those revelers of old in cracked paintings whose names or makers she'd never known, would never know" (106). If, as June Howard has observed, contemporary society tends to "disguise" or "encode" the boundary lines between social classes, Brown strips away such euphemism. Like the canonical naturalists, he depicts "a world in which actions and meanings are constantly seen in terms of class, in which omnipresent class conflict is virtually assumed" (Howard x). Connie's ignorance of higher culture and her trapped status in a low social position are but two examples of the determinism that pervades the novel.

Through such passages Brown depicts an impoverished subculture of the South as thoroughly as Stephen Crane explored the New York Bowery in *Maggie*. Brown uses the common people of *Joe* as a lens through which to view the entire South; he employs a larger cast of characters than in his first novel and consequently examines the entire social fabric of the region. Accordingly, *Joe* is a more rigorous social novel than *Dirty Work*. Even more than Crane, Brown moves upward through the social strata from his central characters toward the source of economic exploitation of which the Joneses and Joe Ransom are merely symptoms. For example, Gary notes that the couple who took Calvin "weren't like them," that they wore nice clothes and diamond rings (133). Class conflict is such a key component of the novel that it becomes one of the work's main themes; a web of social determinism appears to be concomitant with the increasing number of characters in Brown's second novel.

The clearest evidence of Brown's evolving social consciousness resides in his depiction of a liquor-store owner who comes into contact with Wade. The scene is Brown's most explicit indictment of a society that helps to shape creatures such as Wade. The store owner's response to Wade and his fellow vagrants is a trenchant depiction of middle-class complacence, for in the businessman's reaction to the derelict one sees, in naturalistic terms, the chasm between social classes: "The owner sighed. Dealing with these people over and over. With the depths of their ignorance. The white ones like this were worse than the black ones like this. Where they came from he didn't know. How they existed was a complete mystery to him. How they lived with themselves. He tossed his list on the counter without ever thinking he might have helped make them the way they were" (178). It is an interaction in which little is communicated between the two men other than the prices of merchandise, in which any sort of meaningful connection is never established, making it clear that the social differences between the two are insurmountable. In true naturalist fashion, class conflict is at the forefront of the exchange; Wade deceives the owner and flees the store with a stolen bottle. The sentences that follow, with their combination of fastidious attention to detail and underlying social theme, are a powerful expression of naturalist technique:

He took out his pipe and reached for his tobacco and slowly put it in, tamping it lightly, sighing to himself with enormous lassitude. . . . He didn't know where the man had gone. There was nothing but kudzu across the road, an apparently impenetrable jungle of green vegetation that crept softly in the night, claiming houses and light poles, rusted cars and sleeping drunks, the old and the infirm, small dogs and children. He wondered if maybe the old man lived in there and had trails like a rat, like the slides of a beaver or the burrows of a rabbit. Perhaps it was worse than he thought. Perhaps there was a whole city of them under there, deep, sheltered from the rain and shaded from the sun, with tents and canopies pitched beneath, cooking fires, camps where the children played and where they hung their wash. . . . Maybe one day he'd look. Maybe one day he'd lock the store and walk across the road and peer over the edge of the creepers and look down, to see if he could spot a wisp of smoke, to see if he could hear their radios playing, their TV sets. Maybe they had Honda generators and refrigerators. But he knew, really, that he wouldn't look. He wouldn't look because he didn't really want to know. He didn't want to be right. (182–83)

Here is naturalism par excellence as it has been defined by Pizer and other critics. With its attention to detail and local color, the passage builds upon the verisimilitude of realism. The southern landscape is accurately rendered, and the specific details the owner imagines (Honda generators, tents, refrigerators) are characteristic of realist fiction. But naturalist themes intrude, augmenting the realistic style with a consideration of the Other so endemic to naturalism, using realist technique as a springboard to deterministic social considerations. In the manner of Norris or Dreiser, Brown moves from the quotidian to the subterranean, from the normalcy of the business sphere to the underworld of society. Social tensions are obvious here, especially in the owner's comparison of the derelicts to animals and in the clear demarcation between society at large and the subculture beneath the vines. Like much of Crane's *Maggie*, this passage is an indictment of the middle-class morality that helps to create a determined existence for the poor (Pizer 149). Brown makes it clear that the social anxiety that largely catalyzed the American naturalist movement—bourgeois fear of the enigmatic lower classes—is alive and well in his contemporary South.

Out of this tension arises the strongest expression of otherness in the novel: the atavism of the Jones family. Wade Jones resembles Norris's McTeague and Vandover in his tendency toward regression, and his effect on his family is to create an animalistic community that operates outside most of the mores of civilization. Among his first words in the novel is his declaration of the ethics of primitive aggression. Imparting the fatherly wisdom of a Neanderthal man to Gary, he says, "Finders keepers. They ain't a fucking thing wrong with it" (4). He has conditioned his family so thoroughly to violence that they take his beatings silently, conserving their energy for the familiar routine of surviving each outburst. When violence intrudes from other areas, they know that they must rely on their own abilities to survive, without Wade's assistance: Gary thinks of his father during one conflict, "No help from that quarter, never had been, never would be" (92).

The family has learned well from Wade's example. Each meal is a struggle, a bitter contest over what small food they manage to acquire. By the supper fire on an evening that finds Wade "halfway through a bottle of Old Crow," they enact an atavistic scene of predation more animal than human:

The breadwinner was sitting crosslegged on the ravaged grass, the whiskey upright in the hole his legs formed. He was weaving a home-rolled cigarette back and forth from his lips, eyes bleary, red as fire. He was more than a little drunk. His head and chest would slump forward, then he'd jerk erect, his eyes sleepy. . . . The plate of beans before the old man steamed but he didn't notice. A candlefly bored crazily in out of the night and landed in the hot sauce, struggled briefly and was still. The old man's head went lower and lower onto his chest until the only thing they could see was the stained gray hat over the bib of his overalls. He snuffled, made some noise. His chest rose and fell.

They watched him like wolves. . . . The old man toppled over slowly, a bit at a time like a rotten tree giving way, until the whiskey lay spilling between his legs. They watched him for a few minutes and then they got up and went to the fire and took his plate and carried it away into the dark. (42–43)

Here we see the naturalist technique of revealing the primitive in contemporary life, of exposing the animal characteristics inherent to human interaction. Like the quasi-primitive street fight that begins *Maggie*, this scene is rendered in small details but adumbrated by larger, and darker, philosophical concerns than its action seems to indicate. Behind the theft of a plate of beans is a very struggle for survival, what Pizer describes as the naturalist's tendency to explore grand struggles through small events (13). This is evident in the parallels Brown carefully establishes between the mien of a contemporary homeless family and a more ancient human community. Like their primitive antecedents, the Jones family huddles around a campfire, and the weakness of one of their number is seized as an advantage. They watch the drunken "breadwinner" like "wolves," awaiting the opportunity to pilfer his portion and carry it away into the darkness like scavenging animals. The philosophical import of this episode is underscored by the death of the candlefly, which illustrates the perpetual struggle for survival, even down to a miniscule scale. It represents the pervasive need for sustenance, with the deterministic flourish of ultimate futility—and within the context of the scene, it obfuscates the distinction between human and animal as well. The passage demonstrates that regression is never far from the surface of human interaction; Brown simply presents an opportunity for it to reveal itself in contemporary life.

The most persistent conduit for atavism in *Joe* is alcohol. As in the novels of Norris and Crane, alcohol figures prominently in Brown's work as a regressive element, a catalyst to violence. The sum of Joe's wisdom about drinking can be expressed in a cogent observation: "A man did things he normally wouldn't do when those little devils were running loose in his head" (*Joe* 210). This statement could very nearly serve as an epigraph for the novel, for it is the "little devils" that accompany alcohol that drive Wade Jones. Like Norris's McTeague, Wade drinks "a good deal of whiskey," and like McTeague, "the only effect it had on him was to increase [his] viciousness and bad temper" (Norris 519). While Brown treats some of Wade's drinking bouts with the bawdy tone of the Southwestern Humorists, his general aim is to illustrate the regression that accompanies it. Alcohol speeds Wade's decline to such an extent that he begins to operate outside any moral sphere. He becomes the naturalistic brute, following a pattern of devolution similar to Norris's McTeague and Vandover. Initially Wade is cunning (he defrauds a kindly farmer by taking money from him under the pretense of buying medicine for his sick daughter), but as the novel progresses his actions become more animalistic. The fabliaux of a shambling town drunk become by degrees a consideration of the brutish atavistic man.

Wade's devolution is completed when he murders a black vagrant, appropriately enough, outside a liquor store. The scene is another example of Brown's ability to integrate the sensational into the mundane: it begins, like many of Wade's encounters, with a petty hustle, another story of a sick relative intended to induce sympathy. But the black man, his "countenance ruined with the scars of small drunken wars," is more wary of Wade than middle-class people such as the sympathetic farmer (*Joe* 150). Wade gains the man's trust only by declaring that a "little drink never hurt nobody" (151). Yet the action that follows is utterly sociopathic. Capitalizing on some diminished sense of community between two outcasts, Wade kills the black man as he is "in the act of passing the bottle" (153). He nets thirteen dollars, three food-coupon booklets, and a bottle of Fighting Cock from the murder. The meager rewards of the killing underscore the primitive level to which Wade has sunk.

The murder signifies Wade's disintegration into an amoral creature of primitive drives. Shortly thereafter he decides to prostitute his youngest daughter, Dorothy, to Willie Russell and a friend for thirty dollars "Apiece" (330). Joe's knowledge of the transaction puts him on the horns of a moral dilemma such as Walter James faced in *Dirty Work*. As he reflects on the necessity of action, he remembers the violence he witnessed in the penitentiary, thinking "about the old cons in the pen who would take the young and pretty boys down and how they would muffle their screams while they raped them. How everyone turned their heads and looked away because it didn't concern them and it wasn't them" (342). The need for violence predicated on ethics appears again in the moral triage of Brown's naturalistic world. It is a signal moment in Joe's life: he has committed acts of violence before, but these acts were always personal in nature—indeed, his previous conflict with Willie Russell transpired over money. Yet this time Joe acts (like Walter James) without personal motive. He has resisted killing Russell because of a personal vendetta, but circumstances have changed and made violence compulsory. Aware of his sacrifice, he knows that this time he will be sent to the penitentiary for many long years. As Wade escapes into the wilderness with the "wild and pawing energy" of an animal, Joe faces Russell as he climbs off Wade's daughter. He aims his pistol at Russell and "started to tell him a few things first, then decided there was no need of that" (342–43). The execution is a grim conclusion to Joe's life as a free man, lacking entirely a transcendent sense of closure. Once again, communication is nonexistent—action is the only medium. But the violence of Joe's act is not atavistic. In contrast to the murder Wade has committed, it is unmotivated by self-interest and in fact runs counter to self-preservation. Joe kills not for survival but in the service of some higher, if unexpressed, motivation.

The parallels between the conclusions of *Dirty Work* and *Joe* go to the heart of Brown's concept of sandbagging. Each of these novels focuses on a conclusion in which a character, plagued by the unseen forces that govern his life, chooses to transcend them, to act in a manner higher than the indifferent baseness of his surroundings. These characters, in Brown's words, "proceed out from calamity" with a grace and selflessness that defy the indignity of their environments (Ketchin 129). In a fallen world with precious few options, they choose sacrifice. While the concept of individual choice would seem to be at odds with the theme of determinism, its very paradox is central to naturalism, for behind the deterministic and atavistic depictions of the genre lies a tenacious, if embattled, belief in human dignity. In Pizer's words, the naturalist's ultimate goal is "not to demonstrate the overwhelming and oppressive reality of the material forces in our lives," but "to represent the intermingling in life of controlling force and individual worth" (28). Such is the nature of Brown's sandbagging and of Joe's decision. As Brown has said, Joe acts on a "moral imperative" that requires him to "do something bad to get rid of the evil in his world" (Ketchin 135). Superficially, his act of violence appears to be a product of his environmental conditioning, but at a deeper level it is a moral expression of his individual worth. Because Joe's environment has taught him that "evil is real, not some abstraction," he knows that "whatever good is in this world has to have teeth in it if evil is to be dealt with" (135). It is a last-ditch faith in the value of humanity, a desperate belief that the crude materials of the known world may furnish the means of achieving a personal dignity that is hard-earned but real. Brown's view of human worth represents an evolutionary stage in American naturalism, a new phase of the embattled humanism of his predecessors in the genre.

LARRY BROWN AND THE NATURALIST TRADITION

While in many respects Brown's fiction seems firmly within the traditional criteria of naturalism, it also deserves consideration for its innovations to the genre. Brown's work represents significant advances or refinements to literary naturalism in the areas of comedy and form. As many critics have noted, these are problematic aspects of naturalist literature; the former is seldom explored, and the latter is a key weakness of the typical naturalist novel. In *Dirty Work* and *Joe*, both are fully realized as never before, additional evidence of Brown's importance to the naturalist tradition in American fiction.

While comedy has never been considered a staple of naturalist fiction, it is nevertheless often present in the canonical naturalist works; the humorous eccentricities of Maria Macapa, Old Grannis, and Miss Baker in Norris's *Mc-Teague* and the childlike gunfighters of Crane's "The Bride Comes to Yellow Sky" are fitting examples. The technique central to traditional naturalist comedy is tied to the philosophical approach of introducing the sensational into the commonplace. The ordinary is often rendered in such grand, epic terms that it becomes humorous—a mundane action described in heroic language is amusing because of the incongruity between the action of a scene and the rhetoric with which it is described. This technique of "ironic deflation" (Pizer 25) allows the naturalist to introduce comedy to a fatalistic novel without sacrificing an essentially bleak view of humanity.

Brown brings a formidable comedic talent to the genre, and as such he raises the comedy of naturalism to a new level. The humorous episodes in his novels far exceed the best of the naturalist comedy that has preceded him, even while he operates within the same paradigms of humor as Norris and Crane. Witness, for example, the miniepic of Walter James's recollections of the evil Matt Monroe in *Dirty Work*. Like Crane or Norris, Brown recounts the story of a childhood bully in deftly ironic terms, describing an incident of cruelty with a detached comedic tone. Walter remembers one of Monroe's victims, Thomas Gandy, as "a little bitty kid with glasses and a crew cut" whose "glasses could blind you in the sun if he bounced the light on you just right" (29). At the time of the narrative, Thomas Gandy has become a brain surgeon, but as Walter recalls, "he didn't always occupy such a lofty position in the world. No sir. At London Hill, Mississippi, a long time ago, he was once forced to *eat* a large piece of dried cowshit and then say it was good and almost say that he'd like some more please, with sugar on top" (29–30). Like the street-urchin scene in *Maggie*, the Matt Monroe episode functions effectively as comedy, yet its thematic import uses the humor of childhood to comment on human nature through the naturalist's lens. Thus when Monroe turns his attention to Walter, the primitive survival instinct surfaces. Like the wrestling scene in *McTeague* that erupts into real violence, Walter's response betrays the atavism just beneath the surface of everyday life: "Everybody in London Hill was real surprised when I stabbed Matt Monroe one inch to the left of his heart. . . . I know Matt Monroe could hardly believe it" (48).

Much of the comedy in *Joe* avoids such violence, but it works in a similar manner to undermine an ersatz sense of human dignity. Irony is prevalent in the treatment of Wade, whose misadventures are related in an epic quotidian style. Wade finds himself, for example, "trapped in a living hell of steaming green timber" on one of the few days he manages to show up for work with Joe's crew (127). His competition with the forces of nature—rendered in the sweeping rhetoric of military conflict—is little more than a series of mishaps with ants and bees. Yet if the comedy of Wade's accidents seems to resemble the traditional burlesque of southwestern humor, the narrative approach to them does not; in these passages Brown remains firmly within the ironic tone of the naturalist narrator.

When Wade ventures into town drunk, the epic quotidian style reaches its apotheosis. Wade is turned away from a bar and perceives the event in biblical terms ("Turn back, old man, begone. There is no room at the inn" [136]). This incident evokes from him an uncharacteristic moment of philosophy: "Into each life a little rain must fall but perhaps it monsooned in his" (136). Throughout the passage the accurate language of realism struggles with metaphor, with the larger scale, as it does in most naturalist comedy. The interweaving of the commonplace and the sensational in Brown's description of police coming to arrest the "inebriated senior citizen whooping out great obscenities on the town square" is grotesque, depicting Wade as "either passed out or . . . using a marsupial's ruse," the " assault of his body odor" indeed epic: "Chickens dead three days in the sun had never smelled so rank. Ruined elephants on the plains of Africa paled in comparison. The cops gagged and tried to lift him. He lay limp as a hot noodle, quietly exuding a rich reek, a giddy putrefaction of something gone far past bad, a perfect example of nonviolent protest. They went across the square in the dead of night, dragging their prisoner, hapless victims themselves of circumstance . . . struggling along with his unwashed wasted carcass like exhausted mules" (140–41). As with the Matt Monroe passage in *Dirty Work*, this episode works well on a purely humorous level. Yet it is also subtly pervaded by the naturalist perspective, from its many comparisons between humans and animals to the deterministic depiction of the police as victims of circumstance, inconspicuously integrating such philosophy into a comic passage. Here the reader does not sense that the comic is being made to serve the theme, as in much of Norris and Crane. Rather, the comic elements of Brown's novels are integral components of a vision that does not subjugate the craft of fiction to a dogged adherence to philosophy. In this regard Brown is major innovator, a major figure in American naturalism.

Brown seems to have surmounted the central problem of naturalist fiction—that of form. He writes well-constructed, tightly plotted novels that manage to depict deterministic circumstances without reducing characters to ideological mouthpieces or philosophical pawns. Traditionally, the style of naturalism "falls woefully short of the standards deemed appropriate for art" (Mitchell vii) because naturalist works tend to "fail signally to be well-made novels" (Howard xi). Not so for Brown's fiction. He writes with the sensibility of a naturalist and with the style of his venerable forebears in southern fiction. In doing so, he occupies an interstice between two important traditions in American letters.

And who could speak better as the South's preeminent naturalist? Brown is thoroughly acquainted with the poverty and class struggles he presents in his fiction; he is one of the region's self-taught writers who speaks from outside the ideology of his Vanderbilt- and Kenyon-educated predecessors. He is an author who once wondered if learning to write "might be like learning to build houses, or lay brick," and consequently his authority on naturalistic social conditions is hard-earned and immediate—he is a southern naturalist by birthright ("Late Start" 4). Writing at the end of the twentieth century, Brown brings southward the tradition of American naturalism that began almost exactly a century before he first took up his portable typewriter. The epilogue of *Joe*, with its mix of pastoral and determinism, is a cogent expression of his perspective: "They'd stand looking out until the geese diminished and fled crying out over the heavens and away into the smoking clouds, their voices dying slowly, one last note the only sound and proof of their passing, that and the final wink of motion that swallowed them up into the sky and the earth that met it and the pine trees always green and constant against the great blue wilderness that lay forever beyond" (345). *Forever beyond.* Could a naturalist novel have a more appropriate conclusion? For despite the Faulknerian echoes of this perambulatory sentence, *Joe* demonstrates that Brown has established his own place in American fiction. While the southern soil still abides for Brown as it did for Faulkner, it is now marked irrevocably by Brown's stamp, by the presence of his naturalistic view of the South, by the perspective of an author who continues to question whether man may indeed prevail.

MEDIATION, INTERPOLATION

Bobbie Ann Mason and Kaye Gibbons

So much has been made of Bobbie Ann Mason's status as the "last southern writer" that the distinction has become almost a cliché. In many southern literature courses either *Shiloh and Other Stories* or *In Country* is listed as the last text in syllabi on twentieth-century writing, as if her work readily satisfies a curricular need for an ultimate expression of the southern literary consciousness—either as epitaph or coda to the Renascence. Likewise, Kaye Gibbons occupies an interstitial space in the evolving canon: with their fastidious attention to dialect, place, and local custom, her novels at the very least pay obeisance to the tropes of southern modernism while nonetheless advancing an interpretation of southern culture as the product of an invidious patriarchy. Yet to dismiss this curious sort of double consciousness as ambivalence is erroneous. Like the female authors who precede them, Mason and Gibbons work discretely on the margins of—and beneath—the region's dominant literary aesthetic. Like Eudora Welty, Katherine Anne Porter, and Caroline Gordon, Mason and Gibbons incorporate enough of the familiar to allow the conventional reader to classify them peremptorily as members—perhaps lesser members—of the tradition; unlike Cormac McCarthy or Barry Hannah, for example, they do not declare open assault on the canon. But to read either author as docent to Renascence concerns is to miss half their importance to southern writing. In their fusion of traditional narrative forms and unconventional perspectives (working-class and feminist ones, respectively), Mason and Gibbons proffer an artistically legitimate middle road between obsolescent convention and the social concerns of the late twentieth century.

The description of Mason and Gibbons as mediating figures is not in the least intended to be depreciative. As Patricia Yaeger has amply demonstrated in the case of Welty, southern women's writing has often been met with criticism that condescends to its frequent attention to the domestic sphere as de facto evidence that it lacks the historical sweep of great fiction.[1] Mason and Gibbons explode such assumptions—particularly in the latter's most recent novel, which depicts the crucial struggles of the Civil War (the classic historically sweeping southern topic) not on the battlefields but on the home front. Both authors use the domestic community to depict the uneasy relations between poor and female southerners and the dominant ideology of the region. In the process they follow Welty's dictum that writing should move from the particular to the general—a progression opposite the predominant schematic of traditional male southern writing. The duty of the critic, then, is to avoid reading their work solely with an eye to tradition, looking for the past in the present, the canonical in the contemporary. Rather, one should seek out the interpolated subversive elements beneath the surface of writing that may initially appear placid.

For Mason, this tension is effected by constructing novels and short stories that are obversely Agrarian. Her characters hail from regions of Kentucky amenable to Agrarian poetics, where agriculture is on the wane and tradition is in the process of giving way to mass culture. But the class perspective of Mason's characters complicates the familiar Agrarian dynamic of an elegiac rebuke to modernity. Given their limited role near the bottom levels of rural culture, progress can hardly be reckoned anathema to them; the working of the land has already rendered characters like Spence and Lila Culpepper nearly as proletarian as those industrial workers the Nashville group were fond of invoking as a warning. Mason is well aware of the irony at work here. Her people turn their aspirations to the future; contrary to Agrarian prognostications, it is the past that is debilitating to poor southerners who have no regenerative traditions to lose. Consequently, a novel such as *Spence + Lila* questions the value of agricultural heritage, while *In Country* depicts the exploration of personal history and family as a process in which popular culture plays a crucial role in self-discovery—becomes a tool, in fact, rather than an impediment in the rural southerner's quest for definition. The class issues adumbrated in Mason's first two novels become manifestly clear in *Feather Crowns*, a painstakingly accurate historical novel that uses the milieu of the Agrarians to reveal the class hegemony inherent in their conception of the lost southern Arcady.

Gibbons has perpetrated a similar intrusion of subversive themes throughout her career, beginning with the vernacular bildungsroman *Ellen Foster*. Despite appearances, Gibbons's first novel does not buttress Hemingway's famous claim about *Huckleberry Finn* and the literature that came after it. In addition to changing the protagonist's gender, Gibbons alters the trajectory of the hero(ine)'s quest from striking out for the territories to striking *in* to the heart of the community. The fiction with which she has followed her debut continues to modify the traditional depiction of the American individual by reversing the narrative pattern that Nina Baym calls "the melodrama of beset manhood" (14). In Gibbons's treatment, the gender emblematic of constricting and repressive culture is not female (as in *Huckleberry Finn* and other canonical works) but male. Arising from Gibbons's exploration of this theme is the matriarchal ideal predominant in *Charms for the Easy Life* and *On the Occasion of My Last Afternoon*, which fairly reverberate with covert frisson between their conventional narrative structures and their iconoclastic undercurrents. As Gibbons's communities of women enact dramas of beset womanhood in a patriarchal South, the lineaments of southern cultural mythology are systematically exposed. A new narrative form for southern women's writing—part Faulknerian gothic, part popular romance—results, in which the South emerges as a repressive culture from which the enlightened individual must effect an escape more subtle and mature than that of the Adamic hero heading west.

Perhaps the most distinct characteristic of Bobbie Ann Mason's writing is the sense of dissonance that pervades it. She appears to be writing a version of late Agrarian fiction in which waning farm communities are contrasted with the emptiness of an ascendant commercial culture—where the local strip-mall Kmart stands in a kind of cultural chiaroscuro with the cornfields behind it. Yet those readers inclined toward contextualizing Mason within the southern tradition cast about vainly for authorial commentary, for some controlling ironic perspective, on the cultural state of affairs in her work. Absent from her juxtapositions of urban and rural, commercial and local, is the figure of the author herself. One encounters the materials of a neo-Agrarian vision but none of the polemic that should accompany it.

This peculiar objectivity is due in part to Mason's minimalist technique and the generic conventions of realism, but its origins run deeper than the matter of literary style. Given her subject, one must question why Mason has not adopted the tenor of her predecessors, why her work does not more resemble that of authors taking up similar cultural transitions, from William Faulkner's *Go Down, Moses* to Fred Chappell's *I Am One of You Forever*. The answer lies in biography. Although Mason possesses many of the credentials of an Agrarian writer, her experience with the agricultural life precludes the nostalgia that lends poignancy to the pastoral as practiced by other southern writers. Mason never experienced acute poverty, as did Harry Crews, but she has described her childhood as one marked by "isolation" and her family's memories of privation in the not-too-distant past (Mason, "Interview," Wilhelm 27). These come to the fore on the first page of her memoir, *Clear Springs* (1999), with the declaration: "I grew up on a small family farm, the kind of place people like to idealize these days. They think the old-fashioned rustic life provided what they are now seeking—independence, stability, authenticity. And we did have those on the farm—along with mind-numbing, back-breaking labor and crippling social isolation" (ix). The farming life is for Mason an existence "in steady conflict with nature," and the author claims to have "hated the constant sense of helplessness before vast forces, the continuous threat of failure"—"especially" rural "women's part in the dependence" (95, 83). From a class and gender perspective omitted from *I'll Take My Stand*, Mason offers a newly balanced accounting of the agricultural South.

Given such a stance, Mason declines to interpret the intrusion of mass culture into the rural community solely in terms of cultural deracination. Consider her view of the southern tradition: "I'm not sure all those qualities of the Old South were all that terrific. . . . I'm not nostalgic for the past. Times change and I'm interested in writing about what's now. To me, the way the South is changing is very dynamic and full of complexity. . . . My characters have more opportunities in their lives than their parents did, and even the parents are more prosperous in their old age than they ever were before. That is what's changing about the face of the South—that more and more people are getting in on the good life" (Mason, "Interview," Wilhelm 37). Here is explanation for the lack of elegy in Mason's fading communities. These comments go to the core of the dominant ideology in southern letters and expose the class hegemony inherent in, among others, the Agrarians' South. As in the work of Crews, Allison, and Brown, Mason's people cannot afford nostalgia and, even more to the point, have no material reason to interpret changes to the South in negative terms. Hence, the progress the Agrarians decried must be reckoned as something other than the death knell of an ideal culture. That Mason's stance toward the historical South is determined by a class perspective not incorporated into the canonical literature explains why her treatment of conventional southern material fails to satisfy conventional southern readings.

In this manner Mason's fiction participates in what Fred Hobson has happily termed "an expansion of the franchise" (23). She demonstrates clearly Hobson's observation that "some of those qualities of southern writing and southern life identified and celebrated by the Southern Agrarians—who were by and large from landed or educated families, and usually both—were not representative of *all* Southerners" (22). Mason is instead from a class of southerners "whose families had little past to hold on to, little history in which ancestors played important parts, little reason to live dramatically, little high culture to protect" (22). Thus when Mason brings her perspective to the familiar topos of the traditional South giving way to modernity, the result is not an update of conventional themes in minimalist prose or adherence to the literary conventions of the region but substantial revision.

An apt starting point for assessing this contribution is with the work most agrarian in conception, *Spence + Lila* (1988). Mason's second novel takes place in and around a seventy-three-acre farm threatened by the turbulent economy of the 1980s. The era that saw corporate agriculture consuming the small farmer on a massive scale—the period leading to the Farm Aid benefits—seems a perfect choice for applying Agrarian concepts to the contemporary South. The title characters live close to the land and "have spent a lifetime growing things together" (143); Lila maintains a garden that supplies a portion of the family's food, and Spence is a small farmer almost Jeffersonian in his self-sufficiency and disdain for authority. Unlike most of Mason's characters, Spence tends to be critical of the commercialism around him. He observes that "these days, with all the new money, everyone has gone wild" and is disgusted by the consumerism he finds on a trip to town: "All the coffee makers and video games and electric ice-cream parlors in the Wal-Mart are depressing. People are buying so much junk, thinking it will make them happy. And when they can't even make a path across the floor through their possessions, they have a yard sale" (57). Reading the crime report in his local newspaper, he "can't imagine what the world is coming to" (58). Lila, too, is affected by the changes in the community: "It still hurts her to see liquor kept in a house where there are children, to see farmers out spreading manure on their fields on Sundays, to see young people fall away from the church" (139). These passages alone seem to suggest that Mason is operating within the Agrarian tradition, if not taking up its concerns consciously. Spence's criticism of the consumer detritus at Wal-Mart, for example, recalls John Crowe Ransom's prediction of "satiety and aimlessness" as the natural result of the "infinite series" of industrial consumption (xlii, 8). In their dismay over the disintegration of traditional mores, Spence and Lila resemble the archetypal agrarian figure of the rural individual as the helpless observer of his or her own progressive obsolescence, rendered antique by a culture that will not accommodate what it judges to be an outmoded way of life.

The changes wrought by progress are embodied in Spence and Lila's son, Lee, who "works at Ingersoll-Rand" and "has lines on his face and he is only thirty-two" (20). The couple's only son, he has abdicated his farm inheritance, not wanting to learn farming "because he didn't want to get up at four to milk." Yet Lee "has to work even harder at his factory job. He owes the bank almost four hundred dollars a month for a squatty little brick ranch house on a hundred-foot lot in town with no trees," a fact that "makes Spence sick" (98). Spence rejects his son's suggestion that he sell the farm to subdivision developers but concedes that Lee "makes a better living at what he's doing than he ever would on a farm these days" because "[t]here wouldn't be a living in it anymore—not in a place this size" (130, 131). Agrarian prophecy seems to have been fulfilled. Not only has rural youth been corrupted by the empty promises of industrial propaganda, progress has so altered the economic landscape that the small farm is no longer tenable. Accordingly, a sense of loss, of transience, pervades Spence's perspective on his land and the working of it by the novel's conclusion. As he surveys the property, his thoughts cohere around the notion of an organicism lost to people such as Lee: "From the rise, he looks out over his place. This is it. This is all there is in the world—it contains everything there is to know or possess, yet everywhere people are knocking their brains out trying to find something different, something better. His kids all scattered, looking for it. Everyone always wants a way out of something like this, but what he has here is the main thing there is—just the way things grow and die, the way the sun comes up and goes down every day. These are the facts of life. They are so simple they are almost impossible to grasp" (132). A vision of the family farm as a self-contained universe, a place from which abstraction is banished and things reveal themselves in their essence: this is something close to the Agrarian idyll. Spence approximates the Nashville group's ideal agricultural individual. An exemplar of a human being in close contact with the soil, he is connected with "the main thing there is"—the great cycle of life and death— and his knowledge is made the more valuable by the awareness that the younger generation has forsaken it.

Such is the framework of an Agrarian reading of the novel, but to end on this note, however poignant, is too facile. Although we may see Agrarian philosophy in the figure of Spence Culpepper as the small farmer in extremis, the novel resists any effort to extrapolate a larger Arcadian mythology from its pages. Mason is too particular an observer, too much the careful realist, to allow the contours of myth to shape her work. The image of Spence as a latter-day Agrarian—something on the order of Wendell Berry's Old Jack, to cite a roughly contemporaneous example—begins to unravel as his own accommodation of popular culture is revealed. Spence "hates hillbilly music," says "[f]iddles ought to be outlawed" (98, 101), and identifies completely with rock and roll music, which is his primary cultural currency. Rock music "fits the urgency of his life," he thinks, and satisfies his distinctly rural need for "organiz[ing] all the noises of public places into something he can tolerate" (46). In the Agrarian lexicon, this self-recognition within the idiom of commercial music puts him in undignified company—consigned to the level of the "shop-girls" and assembly-line workers reading their comic strips and listening to jazz records in Donald Davidson's "A Mirror for Artists" (Twelve Southerners 35). Lest one read Spence's affinity for rock music as a capitulation to Leviathan, however, in *Spence + Lila* Mason allows her character to express the truly regional sentiment that the "real music is always hidden somewhere, off in the country, back in his head, in his memory" (46). Yet this "real music" is not to be found on the farm or even among the white community. Instead, it can be found "at little places out in the country that people called 'nigger juke joints,' " where rock and roll made its first appearance in the community, and Spence hears "occasional echoes of that raunchy old music he always loved in some of the rock songs on the radio" (46). Thus although Spence expresses contempt for the folk music of his region, what he reveres is in some attenuated sense local, if not indigenous. Nonetheless, his Agrarian profile is compromised in the process.

Mason further problematizes conventional readings in her portrayal of the rural past. The reader tempted to interpret her protagonist as an individual relinquishing the agricultural heritage by degrees need look no farther back than the generation prior to Spence's for evidence that the rural life has its own deleterious elements. During Spence's tour of the Pacific in World War II, Lila lived with Rosie and Amp Culpepper in an unheated and drafty room under conditions severe enough to approximate serfdom. During a bitter winter her first child caught pneumonia and with no money for a doctor had to be treated with "baked onions in ashes" (26). In Agrarian parlance such hardships are ignored or else deemed either ancillary to the cause or salutary in stoic fashion, their edges softened by myth. But Mason presents such tribulations as less than mythic, their cost too steep for them to be judged as beneficial lessons of life on the land. What was largely metaphoric for the Agrarians is all too real here, and these conditions produce a dehumanizing environment quite at odds with any pastoral notions. Amp at one point beats Lila's daughter for disobedience, whipping the child "precisely and fiercely" with a razor strop while remaining detached from her screams (141). The scene recalls Crews's assertion that the lower levels of agricultural work make a rural individual brutal to animals and himself, and, like Crews's people, the elder Culpeppers draw little that is redemptive or regenerative from their environment. Lila finds them to be "so quiet" as to be inarticulate, "their faces set like concrete as they lost themselves in their chores" (25). They embody the anti-abstraction the Agrarians sought, but one must ask at what price, given that the yeoman becomes an automaton, interchangeable with the industrial prole. Once again, the limited class perspective of the Agrarians becomes evident. One finds in Amp and Rosie an agrarian existence unsullied and unadulterated by industrialism, yet the rural life in its pristine state is far from enriching or fulfilling.

From this vantage point, a progression toward the industrial is appealing—not as the product of deceptive industrial propaganda or mere laziness but as a result of immediate experience with the portions of rural life overlooked by Agrarianism. What the Nashville group might cast as a Faustian bargain with progress means, for Spence and Lila, a house with running water and indoor plumbing or hamburgers and Cokes at "Fred and Sue's Drive-in"—the "most delicious meal they ever had" because Rosie "was stingy with meat and cooked the same plain grub day in and day out" (99–100). Later, television fills a similar need, bringing with it "an unexpected harmony [that] filled the house" while providing a welcome alternative to having "no entertainment to work by" (83). It becomes evident that the cultural debasement the Agrarians ascribed to mass culture simply does not obtain for people like Spence and Lila. Despite their agricultural backgrounds, they have no inherent or traditional culture as a legacy of the soil, a fact underscored by the description of Rosie's bland cooking and the consolation of television as contrasted with the impassive silence by which Spence's parents worked. Proceeding out from the cultural vacuum of their origins, Spence and Lila cannot view popular entertainments through the same lens as persons higher on the social scale; what seems vapid or insipid from upper-class or educated perspectives is for them an improvement. Spence, for example, thinks "watching TV is an education" because through programs like *National Geographic* he "gets to see places he'd never go to" (157). His grandchildren "are smart because of all they are exposed to on TV. Sometimes he is flabbergasted by how much they know" (157). Mason makes such statements without irony because they are true for characters lacking a higher cultural register. The changes wrought on them by mass culture cannot be evaluated by the conventional means of lament, of folkways eroded by empty commercialism.

In this manner *Spence + Lila* achieves its dissonance. Counterbalancing the scene of Spence wistfully surveying the land that will pass away with him is the image of the same small farmer studying "unusual animals from all over the world" on *National Geographic*, his husbandman's eyes agleam with the exotic wildlife transmitted through the electric glow of the television (157). The strange hybrid of the past in the postmodern present seems to beg for diatribe on the part of the author, but none is forthcoming. The ambivalence is jarring; however, for Mason and the common southerners of her novel it is the only appropriate response. If the past cannot be romanticized, neither can the present be derided. "Times are better now," Lila tells her children. "You don't know how good you've got it" (87). Southern literature has seldom ascribed much value to the present, and in reversing the familiar dynamic Mason's characters expose the constituent fallacies of the mythic southern past. The import of this new perspective is best expressed by one of Spence and Lila's children, who observes that "things aren't the way they used to be—if they ever *were*" (108).

*I*n *Country* (1985) has been widely read as an important contemporary example of the conventional southern dialectic between the past and the present. In the best of these readings, Robert H. Brinkmeyer argues that "it is just possible that Mason is charting a new direction in Southern fiction, a rebirth of sorts adapting patterns from the past to enrich and comprehend the disorder of contemporary experience" by modifying that "crucial paradigm of the Southern literary Renascence—that to understand the present, including oneself, one explores the past" (21, 31). Owen Gilman has stressed the parallels between the Vietnam War and the Civil War in the novel, suggesting that Samantha Hughes's quest for her father is eminently southern not only as an example of the familiar search for history but also in the legacy of defeat that links the Vietnam War with southern history. From a more feminist perspective, Linda Tate describes the novel in terms of Alice Walker's idea of "prior unity," arguing that Mason fuses "heritage" with the "new space" that Sam makes for herself in the changing community to create a new kind of regionalism (134–35).

Despite their thorough assessments of the historical dialectic in the novel, these readings fail to satisfy completely because they seek to incorporate Mason's work into a tradition to which it has limited connections. As *Spence + Lila* illustrates, in Mason's view the past was never as simple as the Renascence paradigm requires it to be. One encounters difficulties with the terminology of a thesis such as Brinkmeyer's, which implicitly ascribes "disorder" almost exclusively to the present and construes the past as redemptive, "unvexed by the problems of modernity" (22). Gilman and Tate operate on similar assumptions about the past, participating (consciously or not) in the dominant trope of a superior and lost southern existence. But it seems highly unlikely that Mason intended her exploration of history to be appropriated by this tradition. Although history is undoubtedly a central component of the novel, alongside the past-present motif is a subtle and incisive critique of the small southern community that makes *In Country* not so much an expression of literary convention as it first appears.

The initial obstacle to a strictly historical reading of the novel lies in the rural community itself. Hopewell, Kentucky, is hardly possessed of a true historical sense. Although as one character puts it, "everyone's looking backward" to "old-timey days," the accoutrements of the past are reduced to the level of kitsch—flea market spice racks and Confederate memorabilia, farming implements as living-room decor (Mason, *In Country* 79). The Lost Cause survives in a few slight references, among them a man at the shopping mall who "tries to pick Sam up" and wears "a Confederate-flag T-shirt that said I'M A REBEL AND DAMN PROUD OF IT" (201). The fabled southern connection to place receives sardonic reduction in the image of Pete Simms's tattoo, a "map of the Jackson Purchase region of western Kentucky" that the veteran had engraved on his chest during his tour of Vietnam (47). If the regenerative past is not entirely lost, it is at the very least surviving in forms so radically attenuated as to be absurd. The contemporary southerners of Hopewell are vaguely aware that the past is supposed to be important, but like Leroy Moffitt in "Shiloh," they are "leaving out the insides of history."

A traditional reading would quickly point out that such debasements of culture are the product of a corrupted community, that the commodification of rural culture here results from a process of estrangement from vital tradition much like that portrayed by Alice Walker in "Everyday Use." But there seems never to have been any mythic sense of life in Hopewell, any knowledge of the "insides of history"; the a priori foundation of the Renascence paradigm is absent. Dwayne's letters home from Vietnam, for example, thwart Sam's efforts to impose a mythic schema upon them. Dwayne was not, in Allen Tate's sense, consumed by "the vision" of a greater purpose that would link him to the larger patterns of history by which a life may be judged to have consequence. Sam's search for an articulation of mission in her father's written record is clouded by the letters' naïveté and provincialism. Instead of patriotic eloquence she finds the rather prosaic concerns of a young man caught up in historical events beyond his ability to comprehend—a man "hurried beyond decision" in a manner distinctly at odds with the soldiers of Tate's "Ode to the Confederate Dead." Sam is culturally conditioned to seek some mythic stature for her father, but she fails to find it and cannot counter her mother's claim that the war was fought by "country boys" who "didn't know their ass from their elbow" (235–36). The past loses its purported value as an ordering framework for the present; its legacy threatens to be disillusionment instead of fulfillment. Mason is pragmatic in this regard, not nihilistic. Sam hails from a southern background far different from the one presumed by the Renascence paradigm. Consequently, her transaction with the past must be effected through personal and not cultural means.

This point is reinforced by Mason's depictions of what might be termed the old order of the novel. As in *Spence + Lila*, the older generation is remarkable mainly in the way that it has been shaped by hard work and isolation, not for its historical and cultural sense. What Renascence writers characterized as bucolic self-sufficiency, Mason presents as diminishment and limitation. The past, then, is of questionable value, problematic in the search for ideal antecedents in the novel. Witness, for example, the reaction of Sam's paternal grandmother to the Howard Johnson's motel room in Maryland. The room is noteworthy because its "air conditioner doesn't drip water on the curtains" and for its "luxurious shag rug" and "very clean" bathroom with a commode that "doesn't overflow" (19). The room "is large and beautiful, with sliding glass doors that open onto the parking lot. It has dark, striped drapes and two pictures of street life in Paris on the wall above each bed. Even the plumbing is fancy. The commode is beige, and it has a strip of paper across it that makes a satisfying pop when Sam breaks it. 'What's that for?' Mamaw asks, and Sam explains. Mamaw hasn't traveled much" (11). The scene approaches the comic level of similar passages in Crews's *Body*, particularly in the tone that, coming close to mocking the characters' perspective, refuses to ignore their parochialism or present it in terms favorable to the Agrarian dichotomy of country and city. If, as Gilman argues, Mamaw is "crucial" to Mason's expression of the "southernness of the characters," then Mason's views of the region can hardly be considered entirely favorable (50). Yet to structure a reading on the Renascence dialectic necessitates ignoring the critical realism present here. Mamaw's anxiety over sleeping in the same room with Emmett ("What will they think back home?" [Mason, *In Country* 10]) is not a timorous expression of provincialism but rather evidence of her origins in "a culture in which social relationships matter and are closely monitored" (Gilman 50). The solace of good forms is imposed in spite of Mason's understated critique of closely monitored social relationships.

Mason's criticism, however, is outside the lexicon of Gilman's argument. One need only look at the women in the novel to see abundant signs of frustration and repressed energies throughout the southern community: Irene's failed attempt to rebel with Bob and his hippie friends ("There was so much pressure in town for them to get out. They just weren't accepted" [Mason, *In Country* 233]); Anita's first husband, who wanted her "to be a picture," to "just be beautiful" (63); Dawn entrapped by her pregnancy. These limited roles for southern women (including tradition-minded individuals like Mamaw) are the negative corollary of the fixed social relations prized by readings that link *In Country* to Renascence fiction.[2] By neglecting to consider them, traditional readings of *In Country* ultimately falter. The ideal former community that critics are inclined to read into the novel is the kind that Cleanth Brooks saw throughout Faulkner in spite of anomalies like Joe Christmas and Emily Grierson and that other Renascence critics established as representative of the southern experience. But in Mason this critical template obscures the work it would illuminate. It partakes of the dominant ideology that Mason resists and thus fails to apprise the subversive currents beneath the surface—evidenced by Gilman's inability to see that the social network Mamaw represents is less than beneficial. This established conception of southern community reinforces patriarchal assumptions by ignoring, overlooking, or misinterpreting the subtle dissent Mason offers. To acknowledge these countercurrents would complicate Mason's use of history as metaphor and raise problematic issues in situating her within the canon.

The case of one of Mason's apparent influences, Carson McCullers, is illustrative. Although Mason is not so critical of the South as is her predecessor, several motifs in *In Country* are nonetheless reminiscent of McCullers's work. Like McCullers, Mason offers an adolescent protagonist whose nickname obscures rigid gender boundaries (as do "Frankie" Adams and "Mick" Kelly) and who occupies a marginal space in the community. As one of "the baddest girls in Hopewell" (40), Sam thinks of her hometown in much the same terms that McCullers's characters view the various fictive representations of Columbus, Georgia. Hopewell is not an organic and fostering community but a nonplace; Sam longs to be somewhere more cosmopolitan, to be anywhere else. It is a "shitty town," and Sam "would like to move somewhere far away," to "live anywhere but Hopewell" (187, 7). Hopewell, albeit without the grotesque people found in McCullers's work, is not dramatically different from the setting of *The Heart Is a Lonely Hunter*. What Sam thinks of as a cultural backwater, its boutiques and nearby mall, like the New York Café of McCullers's novel, achieve only a faint approximation of the sophisticated urbanity she seeks. Louis Rubin's comments on *The Heart Is a Lonely Hunter* obtain for Mason's novel: "there is little doing" in the local community, and "none of the people involved in the story are either very contented or very hopeful" in a setting that tends to leave them "barren and joyless" (*Gallery* 135). Rubin also observes that the "viewpoint" of McCullers "was not exactly that of the Nashville Agrarians, or even of William Faulkner or Eudora Welty" (136). Finally, McCullers must be dismissed from the pantheon of southern modernists because her fiction is *from* the South but not *of* it, not written "out of its history, its common myths, its public value and the failure to cherish them" (150).

I compare Mason to McCullers not to establish a reductive context for Mason but to point out that her perspective on community, like McCullers's, is hardly within the southern consensus. But where Rubin addresses subversive themes as the basis of exclusion, more recent critics have done the opposite, overlooking Mason's dissent in order to include her. The latter process seems more equable, but it is effected at the expense of Mason's contribution to an evolving, realistic conception of the region: to incorporate her work into the familiar critical schema involves negating her changes to that paradigm. The antecedents of the novel are to be found in traditional works like Tate's "Ode to the Confederate Dead," not in fiction like McCullers's. Mason's stature becomes not so much innovative as custodial. Rather than a revisionist approach to history, *In Country* is deemed a fresh reworking of established technique, and its concerns—despite the depictions of women throughout—are consequently misread as patriarchal. The influence of McCullers is neglected because it has no place in a paradigm that hinges on the South as a regenerative entity. In fact, it threatens it by undermining the foundations of the syllogism that casts the southern past as a better alternative. McCullers depicted conditions similar to Mason's half a century earlier in a South only beginning to be touched by pervasive technology and commercial homogenization. If one acknowledges the echoes of McCullers, then, Sam's disdain for home is not necessarily a product of MTV; postmodernity/technology/progress/mass culture cannot be blamed for the degradation of the community if it was degraded before. Mason is a realist of the postmodern era who places her characters in Kmarts and shopping malls with fastidious detail, but the parallels to McCullers indicate that she does not attribute their dissatisfaction solely to contemporary changes in southern culture. Reading the novel this way, however—as a challenge to the South's traditional topoi of history, common myths, and public values—is to admit of too much revision, too much modification, to the practices of convention.

This muting process has been particularly effective at sanitizing Mason's iconoclasm in the process of explicating her adaptation of Renascence technique. The dominance of the orthodox interpretive strategy is so extensive as to render even Linda Tate's feminist reading of the novel ironically patriarchal. Although Tate recognizes that "Sam discovers that no woman she knows is successful in balancing a sense of cultural heritage with forward-thinking behavior," her reading adheres to conventional critical approaches and fails to question the limitations of that community for its women (142). As Tate acknowledges, remaining in Hopewell means for Sam "taking care of Emmett, dating Lonnie, working at the Burger Boy and going to the nearby state college" (147)—choices that are not really choices at all but an unexamined adherence to conventional expectations much like what her friend Dawn accepts. Nonetheless, Sam must delve beneath "the surface layer of popular culture that threatens to engulf the South" in order to grapple with the "traditional southern questions—questions about past, region, home and family" (134). Tate's reading unravels at this point, contradicting her general definition of southern women's narrative as "subversive in that it seeks to disrupt the prevailing paradigm: it poses a challenge to the accepted story (the master narrative) and seeks to revise and replace that text with the alternative story the master discourse seeks to repress" (177). Her interpretation of *In Country* is anything but subversive: in opposing the popular culture of the novel against "traditional southern questions," Tate negates the very challenges to consensus she would explicate. Here we are back to the cemetery gate of "Ode to the Confederate Dead," back to the tropes of southern modernism, and back to questions posed in a manner that can only be answered in patriarchal terms. McCullers was excluded from the southern consensus; Mason is rendered innocuous enough for admittance. The closed cycle of southern modernism is maintained.

There is an embedded irony about this process in *In Country* itself. From the novel's epigraph to its concluding pages, Bruce Springsteen and his music function as a leitmotif for Sam's quest. Springsteen is an iconic emblem of Sam's concerns—of sexuality, working-class angst, and the desire to escape a quotidian existence; his people are those Sam knows and with whom she interacts every day. In the novel, his ubiquitous presence on radios and televisions is not a shallow popular culture reference but a central component of Sam's milieu, as her discussion with Dawn demonstrates:

"I wish I could buy that new Springsteen album," Sam said. "But I have to save all my money for a car."

"I hear that on the radio all the time at Burger Boy."

"Did you know the title song's about a vet?"

"Yeah. In the song, his brother gets killed over there, and then the guy gets in a lot of trouble when he gets back home. He can't get a job, and he ends up in jail. It's a great song."

"I like the one about the car wash—where it rains all the time and he lost his job and his girlfriend. That's the saddest song. That song really scares me." Dawn shuddered and rattled the ice in her glass. (42)

The scene is a powerful evocation of the subversive discourse of rock and roll. The import of these songs is perfectly evident to Sam and Dawn, from the disillusioned subtext of "Born in the U.S.A." to the bleakness of "Downbound Train" that is so familiar to their experience. The young women are able critics of Springsteen's music, fully conversant with the dissident strains of the blue-collar idiom illegible in 1984 to, among others, Ronald Reagan and George Will—both of whom misinterpreted "Born in the U.S.A." as a jingoist or patriotic anthem. Reagan and Will could not see past the American flag on the cover of Springsteen's album—could not, in fact, interpret Springsteen's engagement with American history except in terms that would incorporate him into the dominant cultural narrative. The analogy to Mason is evident. For southern criticism to subsume Mason and her people under the rubric of tradition entails a similar negation of dialogue and message, a similar loss of inquiry into established cultural forms, and—possibly—the loss of what may be Mason's particular genius.

That one can read a popular figure like Bruce Springsteen as a valuable component of *In Country's* narrative indicates the innovation of Mason's realist perspective in southern letters. As part of her expansive vision of the South, the novel contrasts markedly with common regional views of mass culture by including what has traditionally been left out of southern fiction—by dispassionately observing the changing South without attempting to preserve it as a discrete and mythic region. Whereas Mason's fellow Kentuckian Wendell Berry, for example, argues in the preface to *Sex, Economy, Freedom and Community* that the "duty" of the writer is to resist consumer culture at every turn, Mason takes no such stand (xi). Her realist sense is too committed to verisimilitude to admit the partisan portrayals of tradition.

This ethic is borne out thoroughly in *Feather Crowns* (1993), which dismantles the Agrarian program through the unassuming material of quotidian detail. On one level the novel resembles an Agrarian saga or one of Berry's novels. A reading in this vein can be delineated quickly enough: the novel begins in the early twentieth century on a self-sufficient Kentucky farm that grows more vulnerable to the vicissitudes of a cash-crop economy as its dependence on tobacco increases. With the birth of Christie Wheeler's quintuplets, celebrity and mass culture intrude, and the enticements of progress are heeded by the family patriarch, Wad Wheeler. The babies die shortly after their birth, but through Wad's machinations Christie and her husband take their embalmed bodies on a tour of the South in a combination of Chautauqua and sideshow exhibit. With financial gain comes something close to spiritual death, and the organic culture of the novel's opening—the extended family on the farm—is fragmented.

This is an intentionally reductive summary, yet its very simplicity reflects the consequences of an orthodox reading that would render Mason's complex work familiar. Like *Spence + Lila, Feather Crowns* celebrates portions of rural life, but in a subtle yet important distinction from Agrarian practice, it declines to celebrate it entirely. By taking up the *locus classicus* of Agrarian philosophy—the preindustrial family farm—as its subject, the novel completes Mason's engagement with southern literary tradition. The result is an agrarian novel without myth, rendered in a realistic manner at odds with historical fictions like Stark Young's *So Red the Rose* and Allen Tate's *The Fathers*. Alongside play-parties and fiddle music such as Andrew Lytle described in *I'll Take My Stand* is material less folkloric, from a fan bearing the advertising image of Jesus standing before a tobacco warehouse to trading cards imprinted with the trademark logos of pharmaceutical products. Mason takes pains to depict the racism and material hardships of the culture and has her protagonist conclude on a note resembling Lila's in the earlier novel: "You wanted to know how it was back then, but it wouldn't thrill your heart to know"—"don't ever think we lived in the good old days" (*Feather Crowns* 449, 452). Popular culture, racism, and hard times are present even in the halcyon era of the Agrarian South, and these elements render the characters of Mason's historical novel not very different in their concerns and limited perspectives than the people of her contemporary settings. The novel demonstrates not only the deficiencies of the Agrarians' mythic past but also the shortcomings of a cultural perspective that would locate anomie and disaffection solely within modernity. If Mason's work may in some sense be viewed as a dialogue with Agrarianism, her response here seems to be *Et in Arcadia ego*.

Mason's contribution to southern literature is one of a historical consciousness imbued with an uncommon instinct for realism, and the result is a revisiting of the past without the apologia that has so often accompanied it. Without adopting the mythoclasm of McCarthy or Hannah, Mason manages to achieve similar effects. Mason focuses on those elements problematic to the program of such mythic novels as those the Agrarians wrote, rendering in detail what the Agrarians embellished and deleted concerning southern agriculture. Following Welty's suggestion to move from the particular to the general, her critical realism exposes the mythical contours of the literary past, correcting the Agrarians' tendency to work in an opposite pattern—undermining the grand abstraction of Tate's and Young's fiction by observing a great number of troubling social details overlooked by the sweep of narratives intent on a grander scope.

It is a subtle iconoclasm but an incisive one. As part of the general movement in contemporary southern literature toward realism, it works against the creative process common to Renascence fiction and imperils the consensus on which southern literature has long rested. The threat of verisimilitude such as Mason's is clear throughout Donald Davidson's essay on the region's literary output, "Why the Modern South Has a Great Literature." Like many of the other writers considered here, Mason illustrates that times have changed dramatically since Davidson could claim that "the literature of social protest, represented in the North by such men as Theodore Dreiser, Sinclair Lewis, John Dos Passos, is so uncommon among the distinguished Southern writers of our day as to be hardly worth comment" (*Still Rebels* 169). Mason is not driven by social protest, but neither does she entirely fit the corollary of Davidson's dismissal of social realism. Davidson continues, "At its substantial best—the new literature of the South is not a literature of protest but a literature of *acceptance* which renders its material as *objectively* and seriously as any great literature has ever done" (169; emphasis added). Outside the mythic demesne of Davidson and his Agrarian brethren, simultaneous objectivity and acceptance prove troublesome.

Mason's relation to the southern canon (and the Nashville group in particular) might best be resolved by citing one more piece of Agrarian writing: Allen Tate's "Remarks on the Southern Religion" and its image of the "half-horse." If a slight twisting of Tate's metaphor may be allowed, it seems reasonable to suggest that the Agrarians themselves fell victim to "the enemy, abstraction," and in doing so rendered their program susceptible to theoretical shortcomings closely analogous to Tate's half-horse (Twelve Southerners 167). As Tate wrote in 1931: "Nothing infallibly works, and the new half-religionists are simply worshipping a principle, and with true half-religious fanaticism they ignore what they do not want to see—which is the breakdown of the principle in numerous instances of practice. It is a bad religion, for that very reason; it can predict only success" (158). The Agrarians fell victim to abstraction; Mason has done the opposite. She does indeed praise those portions of rural life that are genuinely redemptive—but she does this alongside her chronicle of the "breakdowns" that invariably accompany it. Her lack of adherence to a programmatic Agrarian platform that can predict only success places her within the "whole-horse" perspective that, quoting Tate again, "takes account of the failures" and consequently is "realistic" (159). The result is a vision of the rural South that is in Tate's terminology "mature" and "not likely to suffer from disillusion and collapse" (159). In focusing on the rural and in delving into the southern past, Mason covers some familiar terrain, but she does so while correcting the "short memory of failure" that has marked that well-traveled landscape (159).

MODIFYING THE MALE PARADIGM: KAYE GIBBONS

Mason's mature work succeeds in mediating between convention and iconoclasm, but such was not always the case for her dialogue with literary tradition.

As she has revealed in several interviews, her vision was thwarted initially by imitation. Most notable among her unpublished apprentice work is a novel "about a twelve-year-old girl, a sort of female Huck Finn" (Mason, "Interview," Lyons and Oliver 454). As Mason describes it, the novel sought to continue the classic American motif of the Adamic quest with a protagonist who rejects society and leaves it, as have many of "our heroes in American literature . . . from Huckleberry Finn up through this century" (Mason, "Interview," Hill 90). Her attraction to the quest—to the "experience of the male," what "females are not allowed to know about"—proved short-lived, however, because Mason found the theme bound up with class considerations beyond her demesne (Mason, "Interview," Wilhelm 30). The Adamic figure can disengage from society because he is "privileged," but the individuals of Mason's experience lacked such mobility; she began to see the motif of escape in its twentieth-century figurations as negatively shaped by "class snobbery" and "elitism." As a result, she turned to the lower classes and to subjects possessing "a whole different frame of reference" (Mason, "Interview," Hill 91). She began "writing about characters who had never been in the center, who had never had the advantage of being able to criticize society enough to leave it" (Mason, "Interview," Lyons and Oliver 454), deciding "not to write about a Huck Finn figure but to write about . . . the average guy—the guy who's struggling to make a living" (Mason, "Interview," Hill 91).

Kaye Gibbons's novice engagement with Twain's archetypal character proved more fruitful. With her first novel, *Ellen Foster* (1987), Gibbons revisited the Adamic protagonist and made the character viable for a new century and a new cultural context, creating in Fred Hobson's words "*Huckleberry Finn* a century later nearly to the year, updated and with a sex change and, in fact, not at all derivative as this description would suggest" (77). Indeed, the parallels between *Ellen Foster* and Twain's bildungsroman are extensive. Like Huck, Ellen is a lower-class adolescent orphaned by a father who "drank his own self to death" and who can claim "for a fact that I am better off now than when he was alive" (*Ellen Foster* 1). Her best friend, Starletta, is, like Jim, an African American who provides an example for Ellen of living outside the mainstream of white culture. And Ellen's gift for plain metaphor rivals Huck's: "You can never be sure about how somebody else thinks about you except if they beat it into your head"; "you look at it that way upside down and the world will start to make some good sense" (84, 87). When Ellen describes her imposing grandmother as a woman "who could make my bones shake and I would think of ghost houses and skeletons rattling all in the closets," the echoes of literary inheritance seem undeniable and definitive (68).

Gibbons also continues Twain's iconoclastic portrait of southern society by positioning Ellen on the margins of black and white culture, avoiding the elitist perspective that thwarted Mason. After the death of her father, her grandmother sends her to work in the cotton fields with the African American workers, where the older woman expects Ellen to "learn a thing or two" about her social position (65). Over a summer of work Ellen serves an apprenticeship outside both the "trash" perspective of her father and the upper-class one of her grandmother, finding sanctuary among the African American community after a short lifetime of exclusion and abuse from both extremes of white culture. By July the field work makes Ellen "like a boy" in physical stamina; it also blurs the racial demarcations by which all the whites of her acquaintance, regardless of social standing, measure themselves: "I thought while I chopped from one field to the next how I could pass for colored now. Somebody riding by here in a car could not see my face and know I was white. But that is OK now I thought to myself of how it did not make much of a difference now" (66). Even more than her fictional predecessor, Ellen discards the ideology of her racialized culture, choosing to abandon the categories on which the South's social hierarchy rests. Eventually she speculates that she "was cut out to be colored" but "got bleached and sent to the wrong bunch of folks," a racial epiphany that allows her to resolve her long-conflicted attitude toward Starletta (85). Her quest does not involve the solitude of a river trek, but her peregrinations through a small North Carolina town nonetheless culminate in a view of society from the outside, free of the constricting ideology that Huck Finn sought to escape.

In her fundamental alterations to the motif, Gibbons succeeds in appropriating Twain's legacy in a manner that eluded Mason—and it is here that one begins to see *Ellen Foster* as the prototype of Gibbons's more powerful later work. Mason appears to have left the crucial element of race out of her failed Adamic novel, but her comments also indicate that she did not see the full implications of the female perspective in her story of "a female Huck Finn." Gibbons derives power from the motif by manipulating its traditional masculine elements, moving beyond a simple gender reversal into a complex alteration to the myths of manhood. It is fitting that Gibbons began her career-long challenge to these myths by using *Huckleberry Finn* as a template. As Baym has argued, nineteenth-century novels (*Huckleberry Finn* foremost among them) played a signal role in shaping the protean canon of American literature—and in defining the participation of women in the mythic American character. In the works of male authors of the American Renaissance (and in the minds of many critics who canonized them), women serve as emblems of the society that the truly individualized American male must escape. Women pose a "threat" to the mythic hero; their connection to the domestic sphere links them irredeemably to the superstructure of society, to the forces of conformity and quotidian existence in which the protagonist of heroic stature has no room to breathe. Consequently, Baym concludes that "the encroaching, constricting, destroying society is represented with particular urgency in the figure of one or more women," and "the role of entrapper and impediment in the melodrama of beset manhood is reserved for women" (12, 14). Thus the appeal of the wilderness in classic American fiction: it is a wild, liberating space untainted by the paragon of societal repression, woman.

Gibbons relinquishes the wilderness in order to orient her critique closer to home, and as her women characters repeatedly demonstrate, it is the men there who incarnate the debilitating aspects of society. Consider first the humorous example of the school counselor who subjects Ellen to weekly therapy sessions. In a scene Twain would appreciate, the counselor queries his unwilling analysand about her "identity problems" and why she is not "a social being" (*Ellen Foster* 87). Although Ellen would "rather be digging a ditch" than be in therapy, she plays along with the sessions because "he will not let go of a word but he has to bend and pull and stretch what I said into something he can see on paper and see how it has changed like a miracle into exactly what he wanted me to say" (86). Like the comic scenes between Huck and the Widow Douglas and Miss Watson, the episode derives its humor from the insipid nature of the character who represents the greater society; the protagonist, aloof and cognizant, cannily complies with the empty ritual. The priggish qualities traditionally associated with the feminine are patently assigned to a male figure here; fatuous authority falls under the purview of the professional man rather than under a domineering mother figure. It is the counselor, with his psychological apparatus and the imprimatur of the school system to validate it, who threatens the heroine's individuality by reducing her experience to a series of "identity problems" (what Ellen dismisses as "chickenshit" [89]) that can be neatly resolved with the blueprint of psychoanalysis. The historical updating of Twain's dynamic is comic in its own right, but it also uses the post-Freudian context of the late twentieth century to touch on profound implications of exactly which gender impedes the other in the search for autonomy.

This shift receives more somber consideration in Ellen's relationship with her father. As Huck does with Pap, Ellen fears the violence imminent in her alcoholic father when he is drunk, and the scenes of his binges in her home recall those in the wilderness cabin to which Pap abducts Huck. Here, however, the gender reversal facilitates a scathing reappraisal of the hero's trials. Ellen has to contend not only with the delirium tremens but also with sexual abuse, not only with a father gripped by terrifying delusions but with one who compares her breasts to her "mama's little ninnies" as he gropes her (43). The survival logic of Huck attains a new level of poignancy in Ellen's observations that "if you push him down you have some time to run before he can get his ugly self up," and "he might grab and swat but that is all he can do if you are quick" (43). Such abuse makes the philosophical concerns of the mythic saga of beset manhood seem trivial. Indeed, it renders the gender conflicts of the classic American hero's quest prosaic: the ability to escape them by lighting out for the territories comes to seem an adolescent resolution—escapist fantasy—when contrasted with the plight of a young woman who cannot effect such a simple migration. The exemplar of "encroaching, constricting, destroying society" embodies those qualities in a sense that is both metaphorical and all too literal, adding to the traditional notion of the restrictive female domestic sphere the image of a leering, incestuous embrace. Given such depictions of males in the novel, it is sensible that the Adamic protagonist of Gibbons's novel seeks to connect with the female sphere, not to escape it. The absence of the mother (an emancipatory condition for Huck) is for Ellen the absence of protection from men such as her father and an obstacle to be overcome. Her adopted surname—which the school counselor sees as a component of her identity problems—underscores Ellen's quest for, not away from, the maternal. The "entrapper and impediment" in the drama of beset womanhood in *Ellen Foster* is male; accordingly, her quest is completed not in the wilderness but in the foster home of her "new mama." Ellen, who "could have been a hobo," declares she will never move from the house full of children in which nobody "drinks or smokes" and the only male presence is a baby, Roger (120, 119).

If such a reading seems tenuous, at least part of its tentativeness stems from the fact that Gibbons's first novel stops short of fully articulating a mythoclastic vision of male southern culture. The novel is, as Hobson describes it, "another triumph of vernacular voice and tone," but it is precisely these areas of triumph that limit Gibbons's debut (77). In the genre of local color *Ellen Foster* is indeed a success, but the scope of regional realism circumscribes the critique that characterizes the author's later work. Her first novel's status as another triumph of southern fiction—a work amenable to tradition—competes with its innovative qualities. Marc K. Stengel's provocative criticism of Algonquin Books (the publisher of Gibbons's first three novels) applies to *Ellen Foster* on this point. Taking Algonquin's 1989 edition of *New Stories from the South* as his subject, Stengel complains that "what passes for Southern literature today . . . is *too much* expected" (8). In its "total effect," Stengel argues, "it's as if contemporary Southern fiction were just another genre literature like bodice-ripper romances and whodunnit detective serials" plagued by "navel-gazing solipsism" (9, 10). Gibbons's first novel fails to break entirely free from the contemporary local-color style practiced by many of Algonquin's authors, falling into a familiar cadence so prevalent in contemporary southern writing that Stengel can term it a "genre." Such stylistic solidarity is appropriate to Linda Tate's description of the press as a "catalyst" in "the second Southern Renaissance" (194). The conflicting aims of *Ellen Foster* make it susceptible—despite its iconoclastic threads—to the long reach of tradition and consensus.

By the time she published *Charms for the Easy Life* with Putnam in 1993, Gibbons seemed aware of her growing abilities as a novelist, ready to move beyond the regionalism of *A Virtuous Woman* (1989) and *A Cure for Dreams* (1991) into more ambitious work seeking a higher position for itself in the context of southern literature. Gibbons's confidence is evident in the opening pages of her fourth novel. In an uproarious satire she declares her willingness to trespass in the sanctum sanctorum of southern writing:

Within days after Camelia's hydrocephalic son died, his wildly sorrowful father wandered out and lay like one already dead across the railroad tracks, to be run over by the afternoon train. Camelia lost her mind immediately. My grandmother implored her sister to come stay with her, but she would not. She stayed alone in her house and handled baby clothes and wrung her hands in the clothes of her husband and baby until these clothes and she herself were shredded and unrecognizable. My grandmother would go each day and change Camelia's soiled dresses and linens while she walked all through the house naked, moaning, "Oh, my big-headed baby! Oh, the man I adored!" (17)

As Michael Kreyling points out, parody is power—especially for southern authors working in and around the long shadow of Faulkner (*Inventing* 156–57). Here the high melodrama of madness and suicide that was Faulkner's reworking of Greek tragedy, along with his characteristic repetition and accretion of detail ("clothes . . . clothes . . . clothes and she herself") is lampooned with a level of bravado possible only for a writer of considerable power. The earlier Gibbons— content to maintain the Algonquin profile and work within the lesser parameters of regionalism—seems by 1993 to have been replaced by an iconoclast intent on serious revision.

The parodic opening of *Charms for the Easy Life* is appropriate for a novel focused on destabilizing patriarchal authority. As the name of Gibbons's protagonist and matriarch implies, Charlie Kate Birch resists conventional female roles, choosing instead to mingle the feminine with active participation in a mid-twentieth-century community that defines autonomy in masculine terms. Her career as a physician is hardly thwarted by her rejection from medical school; abandoned by her husband in the early years of the century, she has built a medical practice among the poor and uneducated who lack the means to pay the licensed physicians of the community. Residents of the mill district and the benighted rural community, individuals who "didn't count as people" to citizens of higher standing, are her clientele, although Charlie Kate also treats members of the aristocracy for ailments outside the accepted purview of their family doctors—a "wealthy landowner," for example, who seeks her treatment for a case of syphilis (21, 19). Her staff consists of her daughter, Sophia (who took a single, valuable lesson from her own failed marriage: "A man will leave you" [25]), and Sophia's daughter, Margaret. The matriarchal arrangement of life in the Birch household is defined in opposition to the patriarchy of Raleigh, North Carolina, which engenders a community within the dominant community that the women create around themselves. Drawing on the romance genre, Gibbons's saga of this subcommunity becomes nearly gothic in its tense relation to the larger culture.

The South of the novel is an environment that necessitates women's banding together for survival. Gibbons follows the pattern of southern women's writing Yaeger describes as a chronicle of "the numinous terrors of the everyday" that "exposes the deforming effects of the southern political tradition upon women, men, and children of color, upon white women and children, and even upon white men" (288–89). From Charlie Kate's rescue of a lynching victim in the novel's opening pages onward, the hierarchy against which she works is depicted as blatantly hegemonic in its arrangement of race and class, the medical profession allowing for a disturbingly literal examination of the "deforming effects" of society.

The place of the white male in this hierarchy becomes clear in Charlie Kate's dealings with a prominent physician in the area. As one might expect, the doctor's knowledge of women's bodies and the health of the poor seems rudimentary compared to Charlie Kate's. She is the only individual in the community aware that in his early years of practice the "real doctor" had blinded a poor infant by spilling silver nitrate in its eyes, and later his misdiagnosis of an elderly African American woman results in her death. To Charlie Kate's suggestion of intestinal paralysis, he replies, "The only thing that goes wrong below an old colored woman's waist is fibroids. That and too much grease" (86). Margaret's account of the confrontation at the doctor's home following the woman's death illustrates how Charlie Kate's position outside the status quo works at times to her advantage: "In these homes lived Raleigh's chief doctors and lawyers and a dying breed of Southerner, white people who seemed to earn a living automatically. She gave me a street address, and she would not listen to my mother's protests that she couldn't go to anybody's house this late in the evening. . . . She said, 'Keep driving. The hour does not faze me.' We drove through what felt like a true maze of affluence before we found the right house. A butler let her in. I remember my mother's saying, 'Remarkable. Truly remarkable. People are hungry three miles from here. A butler. Remarkable.' My grandmother stayed in the house about fifteen minutes, and when she returned, all she said was, 'I took care of the situation for certain this time' " (87–88). The next week's newspaper brings with it the announcement of the doctor's early retirement. The episode is a prime example of what Yaeger terms "carnival moments" of "temporary liberation from the established order" (297). Charlie Kate penetrates the "maze of affluence" to accuse the doctor of his misdeeds in the upper-class heart of the established order. Once again it is a man who represents the destructive facets of society, and Charlie Kate, using feminine knowledge from the lower classes, is empowered to level patriarchal authority.

Such power also exerts itself in her dealings with other prominent white male figures, notably in persuading a factory owner to install sidewalks in the mill district and in convincing the city council to bring the same impoverished area onto city sewage lines. Her strength stems from rejecting the parameters ascribed to women by her culture. Just as Charlie Kate "explained girls' bodies to them, corrected ruinous impressions created by the Baptists," the women of her household, under her direction, revise and reject the roles scripted for them by the dominant patriarchal ideology (40). Convinced that the life of "most middle-class Southern women of the day" amounts to "no more than passing time," she assumes a demeanor often attributed to the masculine sphere, from such gestures as throwing back a glass of brandy "like a cowboy at the end of a bar" to noting the fine points of stock prospectuses "the way other women would've pointed out new fashions in a department store advertisement" (36, 98). Her reversal of conventional roles is completed when her estranged husband appears after years of absence. Charlie Kate enacts the role of the dutiful wife, running into his arms as he approaches the house, cooking for him, and finally accompanying him to the Sir Walter Hotel in Raleigh for what her husband assumes to be a second honeymoon. Three days later she emerges from the hotel with his life savings, over thirteen hundred dollars, having "rolled him" in a premeditated act that reverses the abandonment she suffered decades before. By manipulating the expectations of her role, her act of what might be termed sexual aggression secures autonomy from the man who "had had use of her heart long enough" (76). His death soon after only confirms Charlie Kate's resolution that she would "take a poison pill before I'd take a man" (83). Like the mythic heroes of Baym's inquiry, she effects celibacy after having dispensed with the impediment to her self-development. As in *Ellen Foster*, the gender roles of the paradigm are switched, the absence of the male clearing the path toward womanhood.

From this break between the sexes arises the matriarchal ideal of the novel. Following the example of Charlie Kate, the household of three generations of Birch women draws energy from blurring boundaries, constructing a regenerative environment (like that to which Ellen finally arrives) within the category confusion of "the best house" in "the worst part of town" (20). Free of male influence, the women establish in their home a protracted "carnival moment" of female self-reliance: "My grandmother believed our household was fine as it was. If there was heavy lifting to be done, the three of us did it together. If a picture needed hanging, we tapped the wall to listen for the stud and then drove the nail in with an admirable economy of hits. If anything mechanical broke, for instance the mantel clock from Pasquotank County, we took it apart and spent the afternoon putting it back together. So my grandmother was of the opinion that not only would a man be a threat, he would be an intrusion, wholly unnecessary" (93). The tasks Margaret describes are significant: as what would conventionally be deemed male chores, they underscore the women's autonomy from the opposite gender. More important, they illustrate how the household serves a function analogous to the wilderness in the Adamic narrative that Gibbons began to revise in her first novel. In its very domesticity and distinction apart from the male, the Birch home is a zone liberated from the constrictions of the larger society, an area that fosters the formation of an autonomous identity for the individual. That this identity is collective—the boundaries of "self" between Charlie Kate, Sophia, and Margaret are inchoate—emphasizes Gibbons's modification to the paradigm. If in *Ellen Foster* Gibbons still adhered to the pattern of the individual quest, crafting a bildungsroman, here she alters the foundational assumptions of the mythic quest for selfhood. The self is not to be discovered apart from society, in solitude, but within women's communities of domestic wilderness equally as distant from the dominant culture as the western regions of the male hero. As Charlie Kate puts it, "there *is* no alone here" (218). "Alone" is a condition dispensed by the men who leave; in full flower, Gibbons's matriarchal ideal rejects it as a flawed component of a paradigm that is, in its male formulation, inadequate. To be outside the matriarchy is a negative state that Margaret repeatedly refers to as "the curse of absence"—to be set apart from the regenerative bonds of the Birch matriarchy. Here Gibbons has finally fashioned a complete reworking of the paradigm, shedding the vestiges of male ideology that made the quest motif appealing to the composition of *Ellen Foster*. Baym stresses that "we need to ask whether anything about [the myth] puts it outside women's reach" (11); in addressing that issue Gibbons constructs a myth of womanhood disencumbered of male topoi and so distinctly within women's reach as to render all things male entirely superfluous.

This ideal seems to rest uneasily against the conclusion of Gibbon's novel, in which the neat resolutions of the romance assert themselves. Sophia's marriage to Richard Baines appears to adulterate the self-contained matriarchy, and the basis of Charlie Kate's approval of Margaret's suitor (he is "decent, smart, rich, and everything else" [*Charms* 239]) at least in some measure capitulates to the bourgeois attitudes that function as ideological antagonists throughout the narrative. But perhaps to make such criticisms is to approach *Charms for the Easy Life* from the wrong perspective. As Tania Modleski has noted of the romance novel, its "elements of protest and resistance" abide beneath even "highly 'orthodox' plots" (25). Too, one of the earliest critics of the genre described romance novels as "handbooks . . . of feminine revolt" against "the common enemy, man" in spite of their formulaic elements (Papashvily xvii). To expect Gibbons to articulate a systematically iconoclastic vision in the genre may be to perpetuate the kind of critical chauvinism that, as Baym reminds us, has historically plagued American women authors. The feminine dissent of this "handbook" may be covert and subtle enough to expose such expectations as ironically phallogocentric. The search for a clearly mythoclastic relationship in *Charms for the Easy Life* (tradition/renovation) may participate in the binary thinking that Luce Irigaray attributes to a "phallic economy" of ideas (101)—to a system of categorization akin to those that Gibbons's matriarchal ideal rejects. If so, Gibbons's modified romance novel may well be a more subversive narrative form than any of her male contemporaries' work, the most category-disruptive fiction of the post-modern South.

Considered sequentially, Gibbons's work moves upward through the social hierarchy with each novel, from the "trash" perspective of *Ellen Foster* to the blue-collar milieu of *A Virtuous Woman;* from the vague middle class of *A Cure for Dreams* and *Charms for the Easy Life* to the landed bourgeoisie of *Sights Unseen* (1995). Given such a progression, it seems all but inevitable that her most incisive critique of southern mythology would appear in *On the Occasion of My Last Afternoon* (1998), a Civil War novel centering upon the planter aristocracy of the Old South. Although the novel is flawed in several particulars—its Faulknerian opening tableau of racial violence fails to develop proper thematic weight, and its protagonist seems unlikely to anticipate Eliot in declaring that "humankind cannot bear very much reality" (163)—Gibbons successfully uses history to explore the cultural origins of her unfolding drama of beset southern womanhood. Yaeger notes that "a frequent reprise" in the criticism of southern women writers is their alleged "lack of thematic, stylistic, or political 'largeness' " (288). Gibbons negates the criticism by taking as her subject the nucleus of southern myth, the plantation, and the vast action of the war that arose from it. Exploring such "large" subjects, she operates in territory already mapped by Faulkner, Tate, Young, and others, yet her narrative of a disintegrating feudal patriarchy ascribes blame for the demise of the old order to a source overlooked in the tragic saga of the Renascence: patriarchy itself. In Gibbons's treatment the key battles of the war are waged on the home front, behind the facade of the big house, and the antebellum myth is deconstructed from within.

If Gibbons's aim in the novel is to uncover the historical and cultural bases of her women characters' daunting environments, her choice of patriarchs could not be better. Samuel P. Tate (one notes a rich sense of intertextuality in the name) is a wealthy planter who "had served two terms in the legislature and was known all over Virginia to be an honest, upright, hearty, and earnest Episcopalian" (*My Last Afternoon* 2). In spite of his reputation, Tate is haunted by his impoverished childhood, by the fact that he cannot claim the true aristocracy his culture worships. He is clearly one of W. J. Cash's cotton parvenus, of the instant southern upper class lately arisen from "the strong, the pushing, the ambitious, among the old coon-hunting population" (Cash 14). Throughout her work, Gibbons's men are the practitioners of repression and restrictive ideology; in *On the Occasion of My Last Afternoon* Tate's yearning for social prominence indicates that this tendency is historic. His daughter Emma's description of the rise to such prominence is acerbic:

> In few words, he needed our neighbors, not for political standing, elected and supported as he was during his legislative terms by those men who used him to speak their fears. The families whose ancestors had disembarked at Jamestown were necessary to complete the picture he craved himself part of, just as he had paid dearly for a visiting, reluctant artist to touch up a fox-hunting scene and place him on the one riderless horse. And then there father was, all of a sudden on the library wall, in the lead on a race across a Scottish moor, wearing a full kit. He also had the man render a coat of arms of the Tates of Edinburgh, the place he fancied that he belonged to have come from had his family—as I found out from the greasy letters of passage sent to me when one of his kin died—not swabbed steerage of vomit and human refuse from Liverpool to Mr. Oglethorpe's debtors' colony in Georgia. (40)

Time and frontiers, indeed. The lack of the former is only a slight impediment to a man of Tate's coarseness with the means to purchase the myth he seeks. If one broadens the example of Tate to the larger culture to which he belongs, Gibbons's incisive approach to an ersatz social system once again casts men in the role of socializers. Tate, like his fellow planters, is the architect of a culture preoccupied with false and restrictive roles—what the classic hero(ine) must escape. His other genteel accoutrements—Gainsborough and Copley paintings, Hepplewhite chairs—impart conventionally feminine associations; his masculinity is underscored by his propensity toward violence and his general boorishness, yet his symbolic cultural accoutrements connect him to those "feminine" qualities equated with repression in classic American fiction.

Tate's boorishness fuels his abuse of his family, casting an aura of repression throughout the house over which he presides. Tate castigates the New England family of Emma's fiancé, threatening her engagement with a combination of secessionist rhetoric and the domineering machinations of a martinet. His efforts to fashion Emma's sister, Maureen, into a perfect flower of southern womanhood—a womanhood that he defines—reduce her to a figure reminiscent of Faulkner's Emily Grierson, an unmarried "antique virgin" whose father "had turned away countless suitors because their stations and prospects were inadequate" (144). The greatest victim of his abuse (and the clearest example of Gibbons's reversed paradigm of repression) is Tate's wife, Alice. With her recurrent "sick head-misery" (31), Alice recalls the quailing Ole Miss of legend, a figure targeted by the iconoclastic derision of Old South critics from Harriet Jacobs onward. Yet Gibbons does not attribute her character's ailment to an inherent weakness indulged by a paternalistic society. Rather, it results from the psychological war of attrition fought daily in the Tate household, the product not of a pedestal position in the family but of the incessant hammering of emotional abuse she suffers from her husband. Emma sees her mother as "a lady who could have enjoyed developing her mind and might have found the same pleasure in using it that she did in reading light magazines and chatting at sewing circles with her friends" but whose "survival" in their home "took the place of whatever mind-work she might have accomplished" (96). The portrait of a plantation mistress such as Faulkner's Caroline Compson is tempered by straitened domestic relations akin to those of Charlotte Perkins Gilman's "The Yellow Wallpaper."

Depression emerges as a metaphor for women's repression. The theme of depression is persistent in Gibbons's work, from the suicide of Ellen Foster's mother to Maggie's illness in *Sights Unseen*, both of which, as Gibbons reveals in her memoir, *Frost and Flower* (1995), draw from the author's own life. Throughout Gibbons's work, the victims of depression are exclusively female. The specific connections Gibbons perceives between depression and her gender are apparent in the contrasts between *Frost and Flower* and another southern essay on the same subject, William Styron's *Darkness Visible*. Like Gibbons, Styron traces his depression to the "devastating loss in childhood" of his mother, an "early sorrow" that began a long cycle of illness (56, 79). Yet where Styron, a self-described "autodidact in medicine," explores the causes of the disease in a psychological and biochemical context (9), Gibbons diagnoses it in social terms, in a "farm wife" mother who was "an incredibly smart woman trapped by circumstance" and "surrounded by heat and poverty and the sad certainty that life will not be any other way" (*Frost* 2, 20). The hereditary legacy of the disease takes on another facet. It is indeed, as Gibbons notes, passed down through the maternal line, but in her work its biological proclivities are enhanced and encouraged by social conditions for women that make its maternal origins darkly ironic. Thus when one considers Alice Tate against a description of Maggie in *Sights Unseen*, a historical pattern begins to reveal itself: "Had this been the mid-nineteenth century instead of the twentieth, our farm would have been called a plantation; the house, the Big House; the tenant farmers, slaves; and my mother, a classic nervous matriarch who suffered spells" (44). Alice comes to seem an early victim in a serial disease endemic to the culture. Her deathbed physician speculates that she "must have been a lady of severe emotion and intense study, for such trauma of mind was evident in her drawn face," and he ascribes the cause of her death to "Inflammation of the Brain owing to over-exertion of an organ not constructed by our Maker for life other than that of quiet domesticity" (*My Last Afternoon* 155, 157). As with the "legitimate" doctor of *Charms for the Easy Life*, the myopia of a male physician leads to a fatal misdiag-nosis. Alice's nineteenth-century context merely makes the culpability of men more evident, their role in a repressive society more salient. Given the social range of depressive women in Gibbons's writing—her own mother and Ellen's, Maggie, Alice—the life of "quiet domesticity" appears to be for women of all classes an existence fraught by a quiet epidemic.

This revisionist woman's perspective shapes the account of the Civil War in the novel. The Confederacy is not described in the feminine terms of the histor-ical myth but in the masculine delusions of Samuel Tate. From his "vehement correspondence with every pro-Negro newspaper editor in the South" to his hawkish jingoism, Tate becomes conflated with a social order that represents the apotheosis of repression exerted by white men of power (129). In keeping with Gibbons's conception of patriarchal ideology, the Confederacy thrives on euphemism as an important tool for the maintenance of myth. The culture that insists on substituting the word "servant" for "slave" becomes in the war a patri-archy intent on consciously manipulating fact into propaganda: the southern military initially is depicted as "an army of Natty Bumppos," and casualties are reported with such rhetorical flourishes as "passed at Manassas" (26, 182). After the tide of war has turned against the Confederacy, Tate is "bolstered against all reality by newspaper accounts that diminished truth with such decorous conclusions as: 'Confederate forces were pushed back. Wake County guards performed admirably. Some were lost'" (218). A mythoclastic perspective emerges in Emma's response to such self-delusion. In a room with other women at the announcement of Virginia's secession, she detects an "unspoken agree-ment that martyrdom was for dead saints" and observes that, among the women at least, "nobody was quoting soaring passages from *Ivanhoe*" (173). Her insis-tence that the war "was a conflict perpetrated by rich men and fought by poor boys against hungry women and babies" further separates her from the domi-nant ideology of men like her father (164).

But it is through her depictions of Tate that Gibbons thoroughly decon-structs the mythic stature of the war that became the lodestone of modern southern fiction. As Maureen observes, Tate "thinks he himself is the South" (194). It is in this terse observation that Gibbons's challenge to the modernists' mythic history becomes clear. Tate "is" indeed the South—the South of the Confederacy, of the antebellum slave economy, of the patriarchy that placed landowning white men in a hegemonic position at the peak of the culture. Yet his complete embodiment of the ideals of this culture is used to turn the mythic Confederacy inside out: the trope of a lost organic South is debunked at its foundations. Gibbons does, like Cash in *The Mind of the South*, expose the crass materialism beneath the aristocratic veneer of the antebellum planter, but she also moves her critique into self-conscious literary subversion. As an incarnation of the Confederacy, Tate joins a host of fictive southern characters who epito-mize a vanquished way of life, a vital connection to place and culture that formed the basis of what the dissociated southern modernists saw as "lost" in twentieth-century society. Consider Allen Tate's description of George Posey in *The Fathers* as a fitting example: George is consumed "by an idea, a cause, an action in which his personality could be extinguished . . . it seemed as if George had succeeded in becoming a part of something greater than he: the Confeder-ate cause" (180–81). In Gibbons's revision, the extinction of personality through culture—the *quaesitum* of southern modernism—is exposed as a patriar-chal fantasy. The rewards of being consumed by a historical narrative greater than the individual self are, as the title of Tate's novel makes clear, limited to but a few members of southern culture. Further, the crucial sacrifice of partici-pating in such a cause is reckoned only in patriarchal terms—not, as Emma observes, in the price paid by women, the poor, and African Americans, who have long suffered a different sort of extinction of personality that can hardly be considered beneficial. With Samuel Tate functioning as the avatar of Confed-erate commitment, the Civil War appears as but a sweeping example of the violent damage wreaked at home. Hardly a pitched battle for freedom, indepen-dence, or southern sovereignty, it is a macrocosmic enactment of the male hegemony practiced inside the plantation household. Gibbons's female perspec-tive undermines the foundations of the myth.

The resolution of Gibbons's Civil War novel departs significantly from its southern predecessors, even those focused on the home front of the war such as *The Fathers* and Faulkner's *The Unvanquished*. Despite the trials of Reconstruc-tion, the demise of the old order is more liberating for Gibbons's characters than tragic. Throughout, *On the Occasion of My Last Afternoon* follows with remarkable accuracy the historical conditions chronicled by Drew Gilpin Faust in *Mothers of Invention*, from the ambivalent morale of Confederate women to the hospital work of the domestic war; the novel also reaches similar conclusions about the lasting social effects of secession. Faust notes that the war "undermined the wealth and political power of the planter elite," transforming the hierarchies of race and class "that had so firmly placed white men at the apex of the social pyramid" (4). Samuel Tate's dissolution personifies this shift, symbolizing the less than chivalric tribulations of the planter bereft of his feudal prominence. But the profoundly mythoclastic strains of the novel emerge in Emma's reaction to Confederate defeat. Faust observes that "the desire to cling to eroding status remained strong" for those daughters of the southern aristocracy "who remembered the rewards of class and racial power in the Old South" (254). Emma resists this tendency. Always of "a mind that studied the manner in which people of varying classes dealt with one another," she adapts to the new social order adeptly, seeking to develop and foster in her children the "quick-marrow" that "ignores lines of class hierarchy and race" (Gibbons, *My Last Afternoon* 8, 115). Emma claims to be "tired of the accoutrements of high-toned existence," intent instead on discovering "truth, authenticity" (111). As Gibbons's novel demonstrates powerfully, truth and authenticity are to be found outside the mythos of the Old South and its patriarchal regime. From such a vantage point the Old South's displacement by a new egalitarian society can be reckoned a tragedy only by those orchestrators of the myth that kept them in power.

Faust concludes her study by citing two enormously influential meditations on southern history: C. Vann Woodward's idea of "the burden of southern history" and Gavin Stevens's reverie of Pickett's charge in *Intruder in the Dust*, asserting that "southerners burdened with the past Woodward describes, like the southerners forever poised at two o'clock on July 3, are white southerners and they are male southerners. The weight of southern history is just as heavy for women and for African Americans, but it is constructed rather differently" (256). *On the Occasion of My Last Afternoon* serves a literary function parallel to Faust's history by examining the burden of southern history for those who did not participate in scripting its dominant narrative. Gibbons's historical novel concludes by revisiting a genre generally overlooked in the southern literary canon, the reconciliation romance of the nineteenth century. Her protagonist's marriage to Quincy Lowell of Boston, whose family maintains staunch connections to abolition and transcendentalism, revives the Reconstruction theme of reunion through marriage in the aftermath of war. It is a romance form rejected by the modernists, yet in Gibbons's treatment it is hardly a format limited by generic conventions. The book's epigraphs—passages from Tate's "Ode to the Confederate Dead" and Robert Lowell's "For the Union Dead" juxtaposed—lend ironic resonance to the Tate-Lowell marriage within the pages of the novel, demonstrating that Gibbons's use of the genre is far more subversive than a critic of the romance might allow. Conscious of the ramifications of intertextuality, Gibbons's postmodern reconciliation romance proposes a union not only of North and South but also between the mythic literary history of a patriarchal South and the dissenting voices silenced by it. Quincy Lowell helps Emma Tate to "drag the past into the present," holding her "steady" as she "maneuver[s] amongst the ruins" of history (174). The familiar dynamic of the past in the present perseveres, but from southern women's perspective it accrues Freudian implications of repression and a benighted former existence. Southern history is redeemed only by the outsider's aid—by an accounting of the past outside the terms of southern patriarchy.

Gibbons's interpolation of mythoclasm into the southern historical narrative indicates that her career-long dialogue with the male paradigms of literary tradition has reached a formidable stage. If Elaine Showalter is correct in describing women's writing as a progression toward the self-consciousness of a truly individual voice, *On the Occasion of My Last Afternoon* signals Gibbons's fullest articulation of the women's critique of the South, the completion of her journey toward independent southern womanhood. Showalter interprets women's authorship in three stages, Feminine, Feminist, and Female; her division of British writers applies remarkably well to the development of Gibbons's southern fiction. *Ellen Foster* follows Showalter's Feminine phase of "*imitation* of the prevailing modes of the dominant tradition," including "*internalization* of its standards of art" (13). The Feminist stage of protest against dominant "standards and values," including "*advocacy* of minority rights and values" and a "demand for autonomy," shapes the matriarchal ideal of *Charms for the Easy Life*. *On the Occasion of My Last Afternoon* finally reaches the Female phase "of *self-discovery*, a turning inward freed from some of the dependency of opposition, a search for identity" (13). Gibbons is not unique in using southern history in the search for identity, but the fruition of her evolving quest for autonomous female existence entails dramatic alterations to the template of the past. Nearing the end of her last afternoon, Emma remarks that "a receipt is only as good as its alterations" (266). Her feminine metaphor may well describe Gibbons's legacy to southern literary history.

ATAVISM AND THE EXPLODED METANARRATIVE

Cormac McCarthy's Journey to Mythoclasm

In 1975 Vanderbilt critic and novelist Walter Sullivan, delivering the eighteenth annual Lamar Lectures at Mercer University, assessed the state of fiction in the modern South. His lecture was entitled "A Requiem for the Renascence," and in reviewing contemporary southern fiction he found little cause for optimism. Southern writing, he declared, had lost its sense of the universal and consequently suffered from the "naturalistic excesses" that accompany a loss of faith (*Requiem* 69). In contrast to Renascence authors, southern writers of the 1960s and 1970s offered no organic conception of the region, and the poetics of their works suffered from the lack of a unified vision. In both form and philosophy, they violated the New Critical and conservative principles that Sullivan had acquired and propounded in his many years of association with the Vanderbilt English department. The current scene, Sullivan believed, could be described with the metaphor of the "rainbow's end." Contemporary writers paled in comparison to their predecessors, and many of them seemed intent on undermining the modernist achievement in southern letters. The state of fiction could be described in terms ranging from "decayed" to "barbarous" (50, 72).

The particular target of Sullivan's criticism was Cormac McCarthy. McCarthy seemed to represent each of the literary offenses that threatened southern fiction. While Sullivan admonished Walker Percy for his uncertain faith and rebuked James Dickey for the sensational gothicism of some of his work, McCarthy elicited an almost frantic level of vitriol—as if he posed a threat to the entire achievement of the Renascence. Even if one considers that some of Sullivan's comments may have been grounded in the hyperbolic style that Louis Rubin calls "Vanderbilt apocalyptic," his criticism is revealing. It is indicative of the tensions at work in southern fiction's shift from the modern to the postmodern, a conflict in which McCarthy's work is fully embroiled. Sullivan's comments demonstrate the firm hold that late modernism maintained on southern fiction and criticism well into McCarthy's career, as well as the tribulations faced by the southern writer of postmodern sensibility who departed from the traditional style of the modern southern novel. Sullivan's criticism of McCarthy in *A Requiem for the Renascence* intensifies as he considers this development from novel to novel. His escalating critique represents in microcosm the unwillingness of the old guard of southern literati to accommodate younger writers of iconoclastic vision. At the heart of Sullivan's criticism lies his resistance to McCarthy's mythoclastic strain, an inimical attitude toward southern cultural mythology that has intensified as McCarthy's artistic prowess has developed. In his atavistic depictions of humanity and parodic or critical treatment of cultural fixtures of the southern literary landscape, McCarthy writes against the modernist and humanistic philosophy to which Sullivan adheres. Thus in his career— and in Sullivan's reaction to it—we may observe a clearly delineated struggle between modern and postmodern, old and new, in the evolving landscape of southern literature.[1]

Initially, Sullivan welcomed McCarthy as a formidable new talent. Perhaps because of the Faulknerian prose and pastoral elements of *The Orchard Keeper* (1965), Sullivan perceived McCarthy's first novel as a valuable contribution to southern letters: "His characters come immediately alive. He has a fine sense of dramatic scene and pacing and an ability to reproduce the countryside of east Tennessee where his fiction is set. In *The Orchard Keeper* he pursues a familiar theme: he charts the depredations of time and shows how old ways are doomed by the new. No southern novelist since William Styron has got off to a better start" (70). But this approval was short-lived. McCarthy's meditations on history proved to be far different from Styron's—and much more inimical to the tradition of the Renascence. Sullivan continues: "But in his second book [*Outer Dark*], McCarthy told a weird, almost gothic tale of incest and his third novel [*Child of*

God] is clear evidence of the plane of madness to which our art has finally descended," an "affront to decency on every level" (70, 71). At the time of Sullivan's Lamar Lectures, McCarthy had not yet consummated his southern vision with the 1978 masterpiece *Suttree*, and *Child of God* represented the fullest expression of his mythoclastic vision—and consequently received Sullivan's sternest censure. The sum total of McCarthy's work seemed to Sullivan a "portent of barbarism," the "best example" of a "destructive impulse in contemporary art." Sullivan concluded his remarks with the observation that "McCarthy is the artist not merely bereft of community and myth; he has declared war against these ancient repositories of order and truth" (71–72).

Indeed, McCarthy's artistic vision is an unsettling one that assails the very foundations of humanistic philosophy. The bleak and naturalistic landscapes of his novels are occupied by characters with primitive drives and simian shapes, more homunculi than human beings. McCarthy's world abounds with surrealistic, atavistic depictions of the human race, from the seven drovers of *Outer Dark* who make their way "with no order rank or valence to anything in the shapen world" (227) to the eviscerated cadaver of Lester Ballard, the object of scrutiny for medical students who study his entrails "like those haruspices of old" (*Child of God* 194). In all of McCarthy's work there is a relentless double focus on humanity's ignoble origins and the ineluctable presence of death; in his dark vision, human beings exist not at the pinnacle of teleological development but at some undefined point in a coarse evolutionary process. As John M. Grammer has noted, "it is hard to imagine McCarthy on some platform in Stockholm, assuring us that man will survive and prevail" (28).

McCarthy's use of atavism wrenches a truly ironic twist into a predominant trope of his predecessors: the southern staple of the past in the present. One of the defining techniques of southern modernism, the dialectic with the past presupposes a set of foundational beliefs that McCarthy rejects outright—beliefs that McCarthy's atavism (his own variation of the naturalism Allen Tate predicted in "Narcissus as Narcissus") assails directly. Foremost among them is a sense that the past represents a wholeness lost in modernity, an organic existence that the multifarious incarnations of "progress" have adulterated. As Lewis Simpson observes in *The Brazen Face of History*, this belief has long been prevalent in the southern mind: nineteenth-century "southerners tried to conceive their society as a restoration of the sacred community," an effort that lingered in twentieth-century writers who sought "to represent the South as a unified sensibility" (256). Addressing Sullivan's critique of McCarthy specifically, Simpson describes the critic as heir to this legacy, a proponent of a "mythic system" that "placed the golden age in the past" (258). Sullivan epitomizes the broad tendency to view the modern era through the metaphorical context of the Götterdämmerung, in which the Renascence is considered the "highly fruitful but final epoch of a traditional society which, for all its failings, had a definite and worthy system of values established in a comprehensive vision of existence" (260). But McCarthy's dialectic between past and present serves a purpose antithetical to uses of history that would maintain a sanctified past, turning the tools of this mythic system against the system itself to deconstruct the notion of a bygone golden era. On one level, his use of the past and historical allusion appears to resemble the modernists' deployment of archetypes and mythopoesis by following Eliot's method of "manipulating a continuous parallel between contemporaneity and antiquity" (Eliot 177); McCarthy, too, employs the past to establish continuous patterns of human behavior. But where the modernists used the stability of mythological patterns to inform and order the chaotic present, McCarthy subverts the dialectic. His evocation of the past is antinostalgic; rather than presenting a lost stability, it emphasizes an elemental primitivism that humanity retains, declaring war (in Sullivan's terms) against those venerated "repositories of order and truth" such as cultural mythology and teleological notions of human community. McCarthy inverts the formula of Eliot's mythic method "as a way of controlling, of ordering, of giving shape and significance to the immense panorama of futility and anarchy which is contemporary history" (Eliot 177–78). Indeed, that futility and anarchy constitute the only archetype McCarthy recognizes. Instead of ordering the chaotic present, the sole archetype available to contemporary humanity emphasizes the absence of progress in the present and the very near proximity of a dangerous and benighted human past. One of the epigraphs to *Blood Meridian* demonstrates this perspective with ironic understatement. Excerpting a news account of an anthropological expedition to Ethiopia, the novel takes as its starting point the report of "a 300,000-year-old fossil skull" that "shows evidence of having been scalped." Such is hardly evidence of a golden age in need of recovery: this more distant past debunks the Götterdämmerung at its origins.

McCarthy's atavism, then, shapes his unique deconstructive approach to modernism, his own aggressively iconoclastic engagement with the sacred community traditionally adumbrated in southern fiction. In contrast to a contemporary like Percy, McCarthy's postmodern vision is motivated not by ambivalence but by something closer to a direct attack on tradition. Vereen Bell approaches an accurate assessment of the author's philosophy in noting that McCarthy's novels appear "to resist abstraction on purpose and to move instead toward some more primal epistemology, toward a knowledge of origins before a bicameral brain enabled us—or compelled us—to begin to sort things out" (2). Bell notes that, given such a primitive focus, "conceptual experience . . . is 'bracketed'; eidetic experience flourishes and flashes vivid signals because it is not subsumed into doctrine or ideology" (2). Although Bell neither makes the connection between McCarthy and southern literary history nor identifies atavism as the vehicle of "primal epistemology," his observations are useful in assessing the author's repellence to Sullivan. For Sullivan, the function of fiction lies in its service to doctrine, to an ideology of the past grounded in humanistic and theological beliefs that depend upon a prior unity, a prior order. Whereas an author such as Percy may elicit Sullivan's censure by expressing uncertainty about the soundness of these ideal antecedents in the present, McCarthy's "primal" focus renders him anathema through its subversive attack on these ideals at their source. His forays into an existence that precedes such ordering principles explores humanist philosophy itself in eidetic manner—as a series of disjointed and muddled paradigms that fail to cohere into a valid framework for human experience. The result is a fictional past antithetical to modernism, in which, as Bell states, "not meaning itself but the traditional idea of meaning is made obsolete" (2).

Accordingly, the conventional southern vehicles of constructing meaning—community and myth—receive increasingly critical treatment in McCarthy's novels. By exploring "at a childlike and amoral level of the region's society those impulses that its civilization had done its best to obscure or at least divert into acceptable channels," McCarthy exposes the framework by which the South has been fashioned in literature along classical lines (Bryant 223). As his work and artistic vision have become more postmodern (that is, more diffuse in structure and philosophically skeptical), the development of his atavistic perspective has cohered around a critical trajectory common to post-Renascence authors. Like Richard Ford and others, McCarthy produced a debut novel firmly within the southern modernist tradition. Epistemological in conception, *The Orchard Keeper* uses the conventional motifs of local color to ensconce a modernist quest for a narrative conception of the world. His first novel (like Ford's *A Piece of My Heart*) is therefore conducive to New Critical readings: in the manner of William Faulkner's *Absalom, Absalom!* and Robert Penn Warren's *All the King's Men*, it contains an embedded story that, however concealed, offers the diligent reader the sort of certainty that critics such as Sullivan seek in fiction. Yet with each successive novel McCarthy has delved into the characteristically postmodern arena of ontological uncertainty, requiring one to qualify Bell's "primal epistemology" as an accurate term to describe his work.[2] McCarthy's skepticism of the tangible world's absolute claim to reality is antimodernist in its resistance to narrative configurations of experience and thus runs counter to the aims of most Renascence fiction. It is what Sullivan calls a "destructive impulse in contemporary art," which has led to "the impoverishment of southern fiction under a new dispensation" (71–72, 66). Because of this ontological uncertainty, the southern communities depicted in *Outer Dark, Child of God,* and *Suttree* offer scant sense of order for a fictional cosmos in which the foundations of reality become increasingly suspect. Humanity comes under an escalating scrutiny concurrently, for McCarthy's atavistic vision has developed alongside his growing ontological uncertainty. *Suttree* represents the author's mythoclastic and atavistic strains in full flower. This last McCarthy novel set in the South is a darkly postmodern response to the modernist quest for order; the promise of myth and community is rendered ironic in the work, as McCarthy's atavistic portrayals subvert the myths on which southern culture rests, calling all certainty into question. It is McCarthy's farewell to the southern setting and his most powerful deconstruction of southern cultural mythology. It seems evident now, more than twenty years after Sullivan's lectures, that with the advent of his atavistic vision McCarthy truly came into his own as an artist as he moved toward the unique ontology of later masterpieces like *Suttree* and *Blood Meridian.* McCarthy's mythoclastic temperament may indeed have contributed to the "rainbow's end" of southern modernism, but it has also created some of the most powerful fiction in contemporary southern literature.

M cCarthy's first novel, *The Orchard Keeper,* displays the friction characteristic of the early phase of his work. Throughout, the struggle between a brilliant individual vision and the lure of southern literary convention is evident. On the one hand, McCarthy's proclivity for the grotesque and atavistic expresses itself in the character of Kenneth Rattner, both through his repellent life and his grisly entombment in the orchard's chemical pit. Ultimately, however, literary inheritance dictates the form of the novel. Modernist narrative technique shapes the intertwined stories of Arthur Ownby, John Wesley Rattner, and Marion Sylder, providing an epistemological structure of fragmented viewpoints by which the plot is pieced together. Even more important is the philosophical influence of the Agrarian tradition that, together with the modernist prose style, places the novel in the tradition of Southern Renascence fiction.

Sullivan had cause to applaud the appearance of McCarthy's first book. While evincing a formidable new talent, *The Orchard Keeper* nonetheless remains obedient to the standards of earlier southern fiction. True to Sullivan's formulation of "the old familiar ground" of southern literature, the novel pays close attention to the material of southern regional fiction: "the folk tradition," the "southern penchant for telling tales and creating myths," and the importance of "the land and man's closeness to it" (Sullivan, *Requiem* xiii). The novel's dialogue reproduces the east Tennessee dialect with painstaking accuracy, and the work is replete with tall tales and stories of wild "painters" (panthers) that haunt the hills of the countryside. McCarthy's attention to the region's folk traditions extends to descriptions of raccoon hunting and its attendant misadventures in passages strongly reminiscent of southwestern humor.

The pastoral mode is present throughout the novel as well. Arthur Ownby moves through a rural world much like the one the Agrarians conceptualized, and McCarthy's descriptions of his perambulations comprise an evocative mix of dialect and lyrical language. As Grammer points out, McCarthy even echoes Yeats's famous pastoral "The Lake Isle of Innisfree" in Ownby's reveries of building "a log house" by "a clearwater branch" where his "bees would make black mountain honey" and he "wouldn't care for no man" (55). Through such expressions Ownby functions as an avatar of pastoral existence. He is the orchard keeper of the novel's title: a keeper of rituals, an oral historian of the region, a yeoman with visceral ties to a natural world that is fundamentally regenerative. His symbiotic relation with the land is quintessentially pastoral: "The glade hummed softly. A woodhen called from the timber on the mountain and to that sound of all summer days of seclusion and peace the old man slept" (195). Like Faulkner's Boon Hogganbeck or Andrew Lytle's Duncan Cropleigh, Ownby is a nearly anachronistic figure from an earlier South, an Adamic figure sustained by the soil of a southern Arcady.

The intrusion of modernity into Ownby's world crystallizes the novel's Agrarian themes. The tower constructed by the government on Ownby's territory is a symbol of industrialism, the familiar machine in the garden, and McCarthy describes it in terms that might have been used by an author of the Agrarian school such as Allen Tate or Lytle. It is "clean," "cold," and "capable of infinite contempt" (93). A symbol of inevitable progress—and thus a threat to the old ways Ownby represents—the tower serves as a harbinger of the end of uncorrupted rural existence. Ownby's resistance to the forces that erected the tower is futile; the onward march of cultural deracination is as inevitable in *The Orchard Keeper* as it is in *Go Down, Moses* and Lytle's *The Velvet Horn*. The sole hope of cultural preservation in the novel resides in John Wesley Rattner, Ownby's pupil, who makes the symbolic pastoral gesture of returning government bounty money he had collected for a dead hawk. Returning the reward, he declares that the hawk—and by implication the nature it represents—"wadn't for sale" (233). The novel's conclusion confirms the transience of regional culture in the twentieth century, sounding an elegiac note for the folkways of the mountains: "They are gone now. . . . On the lips of the strange race that dwells there their names are myth, legend, dust" (246).

Thus McCarthy initially operated within the parameters of the traditional twentieth-century southern novel, exploring the familiar themes of regionalism and agrarianism one would expect to find in a work of the Renascence period. His debut novel could be situated comfortably within the modernist tradition. As what Bell has succinctly and accurately described as "an elegy commemorating a doomed way of life," *The Orchard Keeper* indicated to critics such as Sullivan that the regional objectives of the Renascence had endured to 1965 (10). For his debut McCarthy had published a tour de force of regional literature, but as his vision expanded, so would his critical appraisal of the region.

The beginning of McCarthy's phase of ontological uncertainty is evident in the structure of *Outer Dark* (1968). By initial appearances a dual bildungsroman of Culla and Rinthy Holme, it is ultimately a novel of devolution instead of development that culminates (if that is the appropriate word) in the image of a blind man entering a swamp. McCarthy's dissatisfaction with the epistemological framework of tradition is evident in his use of the working materials of regionalism to fashion prose that might be termed "postmodern local color," creating an uneasy mixture of mountain folkways set against what becomes in this second work a blighted landscape, a southern wasteland. Out of this unlikely amalgam emerges the author's increasingly postmodern—and mythoclastic—treatment of the narratives of the culture. As the novel's rambling structure indicates, the telos of all human endeavor is called into question. McCarthy's nascent mythoclastic vision is best symbolized by the murder of one of Culla's benefactors, an old man who adheres to a teleological configuration of the universe (and who, tellingly, most closely resembles Arthur Ownby of the previous novel). He declares, "I believe they's purpose to everything" (124). Yet within a short span of time the man is disemboweled by the three brigands who haunt the novel's landscape like a grotesque and inscrutable parody of the trinity (129).[3] As he is eviscerated, so, too, is belief in a "purpose to everything." Within the violent world of the novel, uncertainty is the only constant, and a teleological conception of humanity is a dangerous indulgence in naïveté. A philosophical system that would propose an order for the universe is, like the old man, exenterated, its constituent elements extracted and destroyed. It is a violently symbolic episode that indicates McCarthy's departure from the conventions—philosophical as well as literary—of tradition.

Outer Dark may be read as McCarthy's farewell to the southern pastoral; in *Child of God* (1973) he reworks another southern literary tradition: the gothic. The novel is strongly indebted to the work of Flannery O'Connor. The saga of necrophiliac Lester Ballard is rendered, like much of O'Connor's work, in an objective narrative voice that makes the protagonist's appalling actions all the more jarring to the reader by its very impassive tone. Like O'Connor, McCarthy uses the techniques of concentration and distortion to describe persons and events in a manner that highlights their mortality and temporal nature, partaking of what Richard Gray has described as the dark strain from which "the power . . . of so much Southern writing" derives (186). According to Gray, this power "depends on a single-minded, almost obsessive dissection of the human animal's claim to authority and status, a stripping-away of his pretensions and, to some extent, even his dignity" (186). *Outer Dark* hinges on this kind of vision—to an even greater extent than such works as O'Connor's *Wise Blood*. The world of the novel is finally, like O'Connor's settings, an environment in which violence perennially threatens even the most quotidian facets of experience, in which human authority and the certainty of existence are troubled by the omnipresent danger of sudden extinction.

Yet McCarthy's appropriation of O'Connor's technique is characteristically subversive. Where O'Connor used the frailty and indignity of human beings to illustrate the need for spiritual redemption, McCarthy makes no such obeisance to eternity. The only thing that seems eternal in *Child of God* is the debased nature of human beings, of which Lester Ballard is merely an extreme example. This novel is a particularly trenchant illustration of O'Connor's legacy to writers who came after the Renascence, her unwitting bequest to southern literature. Like Harry Crews and Larry Brown, McCarthy seems to have read O'Connor studiously and learned much from her fictional technique without accepting her religious beliefs. The skull beneath the skin so prominent in her work continues to be depicted in contemporary southern fiction but without its implied reference to spirituality. The signifier remains, but the signified has disappeared. The result of O'Connor's influence without its accompanying theology is a novel like *Child of God*, which renders the southern setting in grotesque and gothic terms that have none of the thematic import of O'Connor's fiction, no reference beyond the physical world.

A negative vision of humanity is not necessarily at odds with O'Connor's; she also saw weakness and frailty as inherent to the human condition. But where her unflattering depictions of the human race point the reader heavenward, McCarthy's only direct our attention downward, or rather backward, to an inescapable evolutionary heritage. The frame of reference is not Christian but Darwinian, and McCarthy takes pains to demonstrate the shared ignominy of humanity's simian origins. Any attempt to configure Ballard solely as a misfit, a horrific anomaly, is thwarted by passages that implicate the community in Ballard's transgressive development. McCarthy points out that Ballard comes from a "race that gives suck to the maimed and the crazed, that wants their wrong blood in its history and will have it" (156). Such an assertion is at odds with O'Connor's sense of the grotesque, which casts humanity as disfigured due to a perverted hunger for God. Yet it exemplifies the partial influence McCarthy has gleaned from his predecessor and demonstrates that he has adopted the first part of O'Connor's philosophy (the debasement of humanity) without its Christian corollary. Ballard's status as a "child of God much like yourself perhaps" is rendered ironic, and it also ensnares the reader into the same category—into a human race not merely fallen from grace but permanently barred from transcendence by the limits of the physical world and its own insatiable hunger for blood (4).

The result is gothic naturalism. If writers such as McCarthy have adopted O'Connor's fundamentally pessimistic vision of humanity but declined her theology, what else could emerge from her influence? Hugh Holman has asserted that "the vision [O'Connor] had of man was not of a cloud-scraping demigod, a wielder of vast powers, but of a frail, weak creature, imperfect and incomplete in all his parts" (43). For O'Connor, this naturalistic conception of humanity could only be transcended by religion. McCarthy's distrust of metaconfigurations of existence precludes such transcendence. His characters affirm the Misfit's declaration that there is "no pleasure but meanness" in life, yet they fail to espouse its negation: that such meanness results in "no real pleasure in life"

(O'Connor, *Good Man* 28, 29). Instead, they revel in the animalistic assertion of power and will as naturalistic characters do, enacting atavistic traits in a fictional environment absent of God. Unlike O'Connor's characters, the people of McCarthy's novels are not "grotesque and unnatural" because they "seek to deny [God] or pervert their hunger for Him"; rather, their disfigurement is a primary constituent of the human condition (Holman 39). They buttress Thomas Daniel Young's claim that "after reading any of his books the certainty of man's depravity no longer seems anything less than fundamental truth" (*Tennessee Writers* 106). Yet this depravity is attributable to nothing greater than humankind itself. Human beings are fallen in McCarthy's world, but not fallen from divine grace; the ignominy of the human race takes its origins in biology and heredity, not spirituality. Thus he continues to write the world as O'Connor did—fallen, absurd, painful, violent, and grotesque—but without the promise of escape. He has absorbed her technique but rejected her teleology.

The emblem of this incomplete influence is Lester Ballard, who, like O'Connor's Hazel Motes, exists on the margins of society with a pervasive hostility toward those at the center. Like Motes, Ballard drifts along the fringes of his culture, a displaced agrarian figure in an increasingly urbanized southern setting. He, too, is a perennial outcast from mainstream society, a man who "never was right" by the standards of his community (*Child of God* 21). But his environment contains few of the symbolic references that characterize *Wise Blood*. Motes thinks he sees "Jesus move from tree to tree in the back of his mind, a wild ragged figure motioning to him to turn around" (22). The adumbrations of an alternative world in *Child of God* are very different. They are to be found among the "enormous blocks and tablets of stone weathered gray and grown with deep green moss, toppled monoliths among the trees and vines like traces of an older race of man" and among the "gothic treeboles" that hold "two stones the size of fieldwagons, great tablets on which was writ only a tale of vanished seas with ancient shells in cameo and fishes etched in lime" (25, 128). Here references to a world beyond the present one are rendered solely in biological and geological terms. There is precious little transcendence to be gleaned from them. If they contain any religious import, it lies in the deliberately vague reference to a pagan culture, a pre-Christian community of "an older race of man" that may have erected, in druidic fashion, the monoliths that now lie toppled on the forest floor. The second set of tablets contain even less evidence of human existence; on them is "writ *only* a tale of vanished seas." An Old Testament burlesque, these are the "tablets" of natural law and nothing more. Humanity is not granted even a trace upon this palimpsest of natural history. These fixtures of the environment underscore the insignificance of a race that, in McCarthy's vision, leaves no more record of its passing than the lowly creatures of "vanished seas."

McCarthy continues to emphasize human ignominy through the atavistic depictions of his characters. Ballard is described as "a misplaced and loveless simian shape" that moves through a snowfall looking "like some crazy winter gnome" (20, 107). In a characteristically terse conversation with another man, Ballard and his friend look "like constipated gargoyles" (46). When he is frost-bitten, Ballard finds himself "gibbering" in a cave, his cries echoing back to him "like the mutterings of a band of sympathetic apes" (159).

McCarthy brilliantly encapsulates these atavistic concerns in the novel's concluding pages. As if to demonstrate that Ballard did not exist sui generis, McCarthy describes his horrific tenure as a medical cadaver in precise, bureaucratic prose that obfuscates the boundary between Ballard, the serial-killer necrophile, and the medical students who examine his remains:

His body was shipped to the state medical school at Memphis. There in a basement room he was preserved with formalin and wheeled forth to take his place with other deceased persons newly arrived. He was laid out on a slab and flayed, eviscerated, dissected. His head was sawed open and the brains removed. His muscles were stripped from his bones. His heart was taken out. His entrails were hauled forth and delineated and the four young students who bent over him like those haruspices of old perhaps saw monsters worse to come in their configurations. At the end of three months when the class was closed Ballard was scraped from the table into a plastic bag and taken with others of his kind to a cemetery outside the city and there interred. A minister from the school read a simple service. (194)

Here the very idea of civilized progress is subjected to a powerful irony, for the medical students, performing on Ballard the same sort of violence he enacted on his victims (evisceration, mutilation), are unlikely to lay bare the precise source or character of a degeneracy that McCarthy sees as ingrained. Ostensibly the servants of modern medical science, the students resemble their primitive antecedents, the haruspices of antiquity, who sought an elusive knowledge through the divination of inscrutable organs. The locale of their inquiry—Memphis—carries suggestive echoes as well: to ancient Egypt, where embalmers conducted a similar commerce with the dead. The parallels cast into doubt the question of whether civilization has indeed progressed from that ancient time, whether the apprentice physicians and the "minister from the school" who reads "a simple service" are any closer to full knowledge of the universe than their ancient forbears.

Eliot asked, "After such knowledge, what forgiveness?" McCarthy does not privilege modernity with such an assumption of progress; instead, he deconstructs the foundations of Eliot's question, undermining its syllogism. He proposes that there is no absolute knowledge, nor forgiveness—no myth beyond the perennial primitivism of humanity. Mythopoeia is replaced with mythoclasm. This method is indeed analogous to warfare against the modernist conception of myth, for in denying the validity of culture McCarthy gives the lie to the entire modernist project. Without the benefit of history, the contemporary individual must seek meaning in a landscape lacking metanarratives, with no God, no myth, no progress. If *Outer Dark* may be read as a deconstruction of southern community, *Child of God* is an attack on the myths that underlie community, a depiction of a landscape no longer even Christ-haunted.

Suttree is McCarthy's grandest achievement, a massive novel that combines the philosophical musings of its predecessors into a fully realized postmodern vision of the South. In it McCarthy's atavistic technique reaches its florescence, and his mythoclastic treatment of southern culture attains a new level of incisiveness. The novel is a postmodern rewriting of the modernist quest for order, in which a southern protagonist fixated on the past finds that the confusion of his environment resists his attempts at imposing order on it. As Cornelius Suttree relinquishes his modernist compulsion to order experience through the metanarrative of myth, he indicates a new direction for the protagonist of southern fiction—an odyssey in which the past menaces, rather than informs, the bewildering present. In a series of atavistic episodes McCarthy demonstrates that human history and the attempt to construe it as a teleological narrative are futile. The route to Suttree's deliverance lies solely in relinquishing a quest for metanarratives that cannot be recovered, in turning away from an immoderate past defined by bloodshed, primitivism, and chaos. As the "reprobate scion of doomed Saxon clans," Suttree has no other choice (136).

The novel's enigmatic prologue questions the telos of history and culture. It depicts 1950s' era Knoxville, Tennessee, as a primitive, arcane landscape, a *"city constructed on no known paradigm, a mongrel architecture reading back through the works of man in a brief delineation of the aberrant disordered and mad"* (3). The city is pervaded by death and madness, its existence colored by the deceased pioneers who built it—not intrepid harbingers of civilization but *"old teutonic forebears with eyes incandesced by the visionary light of a massive rapacity"* (4). The passage culminates in a vision of Western culture as a theater of the dead, an appropriate image for both the settlers' fate and McCarthy's atavistic vision: "A curtain is rising on the western world. A fine rain of soot, dead beetles, anonymous small bones. The audience sits webbed in dust. Within the gutted sockets of the interlocutor's skull a spider sleeps and the jointed ruins of the hanged fool dangle from the flies, bone pendulum in motley. Fourfooted shapes go to and fro over the boards. Ruder forms survive" (5). These sentences effectively summarize McCarthy's atavistic technique. Beginning with a grandiose invocation of the drama of Western civilization, they survey the dramatis personae of the dead only to culminate in the flatly emphatic declaration that "ruder forms survive"—collocating beginnings (the curtain rising) with human death and, most important, the persistence of the rudimentary forms from which humanity has sprung. The passage is a succinct expression of what may be the most radically anti-anthropocentric vision in contemporary literature.

Comparisons to the primeval continue in *Suttree* beyond the novel's prologue; the tenor of virtually every metaphor in the novel is the crude, the ancient, the primordial. Knoxville, for example, looks "as must the ruins of many an older city seen by herders in the hills, by barbaric tribesmen shuffling along the roads" (179). The novel abounds with similes that focus on atavistic comparisons: poker players in an abandoned mansion "like shades of older times or rude imposters on a stage set" (22); welts on Doll Jones's face "like a sacerdotal brand on some stone age matriarch" (108); Gene Harrogate studying maps by lamplight in his "little grotto" like a "cherrycolored troll or demon cartographer" (116, 260); the "filthy basilica" of the Knoxville sewers (262); Suttree and the Reeses crouching as if "they could have been some band of stone age folk washed up out of an atavistic dream" (358); possum hunters squatting "in the manner of apes" (359); Suttree sniffing the air "in a gesture of some simpler antecedent" (447).

These passages hardly indicate a project of cultural reclamation such as the modernists undertook, for in them McCarthy characteristically moves farther back in time than the modernists, beyond the Fisher King and back to the caves. Instead of a mythological foundation to culture, these antecedents are remnants of the evolutionary past. Countering the modernists' use of myth and archetype, they do not lend meaning and stability to the disordered present but underscore the perennially primitive nature of humanity—the past provides no refuge from the present. As Eudora Welty once said of Katherine Anne Porter's work, memory here is ironic. Racial memory is not a redemptive entity to be recovered (as in Yeats and Eliot) but an omnipresent handicap passed down to the present generation, whether from teutonic forbears or ancestors simpler still. The spiritual emptiness of the contemporary era, McCarthy indicates, is not a lapse from the organic past but its legacy. For McCarthy, then, the modernist metanarrative—an idea of cultural coherence—is a chimera. The dilemmas of twentieth-century culture must be resolved in new terms.

Suttree, however, begins his quest without this knowledge. As his nihilistic fixation is exacerbated by the milieu of death and atavism that surrounds him, Suttree searches for a narrative framework with which to impose order on his environment. Because he cannot accept the reality of his own death, he attempts to integrate himself into a narrative larger than his own life, a means of transcending extinction. Suttree cannot accept the discontinuity of existing sui generis, and thus the image of his dead twin brother functions as a sort of archetype to him, an essentialist antecedent by which he may achieve connection: "His subtle obsession with uniqueness troubled all his dreams. He saw his brother in swaddling, hands outheld, a scent of myrrh and lilies" (113). Keenly aware of the absence of his replicated form, Suttree seeks out his own reflection throughout the novel. The fact that this "othersuttree" (287) is dead compounds his nihilistic fixation with death and spurs him into morbid reflections on mortality: "What deity in the realms of dementia, what rabid god decocted out of the smoking lobes of hydrophobia could have devised a keeping place for souls so poor as is this flesh. This mawky wormbent tabernacle" (130). His obsession with his twin brother—and the search for connection that accompanies it— hinders his ability to achieve any sort of fulfillment. Only by resolving his "subtle obsession with uniqueness" can Suttree produce meaning within his atavistic surroundings.

Two scenes from Knoxville depict the disparate ordering impulses between which he ultimately charts his course. As polar opposites, these scenes provide Suttree (and the reader) with divergent responses to a daunting cosmos, two different approaches to imposing form on an existence that offers little more than eidetic glimpses of an elusive coherence. Suttree's perambulations through the city present him with one mode of existence: "and he saw an idiot in a yard in a leather harness chained to a clothesline and it leaned and swayed drooling and looked out upon the alley with eyes that fed the most rudimentary brain and yet seemed possessed of news in the universe denied right forms, like perhaps the eyes of a squid whose simian depths seem to harbor some horrible intelligence. All down past the hedges a gibbering and howling in a hoarse frog's voice, word perhaps of things known raw, unshaped by the constructions of a mind obsessed with form" (427). Here is one alternative to the human drive for order—raw knowledge of the universe lacking the deduction and consequence of a priori interpretation, experience without logos. The idiot is McCarthy's supreme atavistic human: even more debased than hominoids like the possum hunters, he seems more animal (squid, frog) than human. Although he possesses perhaps the same "news of the universe" as Suttree, his inchoate mind clashes with that of the protagonist, who struggles to establish a catechism of even the barest and most reductive beliefs (414). Suttree's discouraging compulsion is to order the same experience that the idiot knows raw and unshaped.

Yet the idiot represents an alternative to the conventional life that Suttree has rejected to live in the derelict section of the city; at the very least, he proposes an alternative to the bourgeois values that Suttree's father represents. His father's letters urge Suttree to look for a life "[i]n the law courts, in business, in government"—at the obvious expense of conducting a true quest for meaning (14). The institutions endorsed by the elder Suttree reify meaning through a delusive ordering principle. As the ordering units of society, they operate with a reductive logic that seeks to make the transcendent tangible. The workers who raze McAnally Flats serve the ordering vision of commerce and conventional progress: "He watched the bland workman in the pilothouse of the crane shifting levers. The long tethered wreckingball swung through the side of a wall and small boys applauded. . . . Gnostic workmen who would have down this shabby shapeshow that masks the higher world of form. And left at eventide these cutaway elevations, little cubicles giving onto space, an iron bedstead, a freestanding stairwell to nowhere" (464). In contrast to the idiot, these bland, gnostic workers are obsessed with form. Clearing away the shabbiness of the tangible world, they make way for the abstract, the "higher world of form." Again, however, this approach to form is fruitless. At the end of the day, the workers' efforts—their pursuit of the abstract—culminate in the surrealistic image of a staircase leading to nowhere. Their compulsion to refine the slums of McAnally is nearly as futile as the ravings of the tethered idiot. Beyond the site of their labors, the "fields of rubble" remain, where "black hominoids scurried over the waste" (464). The ruder forms of the "shabby shapeshow" and the black hominoids persist.

Suttree's deliverance results from abandoning both approaches to form. Coming out of typhoid fever, he announces an epiphany: he has realized that "there is one Suttree and one Suttree only" (461). By acknowledging his uniqueness, he relinquishes his fixation with the "othersuttree." The gesture is vital;

both realistic and life-affirming, it is a refutation of the abstract construct that Suttree has sustained like the workers' gnosticism, an acknowledgment that his "othersuttree," like their higher world of form, is an illusory abstraction. The vision makes it clear that teleology and ideal forms are as empty as their nominal opposites: the descent into subhuman oblivion the idiot represents or the nihilistic self-destruction Suttree has practiced in McAnally Flats. As if to undermine the logic of formal systems, Suttree's epiphany results from an accident (his fever) and not from the ascetic journey he undertakes in the Smoky Mountains—a fact that underscores both the naturalistic contingency of existence and the futility of teleological goals. Only by accepting the world as it is, without the imposition of human myth, can Suttree obtain real enlightenment. By accepting the solitude of being "one and one only," he comes to focus on the imminent instead of the abstract. Individual experience supersedes the imposition of ersatz paradigms upon the natural world.[4]

Suttree's new knowledge represents an abdication of mythologizing tendencies that are ultimately, in McCarthy's larger vision, little more than anthropocentric self-delusion in a "paradigmless world" (Bell 8). McCarthy's atavism continuously pushes the reader toward the same conclusion. By emptying the past of transcendent significance, he stresses the contingency of existence—his primitive depictions adulterate the comfortable in order to force us to confront the present without artifice. Even the concept of narrative is attenuated in *Suttree* to such an extent that the protagonist's epiphany is rendered in rather ambiguous terms that cast a revelation as something slight enough to be easily overlooked. The iconoclasm of this approach subverts all traditional means of ordering experience, calling into question the efficacy of societal institutions and even the early part of Suttree's quest. While conventional means of imposing form on existence are familiar and certainly understandable, McCarthy's atavistic vision constantly thwarts our compulsion to privilege such efforts. His focus isolates the individual in the present, forcing the "one and one only" descendant of ruder forms to achieve a singular perception of the world.

This focus on the present—this iconoclastic treatment of history—places *Suttree* at odds with southern literary tradition. As if his movement away from epistemological concerns was not emphatic enough, however, McCarthy stresses his break with southern modernism in a rare moment of clear symbolic allusion. Suttree is the first of McCarthy's protagonists to come from the upper classes, and when he visits the abandoned home of his childhood—a mansion with "tall fluted columns" and an "immense and stark facade"—McCarthy indulges in an emblematic display of his break from literary tradition, bringing southern mythology under the scrutiny of his atavistic vision (*Suttree* 135). The house, along with the culture it represents, is in ruin, its chandelier burst, its walls warped and water-stained, its "great doors of solid cherry split open in long fibrous cracks and plundered of their knobs and hardware" (135). Initially the house seems to be one of the symbolic fixtures of traditional southern fiction, representing, in Grammer's words, "the failure of southern order to preserve itself against time" (28). But because of the mature vision of *Suttree*, its connotations move beyond the conventional. As Grammer points out, McCarthy deploys this symbol in ironic fashion, "asserting [his] particular sort of relationship to the southern literary tradition" (28).

This particular relationship is that of the subversive iconoclast, for McCarthy presents what is almost literally an icon of southern modernism only to deconstruct it at its foundations. The house's disorder is in itself hardly shocking; John Crowe Ransom also portrayed a crumbling southern manor in his poem "Old Mansion." But Ransom, in eminently modernist fashion, contrasted the "richly inhabited" realm of the mansion with the "unseemlier world" of contemporaneity (70, 71). McCarthy inverts this pattern. The tradition of the house is a primitive one, with only a token resemblance to chivalry; its former occupants can be best described euphemistically as the "somewhat illustrious dead" (*Suttree* 136). Suttree imagines "large companies" of them dining in the mansion's banquet hall: "Mad trenchermen in armed sortees above the platters, the clang of steel, the stained and dripping chops, the eyes sidling. Yard dogs and starving palliards contest the scraps among the straw. There is nothing laid to table save meat and water. There is no sound of human speech. . . . The master wipes his fingers in his hair and his rising says the feast is done" (136). Here McCarthy intrudes atavism into the most sacrosanct fixture of southern cultural mythology. Unlike the modernists, he does not dwell on the order of this vanished culture but on its inherent primitivism, once again delving into a distant past the modernists seldom acknowledged. The "unseemlier world" is the older one in which chivalric accoutrements adorned primitive humanity with only the semblance of culture. This world lacked even the sophistication of human speech and was marked by a naturalistic struggle such as one sees among the dogs contesting for scraps—a struggle reflected in the "sidling" eyes of the men at the table. Mythopoesis is here rendered obsolete. The contemporary individual has nothing to gain from the past; rather than a sojourner among a regenerative history, the individual is "a vain figure in the ruins" (135). Suttree may well represent his creator in the concluding sentences of the scene. Leaving the demesne of tradition, Suttree notices that its demarcations have been altered, that the signposts between the old order and the new have been reversed. He observes a sign whose meaning no longer applies: "Old paint on an old sign said dimly to keep out. Someone must have turned it around because it posted the outer world. He went on anyway. He said that he was only passing through" (136).

T he scene at the old Suttree estate is truly one of the portentous moments of twentieth-century southern fiction. As he has passed through the imaginative terrain of southern literature, McCarthy has altered its signifiers, reversed its signposts, to such an extent that conventional uses of the past no longer seem viable. Eliot stressed (and the southern modernists would have agreed) that the mythic method is "a step toward making the modern world possible for art" (178). McCarthy suggests that it is mythoclasm—the inversion of modernist historical tropes—that makes the postmodern world possible for art. A continued adherence to the valorizing backward glance of the modernists, he indicates, threatens to reduce the contemporary artist to the status of a vain figure in the ruins—an impotent epigone seeking scraps from the table of an exhausted culture. It is perhaps no accident that this scene from McCarthy's last southern novel echoes one of the defining works of southern modernism, Tate's "Ode to the Confederate Dead." Like the character in Tate's poem, Suttree is a seeker in a familiar environment, and he finds himself beneath the gaze of "blind parget cherubs" (McCarthy 135) that resemble the "uncomfortable angels" of "brute curiosity" in Tate's ode (*Poems* 20). But Suttree does not stop at the gate, paralyzed by a lack of imaginative connection with the past. He can envision the past all too well, and he rejects it, setting out for new territory. One hopes that McCarthy's similar rejection of the southern past does not mark his permanent exodus from the region's literature—that with his western Border Trilogy completed, he will return to the South to perpetuate the achievement of his first four novels—for McCarthy has demonstrated that art can proliferate even among the ashes of a culture's mythology, that the ruder forms laid bare by a mythoclastic vision may contain the seeds of a vital post-Renascence southern fiction.

INTO THE SUBURBS

**Richard Ford's Sportswriter
as Postsouthern Expatriate**

If you don't know who you are or where you come from, you will find yourself at a disadvantage. The ordered slums of suburbia are made for the confusion of the spirit. Those who live in units called homes or estates—both words do violence to the language—don't know who they are.

—*Andrew Lytle*, A Wake for the Living

I wanted to write about a certain stratum of life that I knew, which was life in the suburbs.

—*Richard Ford, "An Interview with Richard Ford"*

In 1996 Richard Ford received the Pulitzer Prize for fiction for *Independence Day*, the sequel to his successful novel *The Sportswriter* (1986). The award placed him in the company of the other prominent southern writers who had received the prize, among them Robert Penn Warren, William Faulkner, Katherine Anne Porter, William Styron, Eudora Welty, Alice Walker, and Peter Taylor. Yet Ford's portrayal of Frank Bascombe, sportswriter, hardly falls within the parameters of southern fiction represented by his Pulitzer Prize–winning predecessors from the South. The Frank Bascombe novels evince none of the importance of tradition found in the novels of Warren or Welty, depict none of the old social order so important to the work of Porter and Taylor, and take place at a point in cultural history largely lacking the tragedy and social oppression that catalyze much of Styron's and Walker's fiction. In terms of artistic temperament, the Mississippi-born Ford has more in common with fellow recipient John Updike than with any of his southern peers; the protagonist of his sportswriter novels is more akin to Rabbit Angstrom than to Warren's Jack Burden or Taylor's Phillip Carver.

Ford's Frank Bascombe novels are nothing less than a deconstruction of the conventional southern novel. To be sure, their New Jersey setting does not immediately disqualify them as southern fiction; as Noel Polk has pointed out, novels such as Faulkner's *A Fable* and Welty's *The Bride of the Innisfallen* retain a southern sensibility despite their nonsouthern settings ("Southern Literary Pieties" 30–32). But in Ford's recent work one finds a truly exiled sensibility that is more profoundly rootless than the delineations of geographical boundaries would indicate. Ford has not only situated his latest fiction entirely outside the South—in locales as varied as Montana and Paris—he has also abandoned the themes and techniques that allowed Faulkner and Welty to carry southern writing into new environments. The prose style of his later work is clipped and precise—the antithesis of the baroque style that has defined much of twentieth-century southern writing. History is notably absent from his vision as well. His mature novels operate wholly in the contemporary and the recent past, outside the tradition that Warren describes in *All the King's Men* as "the awful responsibility of Time" (438). Further, Ford rigorously questions the value of family and community, exhibiting a marked suspicion of the essentialism inherent in modernist views of these institutions as stabilizing forces. His career altogether repudiates the typical progression of the southern author. Ford has not devoted his career to a lengthy examination of the South; rather, his success has hinged on his abdication of the South as subject and setting.

Ford's ambivalent attitude toward the conventions of southern fiction can be explained largely through that of his character Frank Bascombe. Frank is himself a former author who enjoyed critical acclaim for his first and only book of fiction, a collection of stories entitled *Blue Autumn*. Frank's short-lived career in fiction drew heavily on the South, especially in the story "Night Wing," which concerns "a bemused young southerner" who endures a short stint in the navy before moving into the "hazy world of sex and drugs and rumored gun-running" of New Orleans, where he attempts to reconcile "the vertiginous present" with his guilt-ridden past. The story culminates in "a violent tryst with a Methodist minister's wife who seduces him in an abandoned slave-quarters" and is "told in a series of flashbacks" (Ford, *Sportswriter* 36). As Frank admits, "I seemed . . . to have been stuck in bad stereotypes" (46). While staying in a hotel in Pennsylvania, Frank finds a copy of the book in the inn's library: "And to my wonderment and out of all account, among the loose and uncategorized books, here is a single copy of my own now-old book of short stories, *Blue Autumn*, in its original dust jacket, on the front of which is a faded artist's depiction of a 1968-version sensitive-young-man, with a brush cut, an open-collared white shirt, jeans, and an uncertain half-smile, standing emblematically alone in the dirt parking lot of a country gas station with an anonymous green pickup (possibly his) visible over his shoulder. Much is implied" (Ford, *Independence Day* 319). The cover Frank describes is the dust jacket of Ford's own first novel, *A Piece of My Heart* (1976), the first edition of which indeed bears the image of a solitary young man in a dirt parking lot (looking very much the part of a bemused young southerner), with a green pickup truck and a country store in the background. The description of the fictitious *Blue Autumn* cover corresponds in every detail with *A Piece of My Heart*, save only the name of the gas station—Goode- nough's—which is visible on the cover of Ford's novel.[1]

More than a literary curiosity, this confluence between fiction and reality is the clearest example of the significant parallels between Frank Bascombe's liter- ary career and Ford's own, and it illustrates the choices Ford made as a writer seeking his own voice. Like Frank, Ford initially struggled with the South in his fiction; *A Piece of My Heart* suffers from the same gothic excesses as Frank's story "Night Wing." And like Frank, Ford worked as a sportswriter; after publishing the expatriate novel *The Ultimate Good Luck* in 1981, he left creative writing to work as a journalist for the magazine *Inside Sports*. Ford, too, sold the movie rights to his first book to a Hollywood producer and bought a house in New Jersey with the royalties (Ford, "Interview" 94). But Ford did not completely abandon fiction, as Frank does. He returned from his literary hiatus with a new voice for his fiction—that of the ambivalent southerner in exile—and created a masterpiece of American literary realism. In the voice of Frank Bascombe, Ford finally found the outlet for his best energies as a writer. The mantle of southern literary heritage had very nearly stifled a brilliant and original voice that had little to gain from the tradition. The references to *Blue Autumn* in the Frank

Bascombe novels, then, are indeed symbolic. They demonstrate that, for a contemporary writer with Ford's sensibilities, the struggle lies not in coming to terms with southern history but in escaping it—in moving away from conventional literary patterns that have no more authenticity in the author's personal experience than bad stereotypes.

A rare study in literary influence, *A Piece of My Heart* is the sort of first novel one might expect from a gifted young southern writer steeped in the region's literary tradition. It displays a fastidious attention to detail in rendering the peculiarities of local culture and captures the nuances of Mississippi dialect astutely. Ford depicts the geography of the Mississippi Delta with accuracy, elevating it to a level of importance that place typically achieves in Southern Renascence literature. The action of the novel is violent, developing inexorably from the imminent past. Like Cormac McCarthy's *The Orchard Keeper*, it is a debut in which an innovative artistic perspective competes uneasily with the standard motifs of southern literary tradition.

But ultimately Ford's homage to his influences damages the novel; *A Piece of My Heart* is an impressive rehearsal of southern themes that never quite transcends the epigonic territory in which it operates. Flannery O'Connor's influence is too salient in Ford's gothic depictions of Mark Lamb and his black butler, T. V. A. Landrieu, and in grotesque characters such as Mr. Gaspereau. The novel's modernist structure is finally ill-suited to Ford's novelistic temperament. Its schematic prologue, epilogue, and alternating "Robard Hewes" and "Sam Newel" sections, along with the extensive, italicized flashbacks to Sam Newel's southern childhood, combine to give the effect of an exercise in the structuralist poetics of an earlier era.

And the rumblings of the Dixie Limited can be heard throughout the novel. Like Faulkner's first novel, *Soldiers' Pay*, much of Ford's novel consists of philosophical discussions between godless pilgrims in a torrid southern setting. Its debt to *Absalom, Absalom!* is evident as well. Sam Newel's resemblance to Quentin Compson can hardly be overlooked; he moves from an icy room in Chicago (where he watches his breath fog against a cold windowpane and discusses his "poor tolerance for ambiguity" with his girlfriend [71]) to a quasi-suicidal leap into the Mississippi River, to the Delta, all in an effort to come to terms with the past and "stitch it together into some reasonable train of thought" (228). The terrain of Ford's Delta is also haunted by other Faulknerian shades, including a rapacious farmer named Rudolph whose legend is strongly reminiscent of Thomas Sutpen's:

Buck said that the old man had come down sometime in 1941, from Republican City, Nebraska, had sold his half of his father's pig farm to his brother Wolfgang and moved himself and two steamer trunks on the train to Little Rock and put himself up at a commercial hotel at the foot of the Main street bridge and bought himself a Buick coupe and drove all over the country between Little Rock and Memphis looking for cheap land. And after not very long, Buck said, he bought eight hundred acres of swamp fifteen miles back of Hazen, land that no farmer had even thought to abandon, much less cultivate, since La Fourche Creek ran straight through the middle of it and flooded every spring, leaving a solid counterpane of silt and randy water on top of the entire parcel so that even the rice farmers had given up on it and just kept it for duck hunting. He said that Rudolph, who was in his thirties and strong as a bulldog, had gotten hold of the land and practically gnawed every tree on it with his own teeth and built up a maze of bar ditches and ramparts and iron sluice gates to channel the water out of the lows and into an old dead-tree reservoir he dug out with three World War I scoopers. (48–49)

Here one sees the Faulkner influence in both theme and style, notably in protracted sentences reminiscent of the "refining, supplementing, substituting, digressing" that Donald Kartiganer has described as characteristically Faulknerian (886). The passage effectively demonstrates the central flaw of *A Piece of My Heart*: it is a well-written novel with a secondhand artistic vision.

Ford eventually became aware of the deficiency. As he told Bonnie Lyons in 1996, he realized that his "first book was about the South and was captivated by certain traditional southern themes—search for place, freedom of choice, s-e-x—all inherited literary concerns. And it was also probably directly influenced by Faulkner and Eudora Welty and Flannery O'Connor and God knows who else southern" ("Art of Fiction" 49). Like many other contemporary southern writers, Ford's rite of passage as a creative writer was to exorcise himself of the "inherited literary concerns" of southern tradition. In Ford's words, this meant abandoning the South in his fiction: "all the people who wrote about [*A Piece of My Heart*] said it was another Southern novel, and I just said, Okay, that's it. No more Southern writing for me" (Lee 229). The result of finding Mississippi too crowded for a young writer was an artistic journey that involved striking out for new territory—to the very antithesis of the terrain of the Southern Renascence: the urban northeast.

THE SPORTSWRITER AS SOUTHERN EXILE

Frank Bascombe is a transplanted Mississippian with none of the concerns of an exile; he has no precedent in southern fiction. He not only finds himself in suburban New Jersey, he enjoys being there, fixing his mind on the quotidian concerns of rain gutters, storm windows, and property values while consummating his "pastoral kind of longing" for the suburbs (Ford, *Sportswriter* 312). Like his neighbors, he aims to lead a "steadfast and accountable" life on a small scale, conducting himself with some measure of dignity through "the normal applauseless life of us all" (51, 10). His is a conventional American existence, its only tragic element comprised of the death of his son, Ralph, and the divorce that followed it—events that compel him to burrow even more firmly into the commonplace reassurances of the suburbs.

Frank's resemblance to other southern literary émigrés is superficial at best. Unlike Faulkner's Quentin Compson or Styron's Stingo, Frank cares little for his southern heritage. He brings northward no obsession with the past, no link to a Byzantine family history, no sense of the past in the present. He is more akin to George Babbitt or Silas Lapham than to other fictional southern expatriates—including Ford's own earlier character, Sam Newel. His primary concern is to fit into his present environment and become "an ordinary citizen," not to maintain any link to the South or retain a self-conscious identity as a southerner (13). Witness, for example, his attitude toward his past—most of which, he claims, "can be dispensed with in a New York minute" (35). Posing the question, "Whose history can ever reveal very much?" Frank declares, "In my view Americans put too much emphasis on their pasts as a way of defining themselves, which can be death-dealing. . . . The stamp of our parents on us and of the past in general is, to my mind, overworked, since at some point we are whole and by ourselves upon the earth, and there is nothing that can change that for better or worse, and so we might as well think about something more promising" (24). Frank's attitude is distinctly unsouthern, for he views history as lacking in the narrative patterns that Quentin and Stingo desperately seek. He sees himself as part of no historical continuum and feels no compulsion to integrate himself into a story of his culture.

If Frank's viewpoint is unconventional, so, too, are his origins in the South. He cannot claim a distinguished southern pedigree. His parents were native Iowans who relocated to Mississippi before he was born, and his childhood was rootless enough for him to think of it as "a postcard with changing scenes on one side but no particular or memorable messages on the back" (24). He describes his origins in terms that are antithetical to southern configurations of the family saga: "I was born into an ordinary, modern existence in 1945, an only child to decent parents of no irregular point of view, no particular sense of their *place* in history's continuum, just two people afloat on the world and expectant like most others in time, without a daunting conviction about their own consequence. This seems like a fine lineage to me still" (24). Frank's conception of personal history clashes with those of the fictional southern exiles who have preceded him, even taking into account the fact that his parents were born into the disruptive, chaotic modern era. His legacy is not one of a shattered old order or a banished aristocracy. He views the concept of the past in the present sardonically: "Does it seem strange that I do not have a long and storied family history? Or a list of problems and hatreds to brood about—a bill of particular grievances and nostalgias that pretend to explain or trouble everything? Possibly I was born into a different time. But maybe my way is better all around, and is actually the way with most of us and the rest tell lies" (29). Here is evidence of Frank's status as a new sort of protagonist in southern fiction and of Ford's break with southern literary tradition. The past is not in the present for Frank; it is irrevocably past.

Despite Frank's (and Ford's) pronounced ambivalence for the South, at least one prominent critic has felt compelled to situate the novel in the context of tradition. In *The Southern Writer in the Postmodern World*, Fred Hobson describes Frank as a "southern expatriate for the eighties," a "cousin of Quentin Compson" who, by the very nature of his declared indifference to all things southern, protests too much (49, 50). Hobson argues that Frank, like his Faulknerian predecessor, belies himself in his claims to indifference about the South. It follows that, in spite of appearances, *The Sportswriter* is "a southern novel in a southern tradition"—a "book about New Jersey that is very much a book about the South" (57).

Hobson is correct in describing Ford as an ironic writer and in interpreting *The Sportswriter* as "among other things, a commentary on the traditional southern novel," but his assessment leaves much to be desired (52). Ford's Frank Bascombe novels will not fit a traditionalist pattern, no matter how much irony is applied to the reading of them. Their value as "commentary on the traditional southern novel" lies in their emphatic break from that tradition. A contradiction in Hobson's analysis illustrates this point. Hobson notes that Ford "belongs . . .

quite literally to a different *class* of writers" than the Renascence authors who preceded him; his life, with its blue-collar origins and lack of attachment to place, "is hardly the biography of a Southern Agrarian" (43). One wonders, then, why Hobson goes on to equate Frank—whose background he acknowledges to be quite similar to Ford's—with such protagonists of upper-class pedigree as Warren's Jack Burden, Allen Tate's Lacy Buchan, Walker Percy's Binx Bolling and Will Barrett, and Taylor's Phillip Carver (55).

Frank's similarities to Will Barrett (and to Percy himself) form an example of the dangers of misappropriating literary influence. Certainly Frank's "dreaminess" resembles Will's perpetual sense of dislocation, and echoes of "dark ravening particles" are present in Frank's "coming down with a case of the dreads so thick they seemed to whistle out of the heating ducts and swarm the room like a dark mistral" (31). Frank, like Percy, has written an article called "Why I Live Where I Live," in which he discusses the importance of living in a "neutral" environment (40). Hobson notes similar parallels and in fact goes to great lengths in an effort to link Ford to Percy, but he does not point out that Ford resolves his hero's problems in a manner opposite to Percy's. Although Percy's stylistic influence is certainly present in *The Sportswriter*, thematic and philosophical inheritance is not. It is difficult to imagine, for example, Frank indulging in Confederate nostalgia such as Will's or blowing up a Union monument in New Jersey. Although Frank, like Will, begins to think at one point that "it mightn't be a bad idea to return to the South and discover his identity" (Percy, *Last Gentleman* 79), Frank's southern quest is never fulfilled: he finds little connection there beyond "an imputed and remote" heritage (Ford, *Sportswriter* 371). The sort of epiphany that Will achieves in his interaction with the Vaughts is entirely absent in Ford's vision, which continuously withdraws from such enlightenment. Any attempt to connect *The Sportswriter* with Percy's work ultimately founders on this point. The best one can hope for, as Ford pointed out to an interviewer who compared *The Sportswriter* to *The Moviegoer*, is "secular redemption" (Ford, "Conversation" 613). Unlike Percy, Ford offers us no grand pattern of existence, however elusive or attenuated—be it Kierkegaardian, regional, or Christian. Like his sportswriter, Ford has only a superficial link to such tradition.

An insistent focus on literary lineage therefore does an injustice to Ford's achievement. Given that Ford's development has hinged on his abdication of southern influence, it seems spurious to connect his sportswriter novels with a tradition he has left behind. Worse still, such a connection neglects to consider *The Sportswriter* on its own grounds, as a postmodern novel. The lack of southern qualities in Frank would be only a superficial divergence from convention if it did not represent a fundamentally new envisioning of experience—one that requires the critic to approach Ford's work in new terms. If we are to grant the sportswriter novels their due as "a particular expression of the postmodern imagination" (Hobson 54), we must also acknowledge the post*southern* vision they contain, relinquishing the old method of discerning influence and tracing its origins to Renascence works in talmudic fashion.

An effective way to approach *The Sportswriter* is with a full acknowledgment of the postmodern currents that lies beneath the surface of Ford's otherwise traditionally realistic prose. Ford is what might be termed a postmodern realist: although his work conforms to the conventions of realism in its accurate depiction of everyday life, the world he represents is fraught with the uncertainty characteristic of postmodernism.[2] As an example of what Bill Buford has described as "dirty realism," writing such as Ford's "is not self-consciously experimental" like most postmodern fiction but pared down to such an extent that "it makes the more traditional realistic novels of, say, Updike or Styron seem ornate, even baroque in comparison" (4). Such is the shape of realistic fiction in the postmodern era, where verisimilitude is, as Ford has remarked, a "slippery matter in a slippery world" ("Art of Fiction" 63). The truths it conveys are of necessity small and particular—even minimalist. Due to the cultural climate of what Jean-François Lyotard calls the postmodern suspicion of metanarratives, a contemporary realist such as Ford cannot turn to grand historical and philosophical narratives as the modernists did.

The use of irony itself becomes problematic in such an environment of uncertainty. The reader wants to believe that Ford is satirizing his character when Frank lapses into moments of unabashed Babbittry, yet Ford steadfastly refuses to indulge in the authorial condescension that Sinclair Lewis and William Dean Howells intruded upon their narratives. In Ford's vision Frank's story is not an object lesson, not a parable, but "a novel about a decent man" proffered with an absolute minimum of moral judgment (Ford, "Interview" 83). Even as Frank blithely extols the virtues of rental cars—even as he denigrates the craft of fiction and praises consumer culture—Ford maintains a strict first-person consciousness in his narrative. If the reader senses satire in such passages, it occurs, in Ford's characteristic fashion, incidentally, obliquely—without the salient indication of authorial presence. The saga of "a decent man" in contemporary culture is told solely in the decent man's terms, without deferring to a controlling, moralizing intelligence that a writer such as Ford deems artificial.

Witness, for example, Ford's attitude toward the metanarrative of religion. The time frame of *The Sportswriter* spans the days of Easter weekend, yet as Ford explains, any linkage to Christian mythology that occurred as he wrote the novel hindered his vision: "When I realized that I was harnessing my book up to some provocative Judeo-Christian myths, I really tried to pull back. But suddenly it all started connecting up in ways that I didn't like and I just took out, out. Out, out, out. . . . And I certainly would hate for the book to be read as a book just about Christian redemption, because it's not a Christian book. The kind of redeeming that goes on in that book is entirely unreligious; it's really Frank figuring out ways to redeem his life *based on nothing but the stuff of his life*" ("Interview" 85; emphasis added). Clearly Ford operates outside the modernist conventions of mythopoesis. His fiction works within a postmodern arena that denies the validity of grand narratives such as Christianity and history that are so vital to his southern predecessors. Frank must achieve self-awareness and redemption using only the materials of individual experience, nothing more. This is a fundamentally anti-essentialist philosophy, one that is distinctly at odds with the vision of other southern writers like Percy and Tate. Ford confirms this anti-essentialism when he professes that he has come to think "of characters—actual *and* literary characters—as being rather *un*fixed" and "changeable, provisional, unpredictable, decidedly unwhole" ("Art of Fiction" 46). The antidote to provisional identity, for Ford, does not lie in the traditional routes of self-definition; it resides in a new focus on contemporary and proximate experience—in a distinctly postmodern quest with a new set of philosophical assumptions.

If *The Sportswriter* is considered in light of southern tradition, its break from that tradition—the manner in which it treats the southern staples of place, community, and self with a new set of assumptions—must be examined. It becomes apparent that Ford's departure from the South as setting entails a philosophical departure as well. In his postmodern rendering of the motifs of Renascence fiction, Ford indicates a new direction for the southern expatriate and concomitantly a new style for the postsouthern writer.

The landscape of *The Sportswriter* exemplifies Ford's postmodern realism. The novel unfolds in a welter of settings, from New Jersey to Michigan to New York to Florida. Despite their geographical differences, the settings share a common denominator: all are marked by the presence of a pervasive commercialism that exerts a homogenizing effect on the local culture. Ascendant throughout the novel is the architectural disposition that Fredric Jameson calls "aesthetic populism." In depicting this postmodern tendency Ford treats the concept of place in anti-essentialist terms, through a constant focus on mass culture that is at odds with conventional regionalism. Like Bobbie Ann Mason, Ford uses popular culture to render one locale hardly different from another. What defines a place here is the strength of its adherence to the middle-class Zeitgeist of progress, utility, and comfort, not its unique characteristics. As a result, the place of the sportswriter novels offers little assistance in the quest for individual self-definition; the settings in which Frank finds himself do not facilitate the traditional bond between the southern self and its surroundings. If Jameson is correct in asserting that the postmodern era is at ease with the " 'degraded' landscape of schlock and kitsch, of TV series and *Reader's Digest* culture, of advertising and motels," then Ford is certainly an astute chronicler of his age (2).

The eclecticism of mass culture is evident in nearly all the physical fixtures of *The Sportswriter*. Ford depicts a landscape of "strange unworldliness" in which authenticity appears to have been banished, in which the local and the regional have been subsumed by an anarchic mix of architectural references (7). None of the structures in Frank's environment are indigenous to their surroundings; instead, each building seems to draw on a number of heterogeneous and distant references. Frank lives in a neighborhood "of historical reproductions," and the ex- football player he interviews in Michigan occupies "a little white Cape showing a lot of dormered roof with a small picture window on one side of the front door" (51, 153). Like the carefully manufactured authenticity of Nathanael West's suburbs in *The Day of the Locust*, nothing in Frank's environment is as genuine as it appears; the prevailing architectural mode might be termed Generic Indigenous. Detroit is an anomalous scene of "flat, dormered houses and new, brick-mansard condos" juxtaposed in a "complicated urban-industrial mix" (115). The parents of Frank's girlfriend, Vicki Arcenault, live in a New Jersey subdivision called—in a misguided attempt at euphony—Sherri-Lyn Woods (although "there are no woods in sight"), a place where "all the houses down the street look Californiaish and casual" (243). Vicki's condominium is located in a pretentious development that (perhaps unwittingly) exemplifies an ersatz blending of high and low culture. It is set in a landscape that could only be described as postmodern in its chaotic mixture of rural and urban, old and new:

I make the turn up the winding asphalt access that passes beneath a great water tower of sleek space-age blue, then divides toward one end or the other of a wide, unused cornfield. Far ahead—a mile, easy—billowing green basswoods stand poised against a platinum sky and behind them the long, girdered "Y" stanchions of a high-voltage line, orange balls strung to its wires to warn away low-flying planes.

Pheasant Run to the left is a theme-organized housing development where all the streets are culs-de-sac with "Hedgerow Place" and "The Thistles" painted onto fake Andrew Wyeth barnboard signs. All the plantings are young, but fancy cars sit in the driveways. . . .

Pheasant Meadow sits at the other lower end of the stubble field—a boxy, unscenic complex of low brown-shake buildings overlooking a shallow man-made mud pond, a yellow bulldozer, and some other apartments already half-built. (53)

Here is a place in which a quest for self-definition will prove problematic. There is nothing authentic in Frank's surroundings—nothing with connections to a genuine tradition. The Andrew Wyeth signs and the pond are "fake" and "man-made," not autochthonous or local. They represent an environment that is untraditional and commercial, despite its pretensions to venerable gentility. High and low architectural styles are mixed together disingenuously in a perfect display of the conflation (in Jamesonian terms) of aesthetic and commodity production (4). The "frontier between high culture and so-called mass or commercial culture" is obscured in the appropriation of Wyeth's techniques to decorate street signs whose very Anglophilic names indicate a tradition that was never present in this New Jersey cornfield—a fact that the high-voltage lines underscore with irony (2). It is a landscape that might be described as faux-pastoral.

Perhaps the best example of the postmodern commercial aesthetic is Frank's hotel room in Detroit. It thoroughly displays what Robert Venturi calls "the commercial vernacular" (6)—the characteristically postmodern approach of blending the motifs of high culture with the less lofty aim of commercial gain: "It is four-thirty by the time we get to our room, a tidy rectangle of pretentious midwestern pseudo-luxury—a pre-arranged fruit basket, a bottle of domestic champagne, blue bachelor buttons in a Chinese vase, red-flocked whorehouse wall décor and a big bed. There is an eleventh-story fisheye view upriver toward the gaunt Ren-Cen and gray pseudopodial Belle Isle in the middle distance—the shimmer-lights of suburbs reaching north and west out of sight" (Ford, *Sportswriter* 120). This "pseudo-luxury" is a populist appropriation of high culture writ large. What Frank can see from the window is a landscape Venturi would find congenial: Belle Isle, with its mismatched zoo and casinos, and the Renaissance Center, the "city within a city" designed by John Portman, a paragon of self-referential architecture whose work Jameson calls the epitome of "postmodern hyperspace" (44). If Frank's saga is related in a traditional prose style, it nonetheless is set in an eminently postmodern milieu.

Not that Frank objects to occupying such an environment. Aside from one negative comment ("A hundred years ago, this country would have been wooded. . . . But now it has all been ruined by houses and cars" [Ford, *Sportswriter* 155]), Frank revels in the materialism of his era. He seems to enjoy the self-indulgence of "pretentious midwestern pseudo-luxury" even as he denigrates it, and his comments on the merits of rental cars form a sort of ode to the generic, praising "the first moments inside a big, strapping fleet-clean LTD or Montego" with "the stirring 'new' smell in your nostrils. . . . To me, there is no feeling of freedom-within-sensible-limits quite like that. New today. New tomorrow. Eternal renewal on a manageable scale" (148). Here is an ecological theory for the Reagan era: an arrested adolescence of the perpetually new, a return to the womb by route of the generic. Frank is a firm adherent to the philosophy of consumerism, equating a sense of perennial innocence with the tangibility of consumable goods.

Frank's affinity for consumer culture affects his conception of place to an extent that could hardly be termed southern in any traditional sense. He interprets adherence to the generic, not the local, as the best means of assessing the value of a place. He abjures what he calls the pretentious mystery of places such as New Orleans, along with the "genuine woven intricacy" of cities like New York and Los Angeles (103). What he seeks, instead, is a knowable setting, one without mystery or contingency. He admires Detroit because "[s]o much that is explicable in American life" is made there, and he lives in New Jersey because "[a]n American would be crazy to reject such a place, since it is the most diverting and readable of landscapes, and the language is always American" (115, 52). Frank relishes such settings because they provide him with "[c]hoices aplenty" of the small comforts he seeks—those that mass culture can provide (7). He also praises contemporary society's drift toward homogenization: "I have read that with enough time American civilization will make the midwest of any place, New York included. And from here that seems not at all bad" (115). These are hardly the sentiments of an unreconstructed southerner. Frank's song of the suburbs may be interpreted as the death knell of Donald Davidson's autochthonous ideal: "We all need our simple, unambiguous, even factitious landscapes like mine. Places without change or double-ranked complexity. Give me a little Anyplace, a grinning, toe-tapping Terre Haute or wide-eyed Bismark, with stable property values, regular garbage pick-up, good drainage, ample parking, located not far from a major airport, and I'll beat the birds up singing every morning" (103–4). It is difficult to imagine a landscape in one of Faulkner's novels that could be described as "simple," "unambiguous," or "factitious"—or indeed to imagine any southern modernist novel with a setting not fraught with change and complexity. It is perhaps even more difficult to conceive of a modern southern protagonist yearning for such a place. The type of landscape Frank desires is in fact an antimodernist one in which the quest lies almost entirely on the surface of things, unencumbered by the "double-ranked complexity" inherent in narratives such as Faulkner's. Frank's comments about the dubious "mystery" of certain places reveal an anti-essentialist conception of place, a notion of setting as empty of transcendent or definitive character. Behind Frank's affinity for the superficial lies a deep-seated distrust of metanarratives, a suspicion of the type of abstraction that would construe a place as vital to human character. This sentiment is evident in Frank's praise of his own town: "Haddam is in fact as straightforward and plumb-literal as a fire hydrant, which more than anything else makes it the pleasant place it is" (103). For a postmodern individual such as Frank, a new conception of place is in order: a sense of place as literal, straightforward, and knowable, with no mystery to complicate things beyond the tangible, no character beyond the commercial—in short, a postregional landscape.

*T*he *Sportswriter's* community embodies an eclectic and mobile contemporary social order. No one who lives in Haddam is actually from there. Aside from a cadre of blue-collar workers who have relocated there from New York, the town consists of groups like "a small, monied New England émigré contingent" and "a smaller southern crowd"; perhaps because of his lack of regional identity, Frank has "never fitted exactly into either bunch" (49). Beyond the conventional suburban discourse of consumerism, there seems to be no lingua franca in the community, no common aim. Frank's connection to the community tends to be in the form of friendships such as the one he has with Bert Brisker, the closest acquaintance he has left from "the old cocktail-dinner party days," a man with whom he has no more to say than can be expressed once a week on the commuter train to New York. Such a relationship is, according to Frank, "the essence of a modern friendship" (44–45). This, then, is an urban and partial notion of friendship—tepid conversation within the anonymity of mass transit.

Characteristically, Frank sees no problem in the community's indifference to historical unity, the breakdown of such cultural coherence as might derive from a common past. In fact, he harbors a particular disdain for the only character who clings to such notions: a fellow southern expatriate named Fincher Barksdale. Fincher is "the kind of southerner who will only address you through a web of deep and antic southernness, and who assumes everybody in earshot knows all about his parents and history and wants to hear an update on them at every opportunity" (68). Frank is bored by Fincher's absorption with the New South and lampoons him with an acute satire of the stereotypical southern expatriate: "He is the perfect southerner-in-exile, a slew-footed mainstreet change jingler in awful clothes—a breed known only *outside* the south. At Vandy he was the tallish, bookish Memphian meant for a wider world—brushcut, droopy suntans, white bucks, campaign belt and a baggy long-sleeved Oxford shirt, hands stuffed in his pockets, arrogantly bored yet supremely satisfied and accustomed to the view from his eyrie. (Essentially the very way he is now.)" (69). Not only is southern fraternalism entirely absent from Frank's conversation, it is ridiculed. Regional consciousness and networks of family connections are reduced to the level of petty narcissism in an iconoclastic vision of this southern expatriate and his community. Ford does not depict a latter-day equivalent of Faulkner's archetypal expatriate scene, something on the order of Shreve and Quentin reconstructing a southern history from the neutral ground of foreign soil. Rather, he presents the opposite: a relentless focus on the present and a sloughing-off of the past. Instead of frenetic historical lucubration in a monastic dormitory room, he gives us Frank's encounter with Fincher in the bustling Newark airport. Frank's reaction to the southern community that Fincher represents is also telling. As if to underscore his aversion to such southern types as Fincher, Frank declares, "One of the bad things about public places is that you sometimes see people you would pay money not to see" (67).

Perhaps the closest thing to community in Frank's world is the Divorced Men's Club, a group of five men with whom he meets once a month to "puff cigars [and] talk in booming businessmen's voices" (79). The club "bores the crap" out of Frank and is riddled with the tensions of tentative friendship. The best measure of the bond between the men is hardly essential: "even though I cannot say we like each other, I definitely can say that we don't *dislike* each other" (78–79). Frank claims that the men "hardly know each other and sometimes can barely keep the ball rolling before the first drink arrives"; at each meeting they are "as full of dread and timidness as conscripts to a firing squad, doing what we can to be as chatty and polite as Rotarians" (79). This uneasiness may be the result of the club's incessant focus on the superficial and the mundane; indeed, one of the topics barred from discussion at the meetings is divorce itself. Yet in perfect Babbitt fashion (Frank himself uses the term) the men cling to the quotidian as insurance against the abyss of loneliness, the overwhelming scope of loss. The club forms some sort of imperfect antidote to the isolation all the men know intimately. As Frank puts it, "In a way, I suppose you could say all of us were and are lost, and know it, and we simply try to settle into our lost-ness as comfortably and with as much good manners and little curiosity as we can" (80). Such adherence to the superficial customs of behavior precludes any achievement of community in its metaphorical sense. No legitimate bond can be established when the thorny issue that brought the men together is banished from conversation; communication about a topic as visceral as divorce threatens to shatter the veneer with which they achieve comfort in their "lost-ness."

Frank has a name for such communication—"full disclosure"—and he avoids it assiduously. The stark confessionalism of full disclosure threatens the brittle foundations of bourgeois relationships and, further still, Frank's entire carefully ordered existence. It leads into the dark realm of loss and uncertainty against which the ordinary serves as an anodyne. When one of the divorced men, Walter Luckett, reveals his disintegration, Frank feels the pull of that dark region. Within the fragile community of the club, confessions such as Walter's— that he has had a homosexual relationship in search of some means of overcoming his wife's infidelity—are menacing. They illustrate what Frank calls "friendship's realest measure" ("The amount of precious time you'll squander on someone else's calamities and fuck-ups") and demonstrate the superficialities of the relationships within the club (97). For Frank is not willing to squander much time on Walter's problems and cannot see why the ordinary—hotels, rental cars—fails to soften Walter's malaise. Walter's suicide spurs Frank into desperate praise of the quotidian: "He could've . . . read catalogs into the night; or turned on Johnny; or called up a hundred dollar whore for a house call. He could've hunted up a reason to keep breathing. What else is the ordinary world good for except to supply reasons not to check out early?" (351). "You can't be too conventional," Frank asserts. "That's what'll save you" (335).

Despite Frank's sense of alienation, he is not a misanthrope. What lies beneath his frictional relation to others is a pervasive uncertainty about his own self, not a dislike for humanity. He is a Babbitt for the postmodern era: he enjoys "the freely shared air of the public" yet finds his own identity elusive when he is forced to move beneath the small particulars that camouflage the "savage wilderness of civil life" (66, 276). Like Babbitt, Frank is self-conscious and performative, a man who puts his elbows on his knees, "honest-injun style," in a tight argumentative moment with Vicki (137) and who seems unsure of his own voice in a tense meeting with his ex-wife at his son's grave: "I wonder, in fact, what my own voice will sound like. Will it be a convincing, truth-telling voice? Or a pseudo-sincere, phony, ex-husband one that will stir up trouble? I have a voice that is really mine, a frank, vaguely rural voice more or less like a used car salesman: a no-frills voice that hopes to uncover simple truth by a straight-on application of the facts. I used to practice it when I was in college. 'Well, okay, look at it this way,' I'd say right out loud. 'All right, all right.' 'Yeah, but look here' " (11). A truly "frank" voice? An assessment of that claim depends on which definition of frank one accepts, for at least on this occasion "Frank" Bascombe and "frankness" are irreconcilable. Frank's approach to frankness is a "no-frills," "straight-on" disingenuousness, a rehearsed spontaneity—a circuitous route to self-evident facts that, curiously, requires "practice." The voice Frank claims to be "really mine" is no genuine voice at all but a constructed entity that could almost perform on its own—the stuff of booster pamphlets and Chamber of Commerce mottoes. Like George Babbitt before him, Frank finds that what he is left with at the end of a working day is frighteningly elusive—something for which his tangible world of consumable goods has made no provisions.

These Babbitt-like qualities would result in nothing more than an updated portrait of the American bourgeois if they did not give way to substantial late-twentieth-century concerns. What is fundamentally at issue in *The Sportswriter* is not so much the bourgeoisie as anomie, not conformity but the struggles of the decentered postmodern self. What lies beneath Frank's conventional exterior is a struggle to define that self with limited cultural materials. Absent historical, cultural, and psychological metanarratives, the self cannot be recovered through nonconformity, as in *Babbitt*, or by integration into the sort of historical myths Ford's southern modernist predecessors offered. Such external means of achieving meaning have been delegitimized in Frank's era.

As Frank's performative traits would indicate, the very concept of the self is under siege in the novel. A unique, essential identity proves elusive in an environment without tradition and community. Like the world of Don DeLillo's

White Noise, the ostensible communities of Ford's novel "are spinning out from the core" in a welter of consumer messages that proffer an almost endless series of purchasable roles (DeLillo 50). Identities become very nearly interchangeable. As Frank phrases it, "Anyone could be anyone else in most ways. Face the facts" (Ford, *Sportswriter* 81). Ever present and constantly complicating Frank's difficulty with self-definition is the consumer aesthetic to which he adheres. This consumerism, along with the absence of metanarrative legitimacy, gives Frank a position in his culture no more substantial than whichever one he can purchase; it also renders the individual as exchangeable as currency. Frank seems to bear out Lyotard's claim that the loss of credibility for grand narratives is tied to contemporary capitalism's pervasive focus on the present, on the valorization of "individual enjoyment of goods and services" (38). Within such a culture the ends of human activity become less discernible. Frank is aware of this. He observes that "since there is so much in the world now, it's harder to judge what is and isn't essential," and he asks, "Who'd know that certainty would grow rare as diamonds?" (Ford, *Sportswriter* 51, 107). These exemplary postmodern concerns reflect an environment in which conviction is difficult to obtain, in which a sense of purpose outside the individual lacks authority.

The novel's treatment of religion illustrates this crisis of legitimacy. For Frank, religion has no ultimate authority; it is not something to be taken too seriously. He stops in at Haddam First Presbyterian to participate in a feel-good brand of "spiritual orienteering" among church "regulars" who are there "to be saved or give a damned good impression of it, and nobody's pulling the wool over anybody else's eyes" (104). The dominant mood of the congregation seems to be one of tolerant skepticism—or perhaps a willing suspension of disbelief. Church attendance becomes more of a civic duty than participation in a transcendent narrative beyond the rational sphere. As Frank describes it, the Haddam Presbyterians' "ardent hope is to bring you down to earth by causing your spirit to lift" (104). This approach aptly fits Lyotard's concept of "incredulity." If the central question of postmodernism is, indeed, Lyotard's "Where, after the metanarratives, can legitimacy reside?" (xxiv–xxv), the congregation answers: in the community, "down to earth," in the tangible. Frank corroborates their distrust of the transcendent. Leaving church on Easter morning, he confesses that he has been saved the only way he can: "*pro tempore*" (Ford, *Sportswriter* 238).

Frank's concern over his children not attending church illuminates this incredulity from another angle. He worries about his ex-wife not taking his children to services "not because they will turn out godless (I couldn't care less) but because she is bringing them up to be perfect little factualists and information accumulators with no particular reverence or speculative interest for what's not known" (204). But importantly, his reverence for what is unknown does not extend beyond a tentative acknowledgment of the imminent. He has no concern for his children's belief in grand narrative structures, merely in their interest in what lies immediately beyond the tactile. Frank's only interaction with mystery comes in the rather adulterated form of the palmist he sees twice a month. He is fully aware of the hucksterism of Mrs. Miller but values his participation in the small mystery she provides while he is "semi-reliably assured" of himself and his life (101). His reliance on the palm reader is a trenchant illustration of postmodern skepticism, for it demonstrates his lack of belief in a telos outside himself, even while he maintains a tepid search for it. Mrs. Miller, with her predictions like "Things will brighten for you" and "I see a long life," may represent some kind of debased narrative that Frank is still compelled to seek, but her charlatanry is fully evident to herself and to him; nobody is pulling the wool over anybody's eyes.

Thus without the shaping narratives of religion, history, or community, Frank is isolated in the present, in a contemporary existence that seems to lack direction or a discernible plan. He resists any impulse to view his life as a narrative and seems to rank an acceptance of life's contingency as the foremost lesson of middle age. He claims that a "life can simply change the way a day changes—sunny to rain, like the song says," and that "life will always be without a natural, convincing closure. Except one" (107, 366). His is truly a postmodern conception of existence, for he accepts no linear or narrative patterns for human experience. Such narratives, Frank assures us, do not exist. One of the great insights he has gained from sportswriting is that "there are no transcendent themes in life. In all cases things are here and they're over, and that has to be enough" (16). Any other configuration of existence, he insists, is something like "the lie of literature and the liberal arts" that forced him to abandon his fiction career years earlier (16). He cites James Joyce's epiphanies as a prime example of the "pernicious" falsehood of literature that would reduce existence to a set of tenable, if rare, moments of full knowledge (119). Such epiphanies presuppose an order to the universe that Frank cannot see in his own life. Walter Luckett's suicide note reminds him that *"it's hard to think of your own life's themes,"* and Frank remains extremely suspicious of any external entity that might supply such narrative elements (349). He would in fact go a step farther—to stress that

Walter's fixation on the search for transcendent themes was the catalyst of his self-destruction.

And thence the salvation of the quotidian. The closest approximation to a metanarrative for Frank is, as I have been stressing, the ordinary and the consumable. Ford's most brilliant expression of this commodified quest is Frank's obsession with mail-order catalogs. In Frank's fascination with catalogs one sees the search for meaning on its most reified level. Frank's perusal of catalogs astutely captures the postmodern individual's yearning for assurance beyond the self in an age suspicious of grand narratives—it represents the almost predictable melding of consumerism and contemporary uncertainty. The catalogs counter Frank's fears "that whatever *this* is, is it" by holding forth the promise of a life beyond what is known—while assuring him that some measure of commodified "mystery" can be obtained (83).

In the days after Ralph's death Frank and his ex-wife turned to catalogs to fill the new void in their lives that would-be absolutes such as religion cannot satisfy, buttressed in their belief "that satisfying all our purchasing needs from catalogs was the very way of life that suited us and our circumstances" (195). His thoughts on consumerism are indicative of postmodern escapism: "We all take our solace where we can. And *there* seemed like a life—though we couldn't just send to Vermont or Wisconsin or Seattle for it, but a life just the same—that was better than dreaminess and silence in a big old house where unprovoked death had taken its sad toll" (197). What Frank seeks is a postmodern sort of solace for the contemporary consumer, an existence outside his own that might provide some validity from beyond the individual sphere. He stresses that the catalogs represent more than mere consumption, that they adumbrate a broader existence, even if it is limited to the degraded landscape of popular culture:

For me, though, there was something other than the mere ease of purchase in all this, in the hours spent going through pages seeking the most virtuous screwdriver or the beer bottle cap rehabilitator obtainable nowhere else but from a PO box in Nebraska. It was that the life portrayed in these catalogs seemed irresistible. Something about my frame of mind made me love the abundance of the purely ordinary and pseudo-exotic (which always turns out ordinary if you go the distance and place your order). I loved the idea of merchandise, and I loved those ordinary good American faces pictured there, people wearing their asbestos welding aprons, holding their cane fishing rods, checking their generators with their new screwdriver lights, wearing their saddle oxfords, their same wool nighties, month after month, season after season. In me it fostered an odd assurance that some things outside my life were okay still; that the same men and women standing by the familiar brick fireplaces, or by the same comfortable canopy beds, holding these same shotguns or blow poles or boot warmers or boxes of kindling sticks could see a good day before their eyes right into perpetuity. Things were knowable, safe-and-sound. Everybody with exactly what they need or could get. (196)

This is a new and ironic kind of culture religion. It is not at all the sort that the modernists would have espoused, and yet it serves a similar function on a significantly smaller scale. Although Frank cannot cling to religion and cultural history, he is compelled to seek some kind of order beyond himself. The catalogs assure him that the universe has some stability, that "things outside" his life are somehow stable, that somewhere existence is "knowable, safe-and-sound." In the atomized postmodern era this assurance cannot be found in myth, however: it resides in "the purely ordinary" and the "pseudo-exotic"—in what can be known and appraised on the tangible level. It is a radical reappraisal of the quest for meaning rendered within the confines of a conventional contemporary life—no Leopold Bloom, no Eugene Gant, no Quentin Compson seeking the transcendental signifier, but a bemused postmodern suburbanite looking for generic wholeness in the pages of L.L. Bean.

If Frank's search through the catalogs reminds us of anything in previous southern literature, the echo would be to Ike McCaslin's quest for the past in the present in the yellowed ledgers of his family's plantation. Yet if the reference to *Go Down, Moses* is intended, here, too, Ford is ironic. The "clumsy and archaic" tomes of Faulkner are replaced by glossy magazines that look not to the benighted past but to a consumable, utopian future. What is in Faulkner a quest for legacy and logos is in Ford's treatment an escape; "that chronicle which was a whole land in miniature, which multiplied and compounded was the entire South" in Faulkner (293) receives a different kind of universal overtone in Ford's work. Instead of comprising the record of *a* particular family, Frank's catalogs are the record of *no* particular family; instead of containing a buried tragic history, the catalogs evince a cheerful absence of history altogether. Whereas Ike discovers the fabulous within (and beneath) the typical, Frank seeks the typical alone. Here, certainly, is a postmodern attenuation of depth.

What Frank ultimately indicates with his love of the quotidian is the failure of the modernist project. He is a lapsed modern among the ruins of modernist culture: a novelist who has given up literature, a former college professor who now reads mail-order literature and writes sports—in short, an embodiment of the effacement between high and low culture. Not only have metanarratives failed him, high culture is bankrupt as well; the epiphanies of Joyce and the teleological "lie of literature" represent a pretentious deception that mass culture does not perpetrate with the lofty rhetoric of philosophical ideals. To be sure, the easy escapism of consumer culture is facile and ersatz, but to Frank it also possesses a complicated kind of earnestness. Through its very immediacy, its indifference to any great transcendent themes, it proffers what he perceives as a clearer and less deluded expression of humanity. The catalogs allow Frank to construct a vastly reduced, adulterated kind of humanism for a skeptical era, one that operates on a smaller scale than would be endorsed by the high-modern liberal arts he denigrates. He practices a callow sort of humanism in praising them, a distinctly postmodern appreciation and new interpretation of the value of popular culture for the contemporary period: the pursuit of narrative legitimacy rendered in the form of reductio ad absurdum.

Leslie Fiedler stresses that postmodernism is largely a celebratory reaction to the death of "the Culture Religion of Modernism," an irreverent rebuttal to the academicism, rationality, and gentility of modernism (464, 462). Frank, with his populist aesthetic, bears out this thesis emphatically; his life reflects the tenor of his times. He has rejected academe and the liberal myths that lie at its foundations, but his quest for mystery within the mundane—his aversion to factualism—refutes a purely rational and strictly unromantic view of the world as well. With his catalogs and love of mass culture, he advocates a populism anathema to the moderns. His journey through life follows a course parallel to the larger cultural shifts of his literary generation—from an uncomfortable maintenance of modernist tradition (his fiction career) to the postmodern condition of his current existence. He has turned "from literature back to life, where I could get somewhere," and now finds himself "less sober-sided and 'writerly serious,'" worrying less "about the complexities of things" while "looking at life in more simple and literal ways" (Ford, *Sportswriter* 47, 132). He is a realist for the postmodern era—and a pragmatist as well—who deals with the uncertainty of his time on the best terms that he can, in whose credo we may hear the echo of Thoreau: "Stop searching. Face the earth where you can" (53). Frank may seem indifferent to the decline of modernism, to the death of the quest through grand-narrative means, but he is also willing to accept what the postmodern era has to offer, aware of the truth in Thoreau's maxim, "Only that day dawns to which we are awake" (333).

But is there indeed a dawn or only dusk? Ford is a crafty novelist of veiled intentions, and the sanguinary air of Frank's catalog reveries may be as unwittingly artificial as his environment. The senescence of modernism is evident through his character, but what supplants it—a consumerist metaphysics—is hardly a desirable replacement for impotent metanarratives. Despite Frank's often eloquent protest to the contrary, the catalogs finally represent little more than escape and drift—the cultural "logic" of late capitalism tortuously expressed through one of its individual practitioners. Frank's saga validates Fiedler's declaration that modernism is dead, but in quintessential postmodern fashion it fails to offer a legitimate alternative to metanarratives through its suspect consumer religion. Ultimately the catalogs are not restorative but diversionary, the tools by which a latter-day Virgil of the suburbs passes his time in the limbo of postmodern culture. Contemporary life, Frank tells us, "isn't so bad, when you don't think of it" (Ford, *Sportswriter* 255). The catalogs are the embodiment of such a perspective, the texts of an individual whose ironic frankness may well be as extrinsic as the exotic merchandise of his mail-order metaphysics.

SOUTHERN IDENTITY IN EXTREMIS

Ford's *Independence Day* follows Frank through what he has come to call the "Existence Period" in his attempts to maintain the "high-wire act of normalcy" (94). The manner in which Ford continues to depict Frank's existence in postmodern terms in this second sportswriter novel merits attention. The sequel to *The Sportswriter* finds Frank five years older, still committed to a performative identity ("I smile a reliable, You're in good hands with Allstate smile" [248]), and if anything, more spectral, a man who wonders how he can "breathe air into my ghostly self and become a recognizable if changed-for-the-better figure" (108). But in his Existence Period Frank has abandoned any illusion of the essentiality of place and community and consequently of the individual's ability to connect with them. While such reservations were expressed tentatively in the earlier novel, they are conveyed stringently and almost cynically here. *Independence Day* verifies Frank's ambivalence to the South, confirming his evolution to a completely postmodern, and postsouthern, identity.

The setting of the novel continues postmodern. Frank and his son embark on a trip through a commercial landscape of almost unbelievable crassness. They pass through the Vince Lombardi Rest Area in New Jersey, which "is a little red-brick Colonial Williamsburg-looking pavilion" filled with "Roy Rogers burgers, Giants novelty items, joke condoms" and "families walking around semi-catatonically eating" (178). The Basketball Hall of Fame they visit ("which looks less like a time-honored place of legend and enshrinement than a high-tech dental clinic") offers "basketball-history-in-a-nutshell" via its "Action The-atre" and replicas of Doctor Naismith's signature and the original peach basket (264, 266). Pheasant Meadow makes another appearance, "not old but already gone visibly to seed" in the intervening years, now "abutting a strip of pastel medical arts plazas and a half-built Chi-Chi's," reduced in five years from a new development to "the architecture of lost promise and early death" (141). It is indeed a decadent landscape, poorly versed in tradition yet fluent in the commercial vernacular.

Frank's notion of community reflects the devolution of his surroundings. His former praise of the generic has been augmented with a pronounced sense of relativism. Now he thinks of communities not as "continuous" but as "isolated, contingent groups trying to improve on the illusion of permanence, which they fully accept as an illusion" (386). He notes that "we want to *feel* our community as a fixed, continuous entity . . . as being anchored in the rock of permanence; but we know it's not, that in fact beneath the surface (or rankly all over the surface) it's anything but. We and it are anchored to contingency like a bottle on a wave, seeking a quiet eddy" (439). His skepticism is most evident in the declaration that "community" is "one of those words I loathe, since all its hands-on implications are dubious" (386). Here is confirmation of a postsouthern iden-tity, for Frank not only denies the stability of communities (so vital to regional-ism), he also implicates their constituents in a sort of wide-ranging scheme of self-delusion. There are no bedrock absolutes for Frank, only contingency—the sort of postmodern philosophy that defines community as the "social aggregate" of "a mass of individual atoms" (Lyotard 15). His statements evince an advanced suspicion of narratives. If in *The Sportswriter* he was willing to grant a small mea-sure of legitimacy to a toe-tapping Terre Haute or wide-eyed Bismark, he seems at this later phase to deny any measure of authenticity to community esprit.

Frank has chosen a new vocation that suits both his environs and his evolving conception of community. He has left sportswriting and, in a career move of commercial proportions not seen in literature since Rabbit Angstrom assumed the mantle of Fred Springer's Toyota dealership, decided to pursue another live-lihood: he is now a real estate agent or, as he prefers to be called, a "Residential Specialist" (91). Frank thinks of real estate as the "ideal occupation" because it allows him "the satisfaction of reinvesting" in his community and thus "establish-ing a greater sense of connectedness" with it (111, 27). His duties as a Residen-tial Specialist include "lifting sagging spirits, opening fresh, unexpected choices, and offering much-needed assistance toward life's betterment"—altruistic enterprises that accord with his "plan to do for others while looking after Number One" (47, 112). His new disposition—and the florid rhetoric with which he describes it—would seem to be Babbittry verified.[3]

In fact, real estate is an extension of Frank's penchant for the commodified mystery he once found in catalogs—a natural approach to the concept of place for a southerner of postregional inclination who firmly adheres to the consumer aesthetic. What is real estate, after all, but the reification of place, the packaging of locale? If place holds no more value than the consumer goods it provides, and if community is hardly more than an illusion, Frank's decision to buy and sell these entities is understandable. Like the people who produce mail-order catalogs, he participates in a consensual delusion, a venture toward "life's betterment" in which commercial goods stand as the best indicator of a "good life" that no one seems able to define. The position of Residential Specialist is an ideal one for a literal-minded individual in the postmodern era. Even more than catalogs, it focuses on making the intangible tactile—certainly an appealing process for a person who, no longer concerned with the philosophical "complexities of things," has begun to think of life in "more simple and literal ways."

In an indirect way real estate also illuminates Frank's vanishing southern identity. It may be tied, in an inverted manner, to a "rage against abstraction" and a desire "to link with place"—classic southern traits that Hobson discerns in Frank (50–51). Yet these southern characteristics receive ironic treatment in Frank's praise of the realtor's vocation. Frank feels ties to place as an ideal southerner should, but in a postindustrial, decidedly postagrarian fashion. His attraction to place is filtered through a consumer's view of land as property, as a commodity: he does not till the soil but parcels it. In a postindustrial society, his aversion to abstraction becomes a capitalistic interest in the commercial value of location. Whatever southern qualities he may unwittingly retain are now inverted; the "southern expatriate for the eighties" professes his notions of place and community in the discourse of the Reagan era. He stresses the need "to cease sanctifying places" since they "never cooperate by revering you back when you need it," an attitude distinctly at odds with southern tradition; "place," he says, "means nothing" (Ford, *Independence Day* 151–52). Frank poses the question, "[I]s there any cause to think a place—any place—within its plaster and joists, its trees and plantings, in its putative essence *ever* shelters some spirit ghost of us as proof of its significance and ours?" His answer is telling: "We just have to be smart enough to quit asking places for what they can't provide, and begin to invent other options . . . as gestures of our God-required but not God-assured independence" (442). Frank's statement of autonomy could easily serve as Ford's own declaration of independence from the bonds of literary tradition—its terms lend themselves to a metatextual reading. Ford's postmodern perspective and willful break with the southern past could hardly be stated more clearly than in the call for new options, the notion of "essence" as "putative," and the stress on "independence." In the context of southern literature, his novel's title is truly resonant.

On this score one may lay to rest the connection Hobson and other critics have perceived between Ford and Percy. Those intent on preserving literary lineage may discern some vestige of Percy's "angelism" in Frank's "fear of disappearance," an "overall" feeling of "becoming significantly less substantial"—"not exactly as if I didn't exist, but that I don't exist *as much*" (388, 105, 176). Hobson might maintain (as he does of *The Sportswriter*) that in his later comments on the negligible value of place, Frank protests too much. But in its relentless focus on the present, *Independence Day* confirms that the effort to link Ford to Percy is ultimately a critical exercise of limited value, the younger writer's debt to his predecessor extending no farther than the level of stylistic affinity. This is most evident in Ford's break from the central Renascence tradition Percy maintained with his own postmodern accent, the Götterdämmerung. As in the case of McCarthy, this trope is what Lewis Simpson discerns at the heart of traditionalist criticism, the "proper contextual metaphor of the Southern Renascence" for those who view the contemporary period as a fallen era (*Brazen Face* 260). The Götterdämmerung influences Simpson's work as well, through the "aesthetic of memory" that has been "a formative element in southern fiction" in the prevailing dialectic between a dissociated present and a more organic (and whole) past (233). The cultural ramifications of the metaphor are apparent in Simpson's theory that the loss of a relationship with history in the South more broadly "symbolizes" a "general loss in Western civilization" (*Fable* 206). Percy has made his predilection for the Götterdämmerung clear, claiming that "the world has ended in a sense. . . . We're living at the end of modern times. The end of modern times will be the end of Christendom as we know it" (Lawson and Kramer 280–81). He describes his work as "an attack on the twentieth century, on the whole culture. It is a rotten century, we are in terrible trouble" (209).

Such an eschatological vision is entirely absent in Ford's work, particularly in his latter sportswriter novel. The concept of cultural twilight that Percy maintained allows him to be read as southern—as regional and different, set apart from the general tone of American fiction—despite the generic setting of the "nonplaces" to which he was drawn. Yet any pursuit of a similar apocalyptic sensibility in Ford's postmodern landscape is thwarted by the author's refusal to present the contemporary era as a debased shadow of the past. Ford simply does not view contemporary culture through the pessimistic lens that Percy shared with his modernist predecessors. The motives Frank ascribes to his abandoned fiction career are amenable to the protest of the southern Götterdämmerung, including the Kafkaesque goal of "staging raids on the inarticulate, being an ax for the frozen sea within us, providing the satisfactions of belief in the general mess of imprecision" (Ford, *Independence Day* 320). This credo would hardly be objectionable to Percy, yet its aspirations are those Frank has discarded, for Frank (like Ford) has relinquished the modernist trajectory of moving backward from the present toward some more fundamental and bedrock essence of things—has abandoned even its modified postmodern version present in Percy's quest motif. In contrast to a typical Percy character, Frank is "not one bit preoccupied with how things *used to be*" because "you're usually wrong about how things used to be anyway" (95). The character in *Independence Day* most preoccupied with recovering the past is Frank's surviving son, Paul, a disturbed teenager who seeks to reestablish what he perceives as an ideal former existence. Frank advises his son against thinking that events leading up to his parents' divorce "ruined everything that was fixed back then" because "nothing's fixed anyway" (292). His advice to Paul is at odds with the recovery project of the Götterdämmerung: "You shouldn't get used to not being happy just because you can't make everything fit down right. You have to let some things go, finally" (351–52). If Paul's dissociated philosophy is analogous to that of Lancelot Andrewes Lamar, Will Barrett, or Dr. Thomas More, Frank's reaction to him is indeed indicative of a new perspective in southern letters. The desire to order the present by recovering the past is common to Percy's characters—it is what links them to other formative southern literary figures, from Quentin Compson to the Agrarians, through a trope so persistent in southern literature that it could be stretched to accommodate Percy's postmodern tendencies. But Frank rejects the terms of the Götterdämmerung. There is no prior order, he tells his son, no broad narrative by which the divorce of a suburban couple may be read as a symbolic indicator of a more general and pervasive decline that might be countered, in modernist fashion, by making everything "fit down right" into an abstract schema. Such ideas must finally be "let go" in the pursuit of independence and autonomy, the goals Frank hopes to encourage in his son through

their Fourth of July excursion. In waiving the opportunity to continue the Götterdämmerung in his own work, Ford declares a similar kind of independence—
from Percy and from the southern literary tradition in general.

The final comment on southernness and independence in the novel (and
perhaps on literary filiation as well) emerges during Frank's chance meeting with
another expatriate: the stepbrother he has not seen for more than two decades.
The son of Frank's mother and her second husband, Irv Ornstein is a sibling
from the nonnuclear family that evolved after the death of Frank's father. Irv is
the closest approximation of the dissociated southerner of Renascence tradition
that Ford offers in his sportswriter novels. Unlike Fincher Barksdale, he is a
sympathetic character who seeks to recover a vital tradition beyond the narcissism of self-indulgence. He tells Frank that he feels "detached from his own
personal history" and finds himself obsessed with the lack of "continuity" in his
life; in the fashion of a southern seeker, he hopes to get "a clearer sense of
where I've come from before I try to find out where I'm going" (388, 390). He
clings to the validity of family connections and attempts to draw Frank into a
coherent framework with the past as its basis: " 'I was remembering . . . that you
and I were around Jake's house together while our parents were married. I was
right there when your mother died. We knew each other pretty well. And now
twenty-five years of absence go by and we bump into each other up here in the
middle of the north woods. And I realized . . . that you're my only link to that
time. I'm not going to get all worked up over it, but you're as close to family as
anyone there is for me. And we don't even know each other' " (387). But Irv
finds little solace in Frank, who is as ambivalent about their shared history as
he is about Irv's theory of continuity. Frank can offer his stepbrother no better
explanation for the family's dispersal than the observation that life "is screwy as
a monkey" (387). When Irv shows him a faded picture of "four humans in a
stately family pose, two parents, two adolescent boys, standing out on some
front porch steps," Frank does not recognize the family as his own—can in fact
only think, "Who are these? Where are they? When?" (391). It is a shocking
and illuminating moment: clear evidence of Frank's severance from a southern
past, from family connection, from an identity rooted in personal history. The
"quickening torque of heart pain" he feels is "unexceptional," a reluctant nod to
a "long-gone past" captured in a photograph he is quick to return to its owner
(391). The snapshot Irv preserves in laminated, blurred, and decaying form is
for Frank a memento of an anterior world so long gone as to be unreal and
ephemeral. The past is no longer even past but something farther removed in
time and place from the setting of this postmodern "family" reunion.

SIGNIFYIN(G) IN THE SOUTH

Randall Kenan

Black American culture was always a Creole culture, a mixture of remembered African ways, of European impositions and influences and inflections, of Native American wisdom, and of the stubborn will to survive. Long before the term was coined, black culture was a postmodern culture; folk made it up as they went along.

—*Randall Kenan*, Walking on Water

The tenor of contemporary southern literature is more than ever one of revision and renovation—at least among white authors. Yet the revisionist innovations reshaping white literary expression have long been characteristic of African American writing; the impulse toward repudiating the dominant ideology—the catalyst of the poor-white renaissance—has shaped black American literature since its earliest phase. The close parallels between lower-class white authors and black southerners are evident in one of Zora Neale Hurston's most influential essays, "Characteristics of Negro Expression." If one may substitute ideological categories for racial signifiers, Hurston's claim for black Americans seems almost universal for the marginalized individual: "While [the African

American] lives and moves in the midst of white civilisation, everything he touches is re-interpreted for his own use" (28). Blue-collar writers of the contemporary South have put Hurston's observation into practice by appropriating, and then transforming, the narrative patterns of their upper-class predecessors, moving among the aesthetic structures of tradition in the process of reinterpreting their significance and import.

But what, then, of postmodern reinterpretation within the black literary tradition? Here the economic disenfranchisement depicted by "white trash" authors must be considered against social conditions for black southerners slightly more auspicious than those of the past. The classic African American theme of repudiation of white culture—what Houston Baker has called "one of the most important factors in setting black American literature apart from white American literature" (13)—is less evident in contemporary works, such as John Holman's *Luminous Mysteries*, that depict a different set of cultural challenges than those fundamental to the pioneering work of Hurston and Richard Wright. To be sure, one finds echoes of the injustice of Hurston's *Their Eyes Were Watching God* and *Jonah's Gourd Vine* in Alice Walker's *Meridian* and Toni Morrison's *Beloved*, and Ernest Gaines's *A Gathering of Old Men* continues the traditional depiction of racial tension and violence in the manner of Wright's novellas in *Uncle Tom's Children*. But it seems that Hurston's and Wright's success in attacking the shibboleths of southern culture has allowed their successors to address facets of black experience outside what Henry Louis Gates Jr. calls the traditional "preoccupation" of African American writers, "the great and terrible subject of white racism" (173). Consequently, the sense of solidarity against a common enemy is less urgent in contemporary work, and the twentieth-century forerunners of southern black expression have themselves become established enough to be, like their white contemporaries of the Renaissence, subject to renovation.

As Gates argues throughout *The Signifying Monkey*, revision is hardly a recent development in African American literature and culture. "Whatever is black about black American literature," he points out, is to be found in the process of Signifyin(g), in the ongoing revision of key tropes in African American writing—a process of "repetition and revision, or repetition with a signal difference" (xxiv). The black literary tradition may therefore be viewed as a complex narrative of metaphorical recension, what Gates calls "tropological revision": "By tropological revision I mean the manner in which a specific trope is repeated, with differences, between two or more texts. The revision of specific tropes recurs with surprising frequency in the Afro-American literary tradition. The descent underground, the vertical 'ascent' from South to North, myriad figures of the double, and especially double-consciousness all come readily to mind" (xxv). Signifyin(g), then, is an older and uniquely African American version of the sort of renovation taking place on a wide scale with contemporary white writers. As Gates notes, "intertextuality represents a process of repetition and revision, by definition," and his theory of Signifyin(g), with its lineage of "antecedent texts" and "revised" or "descendent" texts, affords an opportunity for examining an African American perspective on creative misreading (60, xxi, xxvii).

What I have been circling here is the possibility of a nexus between Signifyin(g) and the mythoclastic tendencies common to postmodern white fiction. Such is the case for one of the South's most powerful new voices, Randall Kenan. In Kenan's work one finds the treatment of white racism complicated by the author's doubly marginal status as black and homosexual—a perspective cognizant of prejudice emanating from both sides of the color line. Thus Kenan's description of himself as "a spy in an enemy camp" is in a fundamental sense double-voiced, referring primarily to his status as a black man in a racialized society but also, as his novel *A Visitation of Spirits* (1989) makes clear, to his membership in a subculture denied legitimacy in all quarters of the South ("Spies" 26). Like his contemporaries of the postmodern South, Kenan struggles to clear a place for himself in the region's literature. Through his masterful Signifyin(g) on the recurrent tropes of African American fiction, he revitalizes the impulse of those, like Hurston and Wright, intent on expanding the discourse of southern culture.

THE "DARK PARABOLA" OF THE LYNCHING TROPE

It is appropriate to begin with Kenan's most traditional story, "Tell Me, Tell Me," from *Let the Dead Bury Their Dead* (1992), which comes closest of any of his works to the conventional poetics of southern black fiction by revisiting the topos of lynching violence in Wright's *Uncle Tom's Children*. Kenan's debt to Wright in "Tell Me, Tell Me" seems reductively apparent in summary: the story concerns the murder of an African American youth, an attack precipitated by the young man's unwitting discovery of a white couple having sex on an otherwise deserted beach. The sexual tension between races in the story, coupled with a natural setting in which bloodshed suddenly erupts in a pastoral environment, points toward Wright's "Big Boy Leaves Home" as an influence. Yet Kenan modifies Wright's perspective by allowing his white protagonist, Ida McTyre

Perry, to serve as the story's narrative consciousness and by augmenting Wright's realist/naturalist style with the supernatural motif of the dead boy's return to Ida as a ghost, a revenant of the racist past. Intertextuality here must be considered through the process of Signifyin(g), for Kenan's revisions render "Tell Me, Tell Me" a palimpsest in which the traces of Wright's famous story appear both as influence and as dialogical antecedent to an expanding fictional exploration of white racism.

The signal achievement of Kenan's Signifyin(g) lies in his story's perspective. Reversing Wright's choice of protagonist, Kenan positions a white character as the narrative consciousness of his lynching drama. Like Bertha in "Big Boy Leaves Home," Ida has been a witness, a complicit bystander, to the violence that her husband, Frank "Butch" Perry—like Jim Harvey in Wright's story—inflicted upon an innocent young man as the visceral response to an accidental encounter. But Kenan's revision moves the flat female character of Wright's work to the center of the story; the effect is a profound reexamination of the dynamics of racial violence, a glance behind the racism that Wright, for ideological reasons, presents as basically one dimensional. The dramatic arrangement of characters is reversed fruitfully: it is Butch and Ida (not Big Boy and his friends) who are discovered in "Tell Me, Tell Me," caught in a moment of sexual intimacy in the dunes of Emerald Isle by "a little pickaninny" who "just stands with his eyes wide and his mouth hung open . . . like a scared possum" (266). The situation is akin to Wright's, but it is whites here who are observed in an unguarded moment—the objects, not the subject, of an interracial gaze. Their rage is familiar ("What you looking at, huh? See something you like, huh?" [267]), but it is in dealing with the aftermath of the violence for its white participants that Kenan covers new territory, moving into the white psyche. Ida must contend with the memory of Butch walking out of the surf into which he has thrown the sobbing boy "with a peculiar grin on his face, like he has just made a touchdown or shot a great buck," the image of the beaten body describing "a graceful arc, a dark parabola" etched in her mind (267). Wright's trope is reworked to carry such violence beyond the sphere of protest literature and into the psychological depths of racism—Kenan's story ends not with death and flight but in the haunted present nearly fifty years after the sort of brutal climax with which the novellas of *Uncle Tom's Children* conclude.

Kenan's psychological focus allows him to explore racism in a postmodern South in which institutional and personal prejudices have tended to take cover under less brutally salient forms than in Wright's era. Nonetheless, the decline in physical violence hardly results in a peaceful vision of the contemporary South. In making racism again a viable topic for the postmodern South, Kenan does not retreat from the angry protest of his predecessor. Rather, his portrait of the white interior demonstrates that the brutality Wright observed in tangible forms is endemic and enduring in the psyche long after the abolition of Jim Crow social practices. The narrative perspective of his story seems to answer Morrison's call in *Playing in the Dark* for new depictions that assess "the impact of racism on those who perpetuate it" by exploring "what racial ideology does to the mind, imagination, and behavior of masters" (11, 12). Kenan's inquiry into this nearly uncharted area assesses an ideological pathology that Wright only began to uncover in "Big Boy Leaves Home."

By foregrounding a character analogous to Wright's Bertha, Kenan augments Wright's work with a portrait of genteel racism as devastating as the one limned in its lower-class configuration by Eudora Welty in "Where Is the Voice Coming From?" The result is an indictment of the upper-class white South that would claim immunity from racism. For example, despite the violence of her past, Ida is of the social class that "winces" when the word "colored" escapes her in the presence of a black person, yet she is concerned at "how dark a tan" her friend's grandson "allowed himself" (Kenan, "Tell Me" 241, 255). The only African American with whom she seems comfortable is Joe Abner Chasten, "the Negro man who did her handiwork around the house," a "silly black man" yet "a resourceful Negro" with "character"—what "so many of them" do not have "these days" (243, 253). Joe Abner's status as an "enigma," a "grand and impenetrable mystery," is mitigated by his menial function in Ida's household; he fits the African American profile of an earlier era to which she is accustomed (253). The racial mores of an earlier South endure.

But Ida fares less well with those persons of color outside the anachronistic enclave of her home. Beyond her property she observes a society in which, from her perspective, the margins appear to be swapping places with the center. Her reaction to an emergent class of minority professionals reveals the denial that has shaped her life since Emerald Isle. She doubts the credentials of her Filipino physician, for example, although this lack of trust has "nothing to do with her being Filipino. Nothing at all" (244). Such repression is pervasive in the story. During a visit to a black gynecologist Ida stares at anything in the office except the doctor's "exquisite cornrows" and "broad nostrils," until she eventually looks "Dr. Harriet Bridge, M.D., straight in her brown eyes and [feels] an incomparable sense of goodwill, admiration, largesse, and confidence in both herself and the pretty colored doctor in front of her" (257, 258). Obviously, this kind of "largesse" deconstructs itself—especially so after an encounter with a black minister in her church (an alumnus of Trinity en route to Edinburgh): "She smiled, she applauded herself later, and her smile did not slacken, did not yield to gravity; her composure was maintained; her grace assured"—"she did not once make note or mention [to her white minister] of the fact that he was black" (261). Here the social relations that catalyzed Wright's work appear to have, if not reversed themselves, at least shifted dramatically. The professions and cultural positions formerly open only to the likes of the Honorable Judge Theodore "Butch" Perry have become more accessible, and it is the bourgeois whites with attitudes like the whites throughout Wright's fiction who are being pushed to the margins. The uneasy accommodation of these changes by whites, underscored by Ida's perspective, uncovers postmodern permutations of racism in a prosperous Sun Belt South.

The troubling figure of the racial revenant—the drowned boy—functions as an albatross of racial history in the white southern mind. The repression and denial Ida routinely practices receive a starkly appropriate emblem in the ghost of the drowned boy, who appears sporadically as an irruption from her buried past with either a "placid look on his face . . . as if he recognized her" or a glare "full of accusation" (240, 248). If Ida is angered by the insistence of the past, her unwilling recognition of it is matched only by its long delay, by a truculent denial of the guilt that has followed her through the years intervening between the present and the Emerald Isle of 1937. For years she has "wiped the thought" of the boy from her mind "like wiping mucus from her nose": "within moments of seeing him and reacting, something or someone would come between them and he would be instantly forgotten" (244, 248). His previous appearances have "unnerved her," but eventually his apparition forces Ida to ask herself, "How many times did I see him face to face and not pay him one bit of attention? How many times?" (246). But Ida rejects the opportunity to face and forthrightly acknowledge the past; it is discounted by Ida's genteel repression that subtly mirrors the kind of social determinism pervasive in Wright's fiction. Kenan's indictment of the white community, though effected through the consciousness of a fully developed white character, is finally as damning as Wright's: "And the memory took its place, shrinking, and drifted away, more and more remote, amid the giga-fold angel-sized memory hordes stored over the 34,689,600 seconds contained in sixty-six years of life on this planet. . . . But some things you forget to remain innocent; some things you forget to remain free; some things you forget due to lassitude. Moral lassitude, intellectual lassitude, human lassitude. However, Ida had not cared to remember; not to remain innocent, not to remain free, not to spare herself worry, but because she simply did not care. She did not care to remember" (268). In her last encounter with the ghost Ida learns the necessity of caring to remember, as the revenant demands an accounting of the past. Her reaction to his presence is as emphatic and reflexive as those of the whites in Wright's fiction, her impulsive rejection reflecting as much ingrained prejudice as anything in Wright: "What do you want from me? Why do you just stand there, looking, looking, looking? . . . Get away, you hear me? Get away. Leave me be!" (269). These are Ida's final words, recalling the repetitive, panicked rebuke of Bertha in "Big Boy Leaves Home" ("You go away! You go away! I tell you, you go away!" [Wright, *Early Works* 250]). What is in literary terms repetition and revision is the return of the repressed in a psychological and cultural sense. The contemporary white woman of Kenan's story has progressed little from her counterpart in Wright's Jim Crow South, and the "reclamation, doubt, swirling and opaque obfuscation, nagging presentiments, rooted arrogance, proprietary pride, all thick and treacherous and everpresent" with which she has built a "wall" against the events of the past are ultimately as monologic as the discourse of Wright's white characters (Kenan, "Tell Me" 265).

Kenan's Signifyin(g) exchange with Wright hinges upon his modifications to Wright's brand of realism. Wright's sequence of external, naturalistic conflicts becomes Kenan's mixture of psychological and magical realism, resulting in a tale of racial haunting no less critical of white racism than its predecessor yet more resonant because it plumbs the internal depths of its character's pathology in the manner of Henry James. Thus Kenan, who has described himself as a middle-class "integration baby" ("Spies" 26) and whose autobiographical sketches in *Walking on Water* relate an intimate experience with white culture at the University of North Carolina and elsewhere, uses the materials of his own experience in the post–Civil Rights era to make Wright's themes viable some fifty years later. Wright presented a nightmare world of state-sanctioned violence directed toward blacks; Kenan appropriates Wright's bleak vision to a postmodern South that has ostensibly risen above its ignominious racial history.

The result is a dialectical exchange between race and history that allows Kenan to adapt Wright's intrepid mythoclasm to a later era in which the workings of racial injustice have become more covert. A particularly resonant example occurs in the revenant's appearance at one of Ida's regular luncheons at the

Old Plantation Inn. The inn provides Ida with safe harbor from the rain outside (and perhaps from the problematic facets of history as well), "oozing quaintness and doilied charm, with bright-red gladioli, and cross-stitched pillows on wicker chairs, under portraits of belles and horses posed beneath pines dripping with Spanish moss" (Kenan, "Tell Me" 246). This latter-day Old South demesne is Ida's cultural refuge, into which the ghost intrudes an unwelcome presence mirrored by the absence of his forebears in the portraits on the inn's walls. But the sanctuary provided at the inn by "the warm, light conversation of the ladies in their soft Southern cadences" is punctured by the apparition standing just across the street: "They peered at each other, over the distance, through the rain and glass, and Ida—warm, dry, richly fed, impressively dressed, and comfortable—became unaccountably angry with the boy—probably cold, definitely wet, unshod, black—staring at *her*" (247). The ghost performs a mythoclastic function, needling Ida's "hard-won quietude" of "self-satisfaction and contentment" by trespassing in the sanctuary of what she and Butch "strove to achieve" (246). His presence is patent evidence of the troubled conscience of the class of whites who would claim—either through the mythic tenor of the inn or through Ida's sense of personal struggle and entitlement—to have defined the region through an aristocratic and noble history.

The ubiquitous revenant insists on acknowledging the cost of such a history. He undermines Ida's narrative of bourgeois success, from her memories of her father's working his way up "from nothing" to "send her to school and find her a good marriage" to the late Judge Perry's claim that he has "no fear" of reckoning in the afterlife (243, 245). The ghost bears silent witness to the disintegration of Ida's family, which, despite its prosperity, has become fragmented into an indifferent son and a daughter who renounces her father as "a crooked demagogue who should burn in hell for all his wicked doings" (264). The cancer of racial injustice and white hegemony is evident in the family's "plantation-style house," which Kenan presents as a husk emptied of human connection, an inauthentic monument to a bogus mythology:

It was built in 1969, just before Judge Perry's first appointment to the bench—built from proceeds made through Jones, McPhee & Perry and their long-standing connections to Duke Power, Carolina Power & Light, and the Department of Transportation, among others. The house was designed in the Federalist style of orange-red brick, with tiles in the foyer, a bright, floral-patterned sun porch, a grand mahogany table in the dining room . . . all practically unchanged in twenty years. The house contains five bedrooms, a study, a well-stocked pantry. Yet there is a feeling of emptiness, of long nights full of abandoned wishes for hordes of grandchildren and great-grandchildren, for festive Christmases and Thanksgivings and surprise birthday parties. A weight of nothingness and past disappointments tends to bear down in the kitchen over meticulously prepared meals for one. (244–45)

The trappings of aristocracy are in place, yet the means by which they were obtained—the networks of privileged connection, the implied backroom dealings conducted by men exploiting a rigid hierarchy—have left what Ida and Butch "strove to achieve" so tainted by injustice as to render the accoutrements of success a curse. This is an environment amenable to the presence of a passive black man such as Joe Abner, but it is shadowed by other, less docile, black figures. Its mythic profile is indeed haunted by a past far darker than the one it purports to emulate. Further, in her old age Ida has become as forgotten as the boy who could be hurled into the Atlantic without fear of inquiry or reprisal—equally anonymous, equally expendable. The dark parabola of racial violence has completed its circuit.

Such a conclusion differs significantly from the resolution of "Big Boy Leaves Home," yet its rebuke is no less potent than Wright's. True, the white perpetrators of injustice remain untouched by human law, but by delving into the consciousness of the racist mind Kenan judges his characters by an ethical and supernatural standard omitted from Wright's naturalist and materialist philosophy. As a result, the effects of violence on its perpetrators are assessed at a much greater depth than what is visible in the inscrutable white figures of *Uncle Tom's Children*. Ida's fate in fact recalls not Wright's notion of justice but rather that of James Baldwin, who was ever concerned with the lingering psychological costs of misdeeds, their role as shaping forces in the lives of the perpetrators. As the description of the Perry home indicates, a reckoning of Ida and her family in strictly material terms would miss the point of Kenan's revision. By taking up the subject of a racial murder forty years after the event, Kenan revisits Wright's theme through the lens of Baldwin's sense of justice.

Kenan's debt to Baldwin becomes apparent on this crucial point. Baldwin, as Kenan observes in his eloquent 1994 biography, found that his own work benefited from combining the styles of Wright and Henry James (*James Baldwin* 68–70). Kenan effects a similar amalgam in "Tell Me, Tell Me," following Baldwin's example of augmenting Wright's naturalism with a Jamesian psychological realism that explores the consequences of racism for both its practitioners and its victims—a relation that interested Wright only from the victim's perspective.

Kenan seems to have taken Baldwin's criticism of Wright in "Everybody's Protest Novel" into consideration as he fashioned the psyche of Ida McTyre Perry.
Baldwin says of *Native Son* (and his comments may easily be applied to *Uncle
Tom's Children*) that "below the surface of this novel there lies, as it seems to me,
a continuation of that monstrous legend it was written to destroy" (*Notes* 22).
Baldwin describes Wright's work as a "web of lust and fury" in which "black and
white can only thrust and counter-thrust" (22). "Big Boy Leaves Home" certainly
fits Baldwin's observation, the murder of Lester and Buck begetting the murder
of Jim Harvey, which in turn is used as the rationale for Bobo's lynching. But
this "thrust and counter-thrust," this monstrous violence, is carried into the
Jamesian interior in Kenan's work, modifying Wright's model in the process of
engaging it. The faceless mob of Wright's story is replaced by a culture infatu-
ated with plantation trappings and determined to repress the human cost of its
mythology; Ida functions as but one individual member of that collective amne-
sia. The effect is to implicate the entire bourgeois South, through the consciousness of Ida, in the violence of the past. Kenan's story does not conclude with
a protagonist concealed in a truck headed toward Chicago—away from the
South—but in the final days of a life lived entirely in the South, a life haunted
by past misdeeds and a ghostly voice whispering "tell me, tell me" as it demands
an explanation for the unquiet past.

"More Than One Way to Know": A Visitation of Spirits

The structure of Kenan's first book, *A Visitation of Spirits* (1989), threatens to
subvert one's definition of the novel. A sprawling narrative, it seems more intent
on conveying the collective spirit of Tims Creek, North Carolina, than on presenting any conventionally linear notion of story. The novel partakes of what
Gates terms "the ur-trope of the tradition" (13)—the Talking Book—as it speaks
through the voices of Tims Creek residents of several generations, which are
interspersed with script-format dialogue and, as in Jean Toomer's *Cane*, remote
and elegiac third-person narration. Kenan seems influenced by Hurston in his
creation of an autonomous southern black community and by Gloria Naylor's
Mama Day. Tims Creek, a community with a bifurcated, and parallel, racial
history, is similar to Willow Springs in Naylor's novel. Like the enigmatic Sap-
phira Wade in *Mama Day*, Ezra Cross, patriarch of the black Crosses in *Visitation*,
had in the nineteenth century "somehow amassed over one hundred acres of
land, exactly how no one is truly certain" and by 1875 could claim "title to more

land than most former slaves dreamed of having" (Kenan, *Visitation* 115). But what is at times a nearly utopian separatism in Hurston and Naylor receives more problematic treatment here. Tims Creek remains tainted by the white South's penchant for Old South culture. As in all of Kenan's work, white southerners' fetish for plantation mythology perseveres in anachronistic architectural elements like a new hospital that "had been made to look like an old mansion, with fat columns and marble floors, fine wooden panels and carved ceilings" and a public school fashioned "like an old plantation, a huge Georgian vision of red brick complete with white columns holding up the big roof of the verandah" (126, 39–40). The route to black southern identity lies in traversing the pertinacious symbols of a repressive history, not through membership in a distinctly Africanist community.

The strongest influence on *A Visitation of Spirits*, however, lies outside the South, in Baldwin's *Go Tell It on the Mountain*. Indeed, Kenan's novel is a kind of palimpsest, for Baldwin's is the antecedent text informing Kenan's depiction of homosexuality and religion in the South. Parallels between the novels are abundant. Kenan's protagonist, Horace Cross, is, like Baldwin's John Grimes, a teenager of obscure parentage and budding, if closeted, homosexuality. Two years older than John, Horace is steeped in his community's religion, although his observation that "most people left" First Baptist Church of Tims Creek "as somber as they had entered" (71) recalls John's skeptical query, "If God's power was so great, why were their lives so troubled?" (Baldwin, *Go Tell It* 144). Like John, "who was expected to be good, to be a good example," and who "might become a Great Leader of His People" (13, 19), Horace is an exemplary student and the hope of his family and community. He is variously described by others of the community as "the Great Black Hope," "the Straight-A Kid," and "the Chosen Nigger" (Kenan, *Visitation* 13). Kenan's secondary characters are also descendants of Baldwin's. Horace's cousin, Jimmy Greene, recalls Brother Elisha of *Go Tell It on the Mountain* as a role model and mentor in the faith—each is "not much older" and "already saved and . . . a preacher" (Baldwin 13). Horace's father, Sammy, resembles Roy Grimes—or rather, both Royals—in his cynical attitudes toward religion and the poverty of black people. Like Gabriel Grimes, Horace's grandfather is an elder of the church "who walked and talked and slept with God on his lips, at his side, in his breast," and Horace has for years listened to "his grandfather lecture and spin yarns," much like Gabriel's, "about how black folk had been mistreated at the hands of the white man" (Kenan, *Visitation* 71, 89).

But Kenan carries on the Signifyin(g) tradition by manipulating these similarities to revise the crucial passage of Baldwin's novel: the threshing-floor sequence. What comprises some dozen pages of *Go Tell It on the Mountain* becomes a mystical night journey running the length of *A Visitation of Spirits*. Kenan repeats the motif of a trancelike state that spans a literal and figurative long night of the soul, Signifyin(g) on John's mystical seizure on the threshing floor with Horace's visionary perambulation through the sleeping Tims Creek. The demons that accompany Horace on his surreal excursion are reminiscent of the "malicious, ironic voice" that "scornfully" taunts John throughout his trance (Baldwin, *Go Tell It* 193–94, 197). Following the chiastic pattern of Signification, however, the trope is ultimately reversed. John spends his dark night of the soul inside the Temple of the Fire Baptized; Horace wanders outside that sanctuary literally as well as figuratively naked, turning not to God for solace but to the occult and the ominous empowerment of his grandfather's rifle. Accordingly, morning brings a very different resolution to the later novel, and what is a bildungsroman with a tragic setting in Baldwin's treatment becomes, in Kenan's, a tragedy of thwarted development. The effect of this revision is to foreground the issues of black existence in the South and the tension between homosexuality and the church. Religion fails Horace; he cannot eventually claim, as John does, that he is "on his way," and through his suicide Kenan Signifies on Baldwin's work to indict both the white community that cannot accommodate a gifted black man and the black church that refuses to accept his homosexuality. Through such revisions Kenan uses *Go Tell It on the Mountain* as the template for a reworking of the classic tropes of double-consciousness and the double, broadening Baldwin's focus into a descendant text that fully engages contemporary southern culture as it participates in literary refashioning. Kenan augments the traditional black/white dichotomy of double-consciousness with the tension between hetero- and homosexuality, adopting to his own uses African American materials as well as those of the dominant culture. But at the same time that Kenan carries on a vital tradition, he also Signifies on that tradition, reinterpreting its motifs to modify W. E. B. Du Bois's theory of double-consciousness to suit new circumstances. Finally, Kenan's portrait of the black church sets him at odds with one of the fundamental institutions of black culture, resulting in a postmodern work that uses iconoclasm and intertextuality to fashion a radical reappraisal of black and gay identity in the contemporary South.

Horace's phantasmagoric night journey is really a quest for self-definition, incited by the search in an overwhelmingly white culture for a viable black existence that might combine, as the novel's chapter titles indicate, "white sorcery" with "black necromancy" into a new, "holy science." Thus the novel involves from the beginning Du Bois's concept of double-consciousness, which bears repeating here: "It is a peculiar sensation, this double-consciousness, this sense of always looking at one's self through the eyes of others, of measuring one's soul by the tape of a world that looks on in amused contempt and pity. One ever feels his two-ness,—an American, a Negro; two souls, two thoughts, two unreconciled strivings; two warring ideals in one dark body, whose dogged strength alone keeps it from being torn asunder" (2). Horace does indeed feel this "two-ness," navigating between "the double cultural worlds" that are the basis of Du Bois's theory (Sundquist 3). He is acutely conscious of labels like "greyboy" and "Oreo," which follow him in his academic interests and friendships with his white peers, and his conception of himself is ever tortured by the conflict between white and black. But his sense of double-consciousness is particularly complex, compounded by the fact that Horace oscillates between the poles of black and white and between gay and straight. As Doris Betts notes, Horace "feels very much an outcast, first by race in Southern white society but more seriously by his sexual preference within his religious and orthodox family" (12). Crucial to Kenan's use of double-consciousness from a homosexual perspective is the conventional manifestation of the trope in Horace's relation to the white South, which must be examined before proceeding to Kenan's groundbreaking Signifyin(g) revisions.

The route to self-definition offered by white culture appears in Horace's encounter at the Crosstown theater where he has worked in the locally produced play, *Ride the Freedom Star*. Written by a scion of the white Cross family of Tims Creek, Philip Quincy Cross, the play is a piece of monumental poetastery and ersatz cultural mythology. Horace recollects the drama as a "mish-mash of ill-conceived, ill-wrought, cliché-ridden drivel, the doggerel verse and the melodramatic romanticizing of Southern American history" in which "many of the historical facts were just plain wrong" (Kenan, *Visitation* 213). The one-sided mythology of the South is evident to Horace in a work fraught with "long static

passages of fathers patriotically extolling the virtues of riding off into battle"
and "mothers enumerating the travails of the Civil War–torn plantation system"
(213). As yet another iteration of southern mythology, the play resembles the
architectural fixtures of the community in its dogged adherence to a romantic
past conspicuously fashioned around white experience. If the validity of this
past is suspect to the dissenting white southern perspective, it is even more so
to Horace.

A poster advertising the production embodies such ideology in iconic fashion. Proclaiming *Ride the Freedom Star* at once "the saga of an American family"
and "The American Story," the poster, swathed in the billowing flags of the
United States and the Confederacy, bears heroic images of ancestral white
Crosses—statesmen, planters, and pioneers "hearty and robust like comic book
characters" (210, 211). But the black Crosses fit a different kind of image: "Off
to the right of the group stood three black people. A man, shirtless, horse-
muscled, and bronze, and a woman, her head beragged, both with an out-of-
place grin on their faces. Standing beneath them was a young boy, his eyes
much too big, the smile on his face lost somewhere in the conflagration of
counterfeit glory" (211). Here the historically reduced status of the black American is manifest and salient. Literally on the margins of the poster, black participants in "The American Story" are not only ancillary to the dynamic, unfolding
narrative of American culture, they are also reduced to the stereotypes of Man-
dingo, Auntie, Sambo. The images starkly convey a culture so thoroughly racialized as to be blithely unaware of its bedrock racism, bearing out Houston
Baker's claim that "the white culture theorizer's" notion of America as "the refuge
of huddled masses yearning to be free," a "domain of the boundless frontier,"
and "freedom's dream castle" is distinctly at odds with the black American's
perspective on history (10). Even Philip Cross's "concession to his family's slave-
owning past" partakes of such myopia (Kenan, *Visitation* 213). Despite "the inter-
jection of a speech here and there that reflected the reality of the hard life of
the slaves," Cross nonetheless "had tried to create a picture of domestic bliss for
the house slaves and of jolly camaraderie for the field workers" (213). Ultimately
Cross's gestures toward equanimity devolve into hackneyed—and racist—
images of southern culture: "the blacks were mainly there for buffoonery and
hijinks that brought laughs and chuckles from the audience, for the church
scenes with their raw and dynamic singing, and for the minister's sermon, which
was the most passionate, hell-raising moment in the entire play" (213–14).

In his appraisal of such depictions Horace seems aware of what Eric Sundquist has termed the "contending cultural languages and figurative systems" by which American culture receives its expression (5). Horace is cognizant that the culture-theory underlying *Ride the Freedom Star* is reductive, his instinctive pride in the minister's sermon tempered by an awareness that its power is mitigated by its token role that renders the play's theme—not to mention its title—pregnant with irony. Thus he seems beyond capitulating to, or internalizing, the terms of double-consciousness. But his conversation with one of the apparitions in the theater indicates otherwise—that Horace can recognize the dynamic between subject and object given the distancing perspective of fictionalized history but cannot clearly see its workings in his own life. In one of the novel's many fantastic passages, Horace finds himself in strained conversation with a buffalo named Veronica (presumably derived from one of the frontier props in the play) clad in a prim white dress, gold spectacles, and a yellow hat, sipping tea. In her mannerisms and her Victorian lament for the loss of manners and propriety in modern culture, Veronica sounds a nostalgic note that allies her with a prior generation of southern white culture. Her monologue prohibits Horace from asking her the question he longs to pose ("He wanted to ask her, Do you know why I'm here? but was not given a chance" [Kenan, *Visitation* 214]), and her notion of politeness begins to seem infused with ideas of social hierarchy steeped in genteel racism—to such an extent that she can blithely express wistfulness for the past in the face of a naked and mud-spattered Horace.

Even in her chimerical context, Veronica appears as a surreal emblem of the racial myopia that characterizes the theater in general. She simply does not see Horace; instead, she practices the kind of nonrecognition explored throughout Ralph Ellison's *Invisible Man*. Further, what is encoded in the specter's complaint is not substantially different from the social roles depicted on the poster outside the theater. She longs for a bygone era when people knew their places: "I'm afraid people have lost manners and politeness. They abide by no rules. Beasts is what they have become. Beasts" (209). Yet she is utterly and ironically unaware of her own beastliness, of the fact that despite her affectations she remains a brute animal with a "lionlike, snakelike tail switching from one side of [her] haunches to another" (209). Unfortunately, neither is Horace truly conscious of the incongruity. Ever dutiful and proper, he disengages from Veronica deferentially and apologetically, reluctant to make an exit that in the buffalo's terms can only be interpreted as "rude" (215). Another stage of his quest is hindered by the mores of white society that, like those of Ida in "Tell Me, Tell

Me," conceal the dominance of white ideology beneath an etiquette predicated on fixed social relations.

At work in the encounter is a depiction of double-consciousness filtered through the lens of magic realism. Like the other demons Horace meets, Veronica is intent on deceiving the young man, on reinforcing the terms of the ambiguous existence that has driven him to his night of necromancy. Her harangue intimates to Horace, in a manner more subtle than the poster's caricatures, that his agency is limited and that despite the urgency of his mission, his conduct is constantly measured by standards that are not his own. *Ride the Freedom Star* proffers an obviously abhorrent role for African Americans, but Horace seems powerless before Veronica's forceful affectation. In Mephistophelean fashion, it turns his urbane ambitions against him, feeding the self-destructive process by which he continues to divide himself into the warring factions of internal and external definition. Like the black actors in the church scenes who had "ironically . . . kept the crowds coming back" (213), Horace is scripted into a role penned by white ideology, albeit by a supernatural hand more deft than that of Philip Quincy Cross.

The exterior definition limned by this passage feeds the self-hatred Horace feels for his homosexuality. Horace's confusion on this score manifests itself through Kenan's masterful deployment of the double, which appears first in the curious twinning of the protagonist with a schoolmate, Gideon Stone, a doubling that Horace is reluctant to acknowledge. For many years "the prettiest boy in Horace's class," Gideon is despised by many of his classmates because he has "sugar in his blood" and by Horace because he "was known as the smartest in the class" (97–98). However, the central tension between the boys derives from Horace's realization that Gideon represents a part of himself that cannot be revealed: as the uncloseted Other, Gideon continually serves as a reminder of Horace's secret nature. Gideon's transition to manhood draws Horace to him; their shared interests in academics and "*Star Trek* and science fiction and horror novels" mesh with a sexual attraction that forces Horace to examine his dual nature (153). Through his "infatuation" with Gideon, Horace comes to "realize that he was different and vulnerable and that the simple joy of being in love and expressing it with straightforward passion was denied to him" (153). Horace's double has come to terms with a sexuality that Horace still fears; Gideon "had been taunted and excluded for so long that he had built a world of his own within himself. Other people simply did not matter to him" (153). In Gideon, then, Horace discerns a possible resolution to his homosexual double-consciousness. Gideon's lack of concern for what "other people" think puts him outside the ambivalent state of being measured from without, just as the "world of his own" devising avoids the "two unreconciled strivings" of Du Bois's paradigm. Gideon has discarded the dualism that perseveres in Horace's encounters with Veronica and others, choosing instead to define himself on his own terms.

In rejecting Gideon, Horace sets in motion the chain of events leading to his own demise. He ends their affair when his homosexuality begins to frighten him "beyond reason," and he equates his sexuality with "a disease" (156, 160). Their final confrontation culminates in Horace's striking Gideon, an act resonant with misdirected malice: "Horace hit Gideon. Full square in the mouth, so quickly he himself did not realize what he had done, so hard he could not doubt he meant to do it. But had he wanted to hit Gideon, or himself for not wanting to hit him? Gideon staggered; blood appeared on his lip. . . . Horace noticed the blood and felt sick. Suddenly he wanted to rush to him, to grab him, to kiss him, to rock him and beg him for forgiveness. But he would not. Ever. And he steeled his jaw and looked away" (163–64). Kenan's alteration to the double motif becomes evident. A similar encounter in Ellison, for example, posits the invisible man striking out at Ras the Destroyer in the act of rejecting a deleterious alter ego. What is regenerative violence in Ellison's work, however, is Signified upon here as self-destruction. Horace's anger stems from his lack of anger, his hatred from a lack of hatred for the double so simultaneously similar to and different from himself. The portion of Horace that strikes out at Gideon is the obstinate "straight" self that insists on prevalence within him, the identity provided him by the dominant ideology of his cultures—both black and white. His act of rejection, then, is ultimately directed at himself: not only does he turn away from Gideon, he also denies acknowledging his own true nature.

Horace chooses the extrinsic element of his double-consciousness. His last vision of the night echoes the memory of violence with Gideon with portentous finality. In the costume room of the theater Horace witnesses an apparition that combines all the ambiguities of his existence into an amalgam of the double and double-consciousness: "He pulled back a coat, clutching the gun, and saw someone sitting in front of a mirrored dresser, putting on makeup. He was a black man, dressed in a sun-bright costume, orange and green and blue and red, like a harlequin's. As Horace looked into the mirror, the face appeared more and more familiar, though it was becoming obscured by milky white greasepaint. He realized. Saw clearly. It was him. Horace. Sitting before the mirror, applying makeup. Of all the things he had seen this night, all the memories he had confronted, all the ghouls and ghosts and specters, this shook him the most" (219). Kenan's magic realism presents the double in such a fashion as to conflate the literal and the figurative, using a visionary sequence to make the metaphorical Other manifest. In the haunted "greyboy" consciousness of Horace, the Other appears as a reflection variegated and resplendent, yet choosing for its visage only white, only the lack of color. The doppelgänger's actions are telling as it "deftly, expertly" fashions a "perverted image" of Horace by covering its face with white greasepaint as if to do so "were normal" (220, 221). His moment of "redemption" occurs when the double's image shifts and appears naked and without greasepaint, telling Horace that he can choose "to follow the demon," but urging him, "I'm your way . . . I'm what you need" (234). Although Horace "saw clearly through a glass darkly and understood where he fit," he rejects this last double, turning "his heart away" from his own image with more "self-loathing" than he has ever felt (234–35). He fires the rifle at his double, who dies on the floor with "eyes full of horror," looking up at Horace "in recognition . . . as if to say . . . You actually hate me?" (235). It is a coda to the fight with Gideon, and it is Horace's damnation.

Modifying the conventions of the double and double-consciousness allows Kenan to Signify on Baldwin's work by bringing a similar protagonist and cultural context to a very different resolution. The "malicious, ironic voice" that follows John Grimes is a victorious demonic chorus in Kenan's novel that tempts Horace to turn away from a salvation analogous to the one John experiences. John feels for a moment that he is "the Devil's son," but Horace claims actually to be possessed by demons and never returns "into the land of the living" (Baldwin, *Go Tell It* 198, 201). His being "thrust out of the holy, the joyful, the blood-washed community" is confirmed as permanent, for unlike John, Horace feels a sense of divisiveness that cannot be surmounted (196). The beleaguered optimism of Du Bois's theory—"two warring ideals in one dark body, whose dogged strength alone keeps it from being torn asunder"—is rendered tragic in a protagonist who cannot summon the strength to reconcile the two sides of his antithetical nature. As the encounter with the double demonstrates, Horace can see no resolution except for silencing one "ideal," and the resultant split can end only in death—in a body "torn asunder" by a bullet to the brain.

Perhaps the most poignant element of Kenan's Signification on Baldwin lies not in the fact that he reverses the fate of his protagonist but that Horace comes to resemble the biological father of his fictional antecedent, Richard. Elizabeth's first lover also may properly be termed a victim of double-consciousness destroyed by the conflict between his individuality and the role the dominant culture assigns him. Richard's arrest incites a conflict between his dual and conflicting identities—the first (and internal), a thwarted intellectuality determined to know "everything them white bastards knew"; the second, a stereotype that leads to a presumption of guilt by the white policemen who apprehend him (167). This ordeal and the seething tension of Richard's life culminate in a profound despair that leaves him "dead among the scarlet sheets" of his apartment (174). Richard's suicide confirms his knowledge that he will ever be (in Du Bois's terms) "measured" by the "tape" of a world not his own. So, too, Horace dies by his own hand in an act of self-destruction spurred by society's unwillingness to accommodate his individuality.

Such a violent denouement Signifies on *Go Tell It on the Mountain* by revealing the inadequacy of its sole route to salvation, the church. In effect subjecting the bright and devout protagonist of the antecedent novel with the tragic fate of one of its secondary characters, Kenan empties the church of its capacity to deliver his character. This failure hinges on the issue of homosexuality, which Kenan explores in far more explicit terms than Baldwin. Visiting First Baptist Church of Tims Creek in the early morning hours of his last day alive, Horace recalls the Reverend Barden's sermon against homosexuality. Exuding "an aura, not of holiness, but of wisdom, wry and canny," the reverend preaches against "unnatural" uses of the human body by "men and men, women and women— help me, Jesus—living together in sin. Like it wont nothing. Normal. Tolerable" (Kenan, *Visitation* 76, 78). Citing Paul as his scriptural authority, Barden declares "this filth" to be "unclean"—a word he repeats throughout the sermon and that echoes in Horace's mind like a label with which he has been branded; eventually Horace hears but "one word from those brown lips: Unclean" (78, 79, 82). Spurred by this sacerdotal sanction from the church, the demons encourage Horace to "be ashamed" and hurl a host of epithets at him ("man lover," "sissy," "greyboy") that manipulate the bifurcation of his consciousness in their favor (86–87). Their harangue culminates in a declaration that seals his separation from the church: "There is no other way. You belong" (87). Barden's dogmatic assertion that "when lust hath conceived, it bringeth forth sin; and sin, when it is finished, bringeth forth death," proves to be prophetic (79). In Kenan's treatment, however, Horace's status as anathema to the church bears more cultural than spiritual significance. Horace's death results not from lust and sin but from being cast out by the social institution that has defined his existence. The terms of membership in that organization—adherence to "normal" and "tolerable" sexual conduct—are constructed along heterosexual lines that, foreign to him, exclude him at a fundamental level. Once again, Horace's culture provides him with a resolution to double-consciousness that is binary, but this time within an African American context: either heterosexual and a son of the church or homosexual and a pariah.

The polarities engendered by this binary conception lead Horace to conclude "that I was probably not going to go home to heaven, cause the rules were too hard for me to keep" (251). Given the paradigm of the church, of the Reverend Barden, of his community, he is "too weak" to be among the elect (251). Jimmy Greene's meditation on Horace's suicide makes this distinction—and its sources—clear: "That is finally what got to Horace, isn't it? I keep asking myself. He, just like me, had been created by this society. He was a son of the community, more than most. His reason for existing, it would seem, was for the salvation of his people. But he was flawed as far as the community was concerned. First, he loved men; a simple, normal deviation, but a deviation this community would never accept. And second, he didn't quite know who he was. That, I don't fully understand, for they had told him, taught him from the cradle on. I guess they didn't reckon the world they were sending him into was different from the world they had conquered, a world peopled with new and hateful monsters that exacted a different price" (188). Jimmy's comments effectively summarize the conflict of the novel, along with Kenan's challenge to the orthodox religion of the black community. Horace is created and shaped by his community and exists to serve it yet is hindered by the crucial "flaw" and "deviation" of his sexuality that sets him apart from his culture. His identity crisis stems from not knowing "who he was" because his culture has not incorporated such deviations into its criteria for self-definition—a fact underscored by Jimmy's (heterosexual) bewilderment that being "taught from the cradle on" is insufficient for Horace. Indeed, the world of Tims Creek is different because it has "conquered" such benighted social conditions as those that shape the Harlem of *Go Tell It on the Mountain*, but as an accepted member of its community, Jimmy cannot see that the "hateful monsters" that plagued Horace originate in the community itself. His understanding of Horace is impeded by his internalization of the predominant ideology of Tims Creek, rendering even a sympathetic observer of the young man's suicide unable to comprehend its inevitability. At the beginning of his homosexual awakening, Horace learned "the difference between knowledge and experience, and that there is more than one way to know" (155). Despite his efforts to understand, Jimmy is too rooted in his community to apprehend the possible multiplicity of knowledge, to view that community fully from the perspective of one excluded by its strictures.

Kenan joins his white contemporaries in postmodern southern literature in turning a critical eye toward the iconic institutions of his culture. White writers of the contemporary South have abjured the established practice of directing criticism almost exclusively toward entities outside the South. Within an African American frame of reference, Kenan does something similar. In his work the enemy of black culture is no longer entirely external but is also within the community and inherent in one of the primary vehicles of black cultural expression. The dramatic departure of this critical stance is evident beyond the Signification on Baldwin: the church that reluctantly accommodates Hurston's philandering protagonist in *Jonah's Gourd Vine*, that is ultimately reinvigorated by political activism in Wright's "Fire and Cloud," cannot redeem the black homosexual of *A Visitation of Spirits*. The methods of self-definition it provides, like those offered by the class system to Dorothy Allison's characters or the terms of "southern" identity Frank Bascombe rejects, are exposed as inadequate. The result is the kind of crisis of legitimacy that Jean-François Lyotard views as innately postmodern, to the extent that Kenan has described the setting of his novel as "this very stultified community of Tims Creek" (Ketchin 285). Because it contributes to this stultification, the black church is subject to a new level of criticism. The authority of what the preeminent historians of black religion have called "the central institutional sector in most black communities" is eroded (Lincoln and Mamiya 382). Such a fundamental critique of the church puts Kenan at odds with his literary tradition; in refusing to offer a conciliatory interpretation of black religion for the homosexual, he declines the mediating role that Hurston and Wright accepted. In his particular example, the "web of filiation" that shapes the Signifyin(g) tradition reaches beyond revision and modification to something more radical (Gates xxii). The process of Signification is taken a step farther than in the past—literary recension becomes cultural rejection.

The import of Kenan's appropriation of the Signifyin(g) process is profound. To emphasize his break from convention in a southern context, one need only compare him to the writer with whom Fred Hobson concludes *The Southern Writer in the Postmodern World*, Ernest Gaines. Hobson describes Gaines as a legitimate heir to the Renascence tradition, a writer who shares with Faulkner "a valuing of the old ways" and who "is more traditional, in the best sense of that word," than most of his contemporaries (96, 92). Citing C. Vann Woodward's notion that African Americans may be the "quintessential" southerners, Hobson suggests that "the black Southerner might be seen as the quintessential southern *writer*"—possessing those "well-known qualities" of southern authorship that would render a neotraditionalist like Gaines "the truest contemporary heir to the southern literary tradition" (101). Given Hobson's criteria, Kenan is hardly eligible for such a distinction: to read Kenan through the criteria of literary orthodoxy would subject him to the same kind of process Horace suffers in Tims Creek, subsuming the author into the hegemonic consensus he resists in all of his work. Kenan in fact Signifies on the familiar qualities of white Renascence fiction, reversing those motifs that Gaines adopts in a fashion amenable to Hobson's traditionalist readings. As the dark history of "Tell Me, Tell Me" illustrates, Kenan uses the dialectic of the past in the present as a tool to expose a South seldom accounted for in the literary record of the region, not as an ordering principle used to recover a unified history. One would be hard-pressed to link the community of Tims Creek to Faulkner's Yoknapatawpha, as Hobson does with Gaines's Bayonne and environs. Kenan deploys those rural elements of Tims Creek to undermine the conventional notion of the southern community as "organic," to set agrarian folkways at odds with those members of society who cannot view the solidarity of their "traditional" culture as regenerative. The "old ways," the traditions and mores of the past, are consequently viewed from an iconoclastic perspective that resists incorporation into the dominant narrative of southern literature—whether white or black.

The concluding section of *A Visitation of Spirits*, "Requiem for Tobacco," may be read as Kenan's farewell to the South of that dominant narrative. The evocative description of planting, harvesting, and firing tobacco sounds familiar echoes of a pastoral South, even to the point of depicting the tactile labor of an earlier era giving way to mechanized agriculture. But the traditionalist reader is intentionally misled by such statements as "there was a time when folk were bound together in a community, as one" (254). The narration interjects, "but this was once upon a time," complicating the idyllic portrait with a phrase suggestive of utopian nostalgia, and the second-person address approaches facetiousness in asking, "You've heard of these things, I'm sure? Didn't you see it in a play, or read it in a book or . . ." (254, 256). The uneasy balance between poignancy and parody exposes the constructedness of this Arcadian past. This bygone South, received secondhand by the contemporary reader, is cast as a fable, a mythic entity one has "heard of" but never encountered directly—a legend fashioned by the narratives of plays and books. The passage displays a canny awareness of literary tradition, on which it plays the dozens. The repetition of a model of the past with subtle differences reveals Kenan's awareness of those well-known conventions of southern writing, while his ambivalent appropriation of them calls their legitimacy, their authority, into question. Given his marginal position in the South, Kenan's play with such a dominant ideal is an act of critical irony, an expression of parody derived from a culture that, as his comments in *Walking on Water* indicate, was always already postmodern. "Requiem for Tobacco" epitomizes a perspective that questions the totalizing impulse, aware that a community's being bound together as "one" involves the negation of dissent, the suppression of difference. Kenan's work exposes such singularity as reductive, whether in the context of the South's social order or its literature, insisting that there is indeed more than one way to know for a culture—black, white, southern—that has not yet conceded that fact.

BARRY HANNAH
AND THE "OPEN FIELD"
OF SOUTHERN HISTORY

All the generations of wonderful dead guys behind us. All the Confederate dead and the Union dead planted in the soil near us. All of Faulkner the great. Christ, there's barely room for the living down here.

—*Barry Hannah*, Boomerang

The Civil War has been nearly ubiquitous in southern fiction. As Walter Sullivan has noted, "It is a fact that since 1865 Southern novelists have simply not been able to leave the Civil War alone" ("Southern Novelists" 112). Perhaps the most dramatic event in southern history, the Civil War has served the ideological purposes of generations of southern authors. It has been amenable to the configurations of writers of vastly disparate intent who nonetheless share a common perception of it as an iconic event, an incarnation of southern culture. In the nineteenth century, authors like Thomas Nelson Page and John Esten Cooke used the conflict as a dramatic device to advance a romantic conception of the region—a vision that endured at least until the publication of Margaret Mitchell's *Gone with the Wind* in 1936. The southern modernists were less romantically inclined, but they also turned to the South's military history at a formative period in the region's consciousness. The flurry of war novels with which they greeted modernity (the Agrarian output, William Faulkner, Caroline Gordon) indicates that southern writers found the war fodder for another set of generational concerns into the 1940s, a touchstone of the culture that could be used as an archetype for the modern period as well as for the late Victorian era. John Pilkington has perhaps best described the perception of the war as an incarnation of southern culture in general: "Those who explored the South and its history . . . shared a common belief that the Civil War was the single most significant and symbolic event in the Southern past. Understanding the meaning of the South, its strengths and weaknesses, its glory and defeat, and its present problems, must begin with the war" (356). Allen Tate takes such observations into the realm of myth. He describes the war's place in southern letters in metanarrative terms: "The Southern legend, as Malcolm Cowley has called it, of defeat and heroic frustration was taken over by a dozen or more first-rate writers and converted into a universal myth of the human condition" (*Essays* 592). It is in fact difficult to conceive of a "southern" literature without the war; in one form or another, it has shaped the region's philosophical and literary consciousness—and its cultural mythology—for more than a century.

Yet the postmodern period has produced very little fiction on the Civil War. This undoubtedly stems in part from the fact that contemporary writers, unlike the modernists, have no living access to participants in the conflict; the "resource of memory" mined by writers of the early twentieth century has dissipated (Simpson, *Dispossessed* 86–87). But it also seems evident that the appeal of Confederate history has waned in an age that is suspicious of grand narratives and that has also endured the disillusionment of the Vietnam War. In contemporary fiction martial glory is vastly diminished; the contrast between Vietnam works like Tim O'Brien's *The Things They Carried* and Renascence war fiction makes the saga of southern glory and defeat seem like an antiquated fable, a story pervaded by sentiment and nostalgia, no longer viable. Even the common experience of defeat has failed to take hold in the postmodern southern imagination. The familiar formula of understanding the present through the past, with the qualified exception of Bobbie Ann Mason's *In Country*, is generally absent in postmodern southern letters. The generation of southern writers fresh from the experience of a war such as Vietnam—a conflict with no discernible telos, no apparent shape or function beyond large-scale carnage—abandoned the technique of depicting warfare in mythopoeic terms.[1]

Enter Barry Hannah, who (like the protagonist of his story "Bats Out of Hell Division") has rushed to the fore of the melee with "quill high, greeting their cannon" (*Bats* 44). Hannah has ensured the survival of the Civil War in contemporary fiction but in a manner that the modernists hardly would have condoned. He brings a new irreverence to this sacrosanct topic, an iconoclastic interpretation of history that inverts the conventions of Lost Cause mythology even as his pyrotechnic prose style wreaks havoc on the reader's a priori expectations of syntax. For Hannah, the war does not serve the modernist function of ordering the present. Instead, it fully partakes of contemporary anarchy and futility; its very appeal lies in its status as the apotheosis of these qualities. The general in "Bats Out of Hell Division" provides an example. The Civil War is the "World War of his dreams," a cornucopia of bloodshed that quickens his spirit and spurs him to cry, "Thought I'd never live to see it! There *is* a God and God is *love!*"; "Brother against brother! In my lifetime! Can Providence be truly this good?" (45). Hannah uses the past in a manner similar to Cormac McCarthy's: not as the key to essentialist antecedents that promise to transcend contemporary disorder but as evidence of a lack of human progress, a perennial futility.[2] The ordering potential of myth is a chimera.

Herein lies Hannah's importance to southern literature. His Civil War fiction is one of the clearest intersections between southern cultural mythology and postmodern technique. He approaches the sacred ground of cultural myth with a profound post-Vietnam skepticism of military glory. He subverts the mythmaking tendencies that the Civil War has engendered in the region's literature. In place of the honor and order of a chivalric tradition, Hannah offers such radical discontinuity as: "Then sabers up and we knock the fuck out of everybody. With the cherished dream of Christ in our hearts. Basically, the message is: Leave me the hell alone or give me a beer" (*Ray* 69–70). Nothing is sacred in Hannah's vision of the Confederacy: romantic grandeur, patriotism, and divine endorsement are conflated into a mess of sentimentalism that ultimately amounts to nothing more than a petulant wish to be left alone. (And this in three sentences.) Whatever order and significance the moderns saw in the Confederacy are eradicated at the source. A terse demythologizing wit abounds in Hannah's work—a sort of shorthand mythoclasm that undercuts the lofty rhetoric of Confederate mythology with swift strokes of the irreverent and, often, the scatological. The result is a war fiction that, in Noel Polk's words, is "more deeply indebted to *Night of the Living Dead* and *The Texas Chainsaw Massacre* and to Céline than to Faulkner, Freeman, or Foote" ("Hey Barry" 14).

Polk's assessment is astute, for it highlights the frame of reference that Hannah brings to his new brand of "historical" fiction. Because he is suspicious of a symbolic order that would use warfare as an iconic drama of higher values, Hannah's work denies the reader what Jean-François Lyotard calls "the solace of good forms" (81). It dismantles the universal tendencies of myth by reducing the events of war to the level of the absurd and nihilistic—to such an extent that they cannot be interpreted as part of a larger design. In place of the heroic conflict of tradition, one finds a war depicted with such absurdity as to underscore constantly the constructedness of all myth. Action is not universal but frenzied and chaotic. Instead of affecting transcendent gestures, Hannah's characters participate in violence so grotesque as to be almost comical, with a symbolic register scarcely higher than those of the horror movies Polk cites. Thus Hannah echoes the sort of disillusion expressed by Hemingway's Frederic Henry in *A Farewell to Arms* while presenting it in the narrative forms of his own era. The mendacity of mythic rhetoric is even further rebuked by Hannah's depiction of its attendant carnage in images one might expect to encounter in a B movie.

Hannah's attitude toward the chivalric myth is apparent in his choice of its exemplar, J. E. B. Stuart, who appears at least tangentially in most of his Civil War fiction. In his time, Stuart was seen as "the very embodiment of not only of the fortitude and determination of the Confederate fighting man, but of the ideal of Southern manhood" (Seib 43). Shelby Foote describes Stuart as "square-built, of average height, with china-blue eyes, a bushy cinnamon beard, and flamboyant clothes—thigh-high boots, yellow sash, elbow-length gauntlets, red-lined cape, soft hat with the brim pinned up on one side by a gold star supporting a foot-long ostrich plume" (471). Here is a figure ripe for postmodern parody, a historical persona who seems an anachronism even in the 1860s. Given Hannah's iconoclastic temperament, a man of such outlandish appearance (and who also periodically signed his letters "The Knight of the Golden Spurs" [Seib 43]) represents a fraudulent and inflated code of heroism. Hannah has commented that he sees Stuart as "a glorious fool" and an icon of "all that glory, which was pompous and phony anyway" ("Spirits" 329, 331). Accordingly, Stuart's historical profile receives rough treatment in Hannah's fiction. In a letter to his wife, the Stuart of Hannah's imagination cannot extricate the noble sentiments of his military calling from a vulgar expression of his sexual drives: "The only thing that keeps me going on my mission is the sacred inalienable right of the Confederacy to be the Confederacy, Christ Our Lord, and the memory of your hot hairy jumping nexus when I return" (*Airships* 146). Here is a new sort of exemplar for the Confederate mission—a paragon of valor with the sexual sensibility of an adolescent. In Hannah's treatment the lofty iconography of myth is forever problematized by the base qualities it would deny: the embodiment of Confederate chivalry is cast as the reductio ad absurdum of a turgid and narcissistic culture.

Such an approach would be no more than irreverent—a mocking parody of cultural narcissism—if it did not also entail an incisive inquiry into the compulsion to construct such heroic fables. The mythology surrounding the Civil War provides Hannah with a clearly delineated *grand récit*, an opportunity to draw large and startling figures of his postmodern philosophy of metanarratives for those who would otherwise be unable to see in such a manner. Beneath Hannah's best Civil War fiction lies a dissection of the very impulse to view experience in narrative form, to construct a saga of elevated heroism. Particularly in the story "Dragged Fighting from His Tomb" (*Airships*) and in his novel *Ray*, Hannah demonstrates that a culture predisposed to narrative is especially vulnerable to postmodern scrutiny. The protagonists of "Dragged Fighting from His Tomb" and *Ray*, both southerners, find that cultural mythology offers little consolation in a fragmentary cosmos. Their struggles to achieve order through historical means fail them; unlike the modernist characters of tradition, they find their cultural narratives to be impotent fables. Their stories demonstrate that, while the war may indeed be the dominant fixture in the southern cultural landscape, it is also subject to the irreverent scrutiny of the postmodern South.

"POMPOUS AND PHONY" GLORY: THE SHORT STORIES

Hannah's Civil War stories provide an apt introduction to the postmodern vision of *Ray*. They defy the conventions of historical fiction, mixing historical events with willful inaccuracy to such an extent that the veracity of "historical fact" is called into question. If there is any constancy to them, it lies in what Ruth Weston calls Hannah's proclivity for "deglamorizing" the "mythology of war and the myth of the warrior"—a process that dispels the "illusion" that "cultural ideals" can engender "a truly unified self" through myth (72). Hannah undermines and repudiates modernist uses of the war. He attacks both sentiment and the cultural foundations on which the elusive unified self may be ostensibly constructed. In his treatment, the characters of historical drama exhibit a confusion anathema to modernist conceptions of the bygone era of the

Confederacy. At issue with his iconoclasm is the heroic mythologizing that followed the war as well as the metaphysical assumptions of modernity that would cast history as an ordered antithesis to the present.

Witness, for example, the narrator of "Knowing He Was Not My Kind Yet I Followed" from *Airships*. The homosexual corporal Deed Ainsworth sounds suspiciously ambiguous in his appraisal of Confederate morale: "The truth is, not a one of us except Jeb Stuart believes in anything any longer. The man himself the exception. There is nobody who does not believe in Jeb Stuart. Oh, the zany purposeful eyes, the haggard gleam, the feet of his lean horse high in the air, his rotting flannel shirt under the old soiled grays, and his heroic body odor! He makes one want to be a Christian. I wish I could be one. I'm afraid the only things I count on are chance and safety" (145). One need only think of Tate's longing for the conviction of being "hurried beyond decision" to recognize the iconoclasm of this picture. Hannah's Confederate believes in no such grand purpose. His belief is limited to his sexual attraction to Stuart and his "heroic body odor"; he cannot indulge in any legitimizing schema beyond the immanent. Here doubt is depicted as inherent to the Confederacy—not as the product of a modern era that has fallen from a capacity for belief. The "twilight certainty of an animal" that Tate ascribed to the Confederate soldier is rendered parodically in a soldier whose faith is limited solely to the naturalistic level of fight or flight impulses.

For Ainsworth, the war is a struggle for survival rendered absurd by the trappings of chivalry, not a heroic conflict in which values are writ large. He describes Stuart's foray into Pennsylvania as "lunacy" and thinks, "We are too far from home. We are not defending our beloved Dixie anymore" (145). His view seems particularly trenchant in the post-Vietnam era. The rhetoric of nationalism has carried Ainsworth's portion of the Confederate army, as it did the American military in Vietnam, to foreign soil where the rhetoric of patriotism rings hollow. Like the American forces in Southeast Asia, Ainsworth finds himself fighting for causes beyond rational justification. The entire system of belief—in country, in sacrifice, in valor—is undermined.

Nowhere is this lack of belief better portrayed than in Hannah's story "Dragged Fighting from His Tomb." Captain Howard, an officer in the Confederate cavalry, has begun to doubt his commander ("Jeb has the great beard to hide his weak chin and basic ugliness" [57–58]) and his company's objectives in Pennsylvania. He is a man who has "read Darwin and floundered in him" because he cannot determine that his fellow cavalrymen are more ethical or moral than the horses they ride (51). To Howard, the litany of the patriotic code has grown specious; the war seems to be little more than large-scale savagery embellished with empty slogans. Any higher purpose that the fighting is intended to serve proves to Howard to be not only elusive but false.

The captain's standoff with an elderly Union cavalryman brings these issues to the surface. Holding the old man at gunpoint, Howard commands, "Say wise things to me or die, patriot. . . . Tell the most exquisite truths you know" (51). What follows is an awkward dance of modern doubt and naive, unexamined belief, for despite his age, the Union soldier has acquired little wisdom. He professes belief in "Jehovah, the Lord; in Jesus Christ, his son; and in the Holy Ghost. I believe in the Trinity of God's bride, the church. To be honest. To be square with your neighbor. To be American and free" (51). As the man lapses into platitudes, Howard reminds him that he asked "for the truths, not beliefs." Howard asks, "Where is the angry machine of all of us? Why is God such a blurred magician? Why are you begging for your life if you believe those things. Prove to me that you're better than the rabbits we ate last night" (51). The best answer the man can provide is the assertion that "we're not simple animals," along with the faintly Emersonian declaration that "there's a god in every one of us, if we find him" (53). Yet within minutes the old cavalryman is fleeing rabbit-fashion from Howard and frantically engaged "in a carnal act" with a prostitute in the Union staff house (57). In extremis the old man is no better than a simple animal after all, a slave to the animal drives of survival and procreation. Howard ultimately spares him when the Union soldier acknowledges, "There is no wisdom, Johnny Reb. . . . There's only tomorrow if you're lucky. Don't kill us. Let us have tomorrow" (57).

It is a distinctly minimalist resolution to the debate. The old man's equation of sweeping philosophical systems such as religion with slogans like "being square with your neighbor" reduces true belief to a petty level. Given the carnage of the internecine struggle in which the men are engaged, such ordering principles seem ruefully ironic. God indeed seems like a "blurred magician" and the universe, accordingly, a piece of dubious prestidigitation. Under such conditions, the old man's Epicurean philosophy is logical. There are no transcendent truths to be ascertained, no beliefs to justify the rationale of war. The Union soldier seems actually wise only when he admits the absence of wisdom, when he acknowledges the emptiness of the platitudes he espoused earlier. This lack of belief would seem to be the only legitimate approach to experience.

Yet Howard becomes jaded from the interaction. He turns his attention to horses; the death of a horse had first aroused his anger about the war. The horses represent an antithesis to human violence and abstraction. This disparity is evident to Howard: "What a bog and labyrinth the human essence is, in comparison. We are all overbrained and overemotioned. No wonder my professor at the University of Virginia pointed out to us the horses of that great fantast Jonathan Swift and his Gulliver book. Compared with horses, we are all a dizzy and smelly farce. An old man cannot tell you the truth. An old man, even inspired by death, simply foams and is addled like a crab" (53). Humanity as farcical, "overbrained," "overemotioned," and frenetic as the atavistic crab: this view stands in sharp contrast to the purported logic of honor, duty, country. Humanity, in Howard's vision, lacks the simple dignity of horses because of its insistent adherence to higher causes of dubious origin. The old man, for example, had been prepared to kill Howard in defense of beliefs he could not even define; Howard realizes that he is in the same position.

Howard deserts the Confederate army to join the Union, indifferently donning the blue uniform ("I did not care if it was violet" [58]) and killing Stuart. Stuart seems to embody the fallacious ideals that Howard abhors, and Howard shoots him in the forehead "so that not another thought would pass about me or about himself or about the South, before death" (58). He is rewarded by General Grant with a horse, the "grandchild" of Howard's favorite steed that he had earlier declared "was the Confederacy" (50). The new horse has never been given a proper name, Howard says, "But Christ is his name, this muscle and heart striding under me" (60).

Howard's narrative is the story of a madman, but it is also clear that Hannah uses the captain as an example of epistemic uncertainty. Howard is a sociopath, but so, too, is Jeb Stuart in Hannah's vision. What separates Howard from his colleagues is his awareness of the false ordering systems that sustain men like Stuart and the Union cavalryman. Because Howard cannot believe the narratives that justify the fighting, he subscribes to no cause—he cares little whether his trappings are blue, gray, or violet because he disregards the abstractions these colors represent. His lack of belief in causes or other metanarratives is exemplified in the concepts he associates with his horses. These animals are not the incarnations of the Confederacy and Christ, for Howard ascribes to no such abstractions. Instead, they represent the extent of his belief; they are the closest approximation to transcendent motivation for a tortured figure limited strictly to the immanent—absurd examples of the constructedness of all causes. Through Howard's deranged, antihumanistic devotion to these sentient but dumb creatures, Hannah illustrates a larger insanity inherent in the very concept of warfare. Howard kills for animals that to him represent a higher world; his motivation, however misguided, contains unsettling parallels to the ideologies behind the larger conflict in which he is embroiled. He does indeed fight to defend "Christ" and "the Confederacy." If the sphere of human action is limited to the tangible world, Hannah intimates that Howard's insanity is hardly greater than his leaders'—lacking only the legitimation of consensus that the Confederate cause enjoys.

"Bats Out of Hell Division" may be read as an allegory of Civil War mythology in southern literature. Like "Dragged Fighting from His Tomb," the story presents the war as a disordered conflict, a parody of chivalry. Instead of a cavalryman, however, the narrator of "Bats Out of Hell Division" is the historian of his unit, a scribe reduced by the brutal fighting to little more than a pair of eyes and a writing arm. As a kind of analogue to the southern writer, he self-consciously addresses his readers directly as "my posteritites" and stresses the war's importance "because there will never be anything like it again. It will set the tone for a century and will be in all the books" (43, 46). This scribe is acutely sensitive to the war as a defining moment is the region's culture. In the last days of the war, he says, his function has grown more important; he has "become as important as our general" (45).

But his account of events is suspect. He claims to "have license to exaggerate," and his reliability is further sacrificed by being at the service of a maniacal general who "is dead-set on having these battles writ down permanently in ink and will most certainly push me on afterward, whatever befalls, into working up his own biography" (45). He asserts that the "most momentous" theme of his writing is that there is "no plan at all" to events (43), yet as the functionary of an evolving cultural myth he must impose some order on the battles for his narrative. As with the general's biography, his account of the war must perpetuate a certain image, must give a narrative form to the conflict. The scribe is not unlike his fellow Confederate Beverly Crouch, who is also keenly aware of posterity. Crouch rehearses his war tales in a foxhole before the action is even concluded, envisioning his role as an oral historian in postbellum society: "Already he is practicing his posture around a stove fueled only by corncobs in an impoverished, riven home. He speaks his tales to gathered neighbors, family and children. They say he has a mirror down there, long as a tailor's, at which he practices" (46). It is a cogent satire of the mythmaking tendencies of an oral society, for what is foregrounded through both Crouch and the narrator is a historical self-consciousness, an almost prescient sense of their roles in the drama of their times. All action in the story comes to seem performative and staged; war as theater.

The surrealism of the story heightens this effect. Crouch cannot truly know, in advance, the specific benighted conditions of Reconstruction; neither can the narrator nor any of the other ghoulish Confederates actually survive the types of injuries Hannah describes. But the story's fantastic elements serve its theme beautifully. The account of Bats Out of Hell Division, C.S.A, is a ghost story, a fable—a commentary on Civil War fiction from a postmodern perspective, told by a corpse. When the narrator cries, "I tell you we are gaunt! We are almost not there," he speaks of his compatriots and of the literary Lost Cause as well (48). Himself a southern writer, he not only indicates the mythologizing process with which the war is or will be recorded but also foretells its decentering in the contemporary age. He embodies the myth itself in Hannah's vision: riven and plundered, the piecemeal remains of a deteriorating heroic figure.

RAY *AND* CULTURAL *"MEMORY"*

Ray is Hannah's finest work, a novel that may be ranked among the best southern fiction of the 1980s. In it Hannah provides a meditation on history more extensive and fully realized than in his stories. The novel's protagonist, Dr. Ray, is a former jet pilot who saw action in Vietnam and has now returned to Alabama to practice medicine. With his marriage crumbling and his chemical abuse getting out of hand, Ray proffers a nearly schizophrenic narrative of intense confusion and anguish, frequently referring to himself in the third person as if to reify his fragmented personality. Like many southern characters before him, Ray turns to the past—particularly the Civil War—as an anodyne to his personal disorder. Yet the uses of the past are different here from those of Hannah's predecessors. While Ray's situation and his attempts to escape it resemble the crises of the speaker in Tate's "Ode to the Confederate Dead," its resolution represents an epistemic shift toward a foreshortened view of history in which radical subjectivity dictates the shape of a dialogue with the past.

The setting of the novel presents contemporary life as a dystopian experience. Contemporary culture, Ray observes, "is full of crashing jets, carbon monoxide, violent wives, and murderous men. There is a great deal of metal and hardness" (44). Even within the tradition-minded South, historical continuity is reduced to the level of kitsch references—such as the saloon Lee's Tomb—or else consumed by a landscape of Jiffy Marts, 7-Elevens, and AM radio bands transmitted through beepers. Amid such chaos and violence, the doctor has "seen everything dependable go against its nature" in tableaux of "needless death and needless life" (70). Consequently, he entertains few notions of human existence as purposeful or productive. Posing the question, "Why in the hell is there so much cancer today, anyway?" he concludes, "it serves us fucking right" (45).

But counter to the Agrarian protest against modernity, Ray refuses to believe that history might offer redemptive antidotes to the disorder of his age. He is fully aware that history supports his jaded perspective on the present. His friend Charlie DeSoto reads accounts of Hernando de Soto's expeditions "to renew himself with his old perhaps ancestor," yet what he finds in them is an antique version of contemporary events, a record of senseless violence and slaughter (15). The Spanish explorer's commerce with the native Americans contains too many parallels to American experience in Vietnam. Charlie concludes that "it is terribly, excruciatingly difficult to be at peace . . . when all our history is war" (16). Ray harbors a similarly iconoclastic view of the past. Addressing an American Civilization class, he offers a banal accounting of hypocrisy: " 'Americans have never been consistent. They represent gentleness and rage together. Franklin was the inventor of the stove, bifocals, and so on. Yet he abused his neglected family. Jefferson, with his great theories, could not actually release the slaves even though he regularly fornicated with one of them. One lesson we as Americans must learn is to get used to the contrarieties in our hearts and learn to live with them.' Etc." (51). Ray draws little solace from a history of contradiction, however. The concluding remark in his account of this lecture ("Etc.") denotes his full consciousness of its mendacity. He cannot postulate even a theory of contrarieties with any conviction.

Ray is truly a postmodern southerner. He is fully aware of the constructedness of his culture's legitimizing systems. He has rejected religion ("Most preachers . . . are more evil than the rest of us walking pavement" [54]), has an uneasy relation to abstractions like patriotism, and derives only sporadic pleasure from practicing medicine. His skepticism extends to reductive speculation about human origins: "Who was it said we were invented by water as a means of its getting itself from one place to another?" (100). He steadfastly refuses to indulge in transcendental conceptions of his existence. He abjures what he thinks of as facile routes to achieving meaning and has conceived a polarity between his psychological disorder and the "smugness" of adhering to specious and unexamined belief: "And yet without a healthy sense of confusion, Ray might grow smug. It's true, isn't it? I might join the gruesome tribe of the smug. I think it's better with me all messed up" (103).

Ray's challenge lies in charting a course between smugness and unhealthy confusion. His current state, he admits, is one of "Constant Misery," in which he feels his selfhood partitioned into atomized units that reflect the disorder of contemporary life. In contrast to the bewilderment of his present status, he longs for the "glory" of his days as a fighter pilot; he is drawn to the "clean choices" of "either me or them, by God" (102). He perceives the materials of his deliverance in traditional southern terms. His route to wholeness, he thinks, lies in the past. He claims that "you are packed with your past and there is no future" and admits that he "roam[s] in the past for my best mind" (88, 95). He is well equipped for such forays; his memory is capacious. God has "cursed" him, he claims, "with a memory that holds everything in my brain. There is no forgetting with me" (51). His recollection is so precise that one of the chapters of his narrative is composed entirely of flight lingo from Vietnam: "ERD. #92. #Doe4. Utap. At 40–50. Range. In clear. Solid. Ventro" (80). Indeed, for Ray the past is not even past.

Like a modernist figure, Ray turns to the Civil War in hopes of integration into a larger and more coherent scheme of existence. His narrative, already disjointed, begins to include "memories" of his participation in the war that transpired a century before his own. Through six episodes he engages in a curious sort of mythopoesis. Rather than a pilot, he assumes the analogous position of a Confederate cavalryman, and instead over flying over Hanoi and the China Sea among SAM missiles, he charges through rolling meadows singing with minié balls.

Initially Ray's memories are related in sedate, if somewhat romantic, prose. Their historical detail is accurate. Ray is a captain and rides with Jeb Stuart, pitched in battle against General George McClellan's Union troops in Maryland. The valor of the Lost Cause is evident: "Jeb Stuart is as weary as the rest of us, but he calls for sabers out. Our uniforms are rotting off us" (39). Despite the haggard condition of the Confederates, their attitude is hopeful, the tone of the passage optimistic. The battle culminates in a decisive victory and a civil, almost Victorian exchange between Captain Ray and the sole surviving Union soldier. Although the episode hints at darker themes (Stuart weeps after the battle, and Ray notes that there are "[t]oo many dead" [41]), it nonetheless maintains a level of staunch morale, an esprit de corps that carries into the second historical fantasy. Now Ray seems to rely on the high spirits of his pseudomemory to rally himself for a daunting day following one of his drinking binges. Its tone is gallant:

Sabers up! Get your horses in line! They have as many as we do and it will be a stiff one. Hit them, hit them! Give them such a sting as they will never forget. Ready? *Avant!* Avant, avant, avant! Kill them!

Horses gleaming with sweat everywhere, Miniés flying by you in the wind. (51–52)

The disparity between this memory and Ray's earlier commentary on American history is vast. Here he operates in the domain of myth; doubt and contradiction are banished, and the action is charged with conviction and certainty. It is an Eliotic "memory" that uses the past to clarify and order the present. Coming as it does after Ray's admission that he has been spending too much time at Lee's Tomb, this foray into the past lends coherence to his disordered life. It follows Eliot's "mythic method" by "roaming" in history for a sense of order that is absent in the present, by turning to the past for some shape and significance that may serve the purpose of "ordering . . . the immense panorama of futility and anarchy which is contemporary history" (Eliot 177–78). The vanished Confederacy begins to assume the shape of myth for this contemporary southerner.

Ray's flashbacks soon become entirely mythic. In the first severely outmatched encounter of his recollections, facing three thousand adversaries, he and his men experience a vision: "The shadow of the valley passes over our eyes, and in the ridge of the mountains we see the white clouds as Christ's open chest" (Hannah, *Ray* 65). Ray's personality, already confused and multifaceted, has taken on a new mystical quality here. The narrator who has questioned the validity of all things intangible achieves an epiphany, a visionary glimpse of his physical environment as biblical metaphor. With pennants high, sabers drawn, and horses "in perfect line," the Confederates charge in an act of chivalric immolation. The resulting sacrifice is beatific and prompts Ray to conclude, "If warriors had known this story, we would have taken the war to the gooks with more dignity" (66). The episode would seem to indicate that Ray has at last achieved some sense of significance, for despite its concluding epithet, the passage holds forth the promise of transcendent purpose that has eluded the doctor throughout his narrative. Pursuant to the mythic method, Ray realizes a continuous parallel between the present and the past, achieving the consummately modernist objective of recovering a transformative past. It would seem that at the midpoint of his historical exploration Ray has succeeded in connecting with history and fulfilled the quest undertaken by such southern modernist figures as the speaker of Tate's "Ode."

Ray is not a modernist, however, and cannot ultimately maintain this relation to myth. He begins to confuse the transcendent with the tactile, even the base. His schizophrenia returns: "Then sabers up and we knock the fuck out of everybody. With the cherished dream of Christ in our hearts. Basically, the message is: Leave me the hell alone or give me a beer" (69–70). Ray's reference to "the cherished dream of Christ" is not self-consciously ironic, in spite of its incongruence amid the other sentences of the short paragraph. It is simply not his *own* voice; it represents an adherence to beliefs that are not Ray's. The startling juxtaposition results from Ray's combining his own personality with the exterior persona supplied by history. It is truly schizophrenic—a multiple personality of competing identities. The subsequent memory indicates Ray's awareness of this disjointed historical identity. Disillusionment returns: "Your hat's rotting off. It's hot. You're not sure about your horse. Or the cause. All you know is that you are here—through the clover, through the low-hanging branch, through the grapeshot. . . . Your saber is up, and there goes your head, Christian" (96). The tone of this passage contrasts sharply with its predecessors. Fatigue, initially a mere physical nuisance to be disregarded, is sovereign in the prepositional clauses that repeat themselves in a litany of weariness. Morale suffers accordingly from this lassitude. The cause is now uncertain, and the previous notion of sacrifice is rendered fruitless with the flat, ironic concluding phrase. Ray's attempt to achieve an obscurely historical validation has failed. He is left only with physical dissolution for an obscure cause. The grand narratives—whether Christianity or military glory—have lost the scant legitimacy Ray attempted to provide them.

The modernist means of Ray's quest have doomed it from the start. The nature of the mythic method—its linear focus, its attempt at objectivity and rationalism—threatens a personality such as Ray's; the extinction of individual identity is precarious for a borderline schizophrenic. What is necessary is not integration of the self into a grand narrative but the construction of a personal narrative within the subjective self. Ray cannot imbue metanarratives with any legitimacy; instead of a universal narrative, he must seek a local and immanent one. He must somehow embrace the radical discontinuity of his time. His final historical reverie achieves such integration. "Let us meet again," he says, as "cavalrymen of every race and creed" wearing "the wool short jacket with every color of the rainbow on the breast" (108). His vision has become utopian, parahistorical.

Ray moves into the fantastical in this last "memory," abandoning his former historical accuracy. The cavalry is now complemented by the air force, and, as he assures a fearful colleague, the "new pistol" with its heat-seeking bullets is nearly invincible against the "old lead" of the enemy's machine guns (109). His tone becomes ecstatic:

> Their cannon just missed me as my horse started running on the water. We are high on our horses and laughing and I can hear the shrill Rebel yell behind me. They are throwing out phosphorus bombs, and I see some of the men go down. My men just laugh and the horses climb the banks. What an open field. We are laughing and screaming the yell.
> It is an open field. (109)

Here at last a kind of unity is achieved through a postmodern vision of history. Ray's history is antirational; it conflates the ordnance of the Civil War and the Vietnam War into a montage of anachronisms. He is indeed rewriting history from the subjective vantage point of his own experience. Such a perspective is at ease with the impossible and the indeterminate; in fact, it welcomes them as constituent qualities of an existence that is truly immanent. Through them the paradox of smugness/confusion may finally be resolved. A truly "healthy" sense of confusion results from becoming comfortable with the purely subjective, from abandoning the smugness of ersatz ordering principles while refusing to devolve into the bleak confusion of nihilism. Ray achieves this by moving beyond the failure of the modernist dialogue with history and into the imaginative realm of the self, abdicating the kind of closure sought by modernism. His provisional sort of mythmaking abandons the rational traits of smugness for something that is more diffuse yet regenerative. History is for Ray no longer a linear progression but a lateral one; he has relinquished the metanarrative for his own *petite histoire*.

Consequently, he achieves the vista of "an open field." The image suggests forward motion but no singular route—progress without transcendent rationale. Horizontal rather than vertical, the open field represents the resolution of Ray's struggle from a modern to a postmodern perspective. In it one may see symbolized many of Ihab Hassan's oppositions between modernism and postmodernism: closed form/open form, purpose/play, hierarchy/anarchy, centering/dispersal, selection/combination, determinacy/indeterminacy, transcendence/immanence (152). The open field embodies the postmodern portions of these oppositions. As a symbolic construct, it is open in form, playful, and anarchic; the wildly incongruent historical references and the joyful cacophony of the men laughing and yelling combine to create a sense of regenerative chaos. This abandon is evident as well in the combination of all colors and creeds into an irrational amalgam of indeterminate elements. The focus has shifted from the recovery of a discrete past to a fusion of the immanent. In "Dragged Fighting from His Tomb" Howard lapses into nihilism with his claim that his uniform may as well be violet; Ray surmounts such negativism by incorporating all colors into his own banner.

The open field is one of the most significant symbols in twentieth-century southern literature. It is a triumphant reply to the modernist imagery of the walled and gated cemetery of Tate's "Ode." Tate depicted the mordant final phase of southern modernism in images of closure and claustrophobia, in the silence of "brute angels" and "mute speculation" (20, 22). From a different era, Hannah answers with the emblematic expanse of a rolling field and a victorious yell. His field is a symbol of contemporary resolution, however attenuated, of the perpetual southern struggle to connect with the Civil War past. It depicts lateral movement as far less futile than Tate's speaker would have imagined: such motion is not pointless like the "heaving" of the "blind crab" but rather the trajectory of what Tate calls "sustained imagination" in its postmodern incarnation (*Essays* 604). The mythic method of the modernists was doomed (as Tate's character demonstrates) because the origins it seeks are vanished, extraneous. Hannah suggests that, if history cannot be recovered, it can be created within the immanent sphere of subjective consciousness. To seek connections elsewhere is to indulge in smugness or, ultimately, paranoia.

The innovative manner in which Hannah resolves the dialogue with history is best illustrated by comparing *Ray* to Thomas Pynchon's *The Crying of Lot 49*. Like Ray, Oedipa Maas seeks "some promise of hierophany" in her environment, some underlying structure to a seemingly random existence (31). She is driven by a need to order experience and to "create constellations" to explain the inchoate nature of events (90). Yet like Ray, she cannot find a grand framework, and the "patterns" she begins to discern in the "languid, sinister blooming of The Tristero" begin to assume the symptoms of paranoia (89, 54). Oedipa enacts the collapse of modernist epistemology; she cannot find an order other than what she projects. Her paranoia is but the product of a modernist quest that—counter to its intentions—results in solipsism. Like the speaker of Tate's poem, she perpetrates an effort at connection that cannot be fulfilled.

But Ray abandons the search for origins and ultimate causes. In an act of quintessential postmodern irony, he counters paranoia with schizophrenia, replaces an obsessive ordering impulse with an inclusive system. At the nadir of his narrative—at a point of failure in his modernist approach—he has cried, "Oh, help me! I am losing myself in two centuries and two wars" (Hannah, *Ray* 45). Such is the complaint of a paranoid, a person fixated on the discrete and the rational. The quest, like Oedipa's, is obsessed with hierarchies, centering, and selection; dispersal is its nemesis. Ray avoids such dysfunction by accepting the open field of imagination. He finally concedes that the pursuit of hierophany is delusional, that no schema exists to supply a linear progression of history. The parallels between the Civil War and the Vietnam War indicate a lack of teleology in human history. Their similarities demonstrate that, to the extent that history is a narrative, it is a narrative of open forms, of no neat resolutions.

To what extent, then, is Ray's dialogue with the past mythopoeic? Eliot's "continuous parallel between contemporaneity and antiquity" (177) is certainly present in a character who claims to "live in so many centuries" that "everybody is still alive" (Hannah, *Ray* 41). But in Hannah's fiction the parallel no longer serves the purpose that Eliot intended. Ultimately it only reinforces the sovereignty of subjective experience, for if history supplies no logos to the present, it underscores the isolation of individual consciousness rather than supplying personal experience with a larger context. Given Hannah's iconoclastic temperament, history cannot be relied upon to provide transcendent meaning. Although it may contain parallels to the Vietnam experience, the Civil War is not (as Tate described it) a "universal myth of the human condition." Instead it is a lucent example of how humanity constructs what it calls "universal myths" to explain a cosmos that is ultimately contingent. Thus the conclusion of Hannah's novel may well contain a hidden irony. No matter how irrational or dispersed (that is, antimodernist) Ray's penultimate "memory" may be, it nonetheless participates at least tangentially in the sort of narrative constructions Hannah seems to suspect. Ray is, after all, a schizophrenic, and his reliability is questionable. His fusion of past and present may be a wry postmodern commentary on the idea of memory itself, a hallucinatory reflection of the impulse to seek meaning in too many centuries beyond the present.

Hannah's attraction to history places him in a curious position among contemporary southern writers. As Fred Hobson notes, he is a consummately postmodern stylist who is nonetheless more concerned with the past "than nearly any other southern writer of his time" (33). Whereas Richard Ford—an almost precise contemporary of Hannah's who was raised in the same part of Mississippi—treats the southern heritage with marked ambivalence, Hannah repeatedly turns to the region's history as the catalyst of his fiction. This insistent use of the past is also at odds with the technique of Cormac McCarthy, Hannah's closest southern literary relation. McCarthy carries Hannah's iconoclastic treatment of history a step farther, into a nihilistic interpretation of human endeavor that denies the validity of all cultural constructs. Clearly Hannah perceives some value for the southern past in postmodern fiction that his contemporaries do not.

In fact, Hannah's fixation with the Civil War and its attendant mythology has developed as his fiction has become more postmodern. In moving from the picaresque and Salinger-influenced style of *Geronimo Rex* (1972) into a postmodern poetics, he has increasingly used the war as the crucible of his evolving vision; in contrast to Ford and McCarthy, his exploration of southern identity has intensified as he has matured as an artist. If the fiction of the post-Renascence South has focused, as Lewis Simpson observes, on recording the "breakdown" of the cultural reclamation sought by the southern modernists (and Ford and McCarthy support this claim), then Hannah's position is at odds with his moment in literary history (*Dispossessed* 71). Hannah, however, is not an anachronism; he is a link between the disparate movements of twentieth-century southern literature. His work suggests the possibility of a marriage of postmodernity and the southern literary imagination—a movement antithetical to the approaches practiced by his contemporaries. Certainly he rejects the mythologizing of the modernists, for he subjects the very act of looking backward to irreverent scrutiny. Yet he also demonstrates that the past is viable for an artistic vision beyond mythoclasm or emigration—that the mature southern artist of the postmodern era need not leave the South behind.

Such is an intrepid position, and southern criticism has had a difficult time coming to terms with it. In *Writing the South*, Richard Gray describes *Ray* as a vision of life as "fluid to the point of chaos," an impish rebuke to "conventional narrative patterns": "In this book, it seems, it is not only the traditional Southern structures that are rejected but structures of any kind and the actual *idea* of structure—and not just rejected, but openly challenged" (235). Nonetheless, Gray's otherwise astute study of southern myth and literature falters in an attempt to situate Hannah in the context of southern fiction. Gray concludes that writers such as Hannah participate in an irreverent "postmodern consciousness;

in doing so, they have shrugged off their Southern identity" (236). Therefore Hannah "is not so much a Southern writer as a postmodernist one" (235). Hannah is in fact both, and his work presses us to question the impulse to see the two categories as mutually exclusive.

Hannah may well be the contemporary South's version of John Barth's ideal postmodern writer. In *Ray* he offers a novel of replenishment for a topic that, as his own "Bats Out of Hell Division" indicates, is very nearly exhausted. He continues the traditional southern exploration of history but with a new approach to the inquiries of his predecessors; although he is indeed "an heir to several southern literary traditions," he is not a prisoner to those traditions (Hobson 33). In Barth's words, he "has the first half of our century under his belt, but not on his back" (203). His Civil War fiction demonstrates that contemporary southern writing need not be "the next-best thing" to the modernist literature of the Renascence; instead it holds the potential of being "the *best next thing*" in the region's long and distinguished literary dialogue with history (206). Faulkner asserted that the past is not even past; but what *is* the past? asks Hannah. In pursuing that question, he ensures the continued vitality of southern fiction in an era when history is fabulous no longer.

CONCLUSION

No Jeremiad

F or nearly forty years the predominant mood of southern criticism has been, in Walter Sullivan's memorable formulation, melancholy. As the old order has waned and been replaced by a younger generation of writers less captivated by tradition, the shape of southern fiction has become more diffuse and eclectic—to the dismay of those who would interpret southern modernism as the apotheosis of the southern literary imagination. For those of traditional inclination, the region's contemporary fiction represents the certain sign of imaginative decline or, worse still, the very portent of barbarism. To subject the region's cultural mythology to incisive critique is seen as an act of literary treason—apostasy even—in an era when tradition requires ever more vigilant maintenance.

But those who would wring their hands over the current state of southern letters evince a curiously short memory. Inquiry into the merits of the culture was pervasive in the Southern Renascence; even the halcyon era was marked by dissenting perspectives, from the Fugitives and William Faulkner to Katherine Anne Porter, to say nothing of the African American protest. As Lewis Lawson reminds us, a large part of twentieth-century southern literature has always been "a catalogue of disintegration" (15). The writers of the contemporary South have maintained that tradition at least, by recording the disintegration of Renascence mores and methods and by moving the vulnerable icons of convention up a generation. A continued literary Solid South would ultimately result in a return to the quietude of the "Sahara of the Bozart" years; the present generation of skeptical authors ensures that such a devolution will not occur.

Iconoclasm and irreverence, then, have their uses. As another critic has noted, change and revision are intrinsic components of a vital southern literature:

> The point is that if Southern literature is to continue to play so important a role in national letters as it has done since the 1920's, it will have to be constructed on new foundations, based on markedly different conditions of experience, and will thus constitute a recognizably new and different phase of the Southern Literary Renascence. Its writers, forced to find new responses to new situations, cannot write in the forms developed by Faulkner and his contemporaries, without first subjecting those forms to an extensive remodeling and alteration. The new Southern writing will have to be . . . substantially different in its values, its attitudes, its techniques, from that of the previous generation. The age, in Ezra Pound's phrase, demands the image of its own special grimace, and what has sufficed before, no matter how splendidly, will no longer suffice. (237)

The passage is from Louis Rubin's book, *Writers of the Modern South*, published in 1963—before any of the writers considered here had yet released a novel, before the present period of "remodeling and alteration" had begun in earnest. Rubin made these observations four years after Cormac McCarthy debuted in *The Phoenix* with his story "Wake for Susan," a historical reverie with only slight indications of the atavistic vision to come. It was the same year that Harry Crews's first published story, "The Unattached Smile," appeared in the *Sewanee Review*, replete with Lost Generation locutions and cadences that he would not maintain for long. Neither author had quite yet divorced himself from the forms of the preceding generation. The vital work of dissection and renewal lay ahead.

Of course, McCarthy and Crews went on to construct formidable careers and greatly influenced the writers who followed them. The extent to which contemporary southern fiction may be considered the "second Renascence" of Rubin's predictions hinges largely on the achievement of these authors. As the pioneers of "substantially different" values and techniques, they inaugurated new perspectives in powerful opposition to the waning Renascence. Where, indeed, could the southern writer turn after the achievement of Faulkner and Eudora

Welty—what sort of community could be claimed on the order of the Fugitives or Agrarians? McCarthy and Crews ensured the continued relevance of southern fiction by rejecting an epigonic relation to these forebears. McCarthy answered the Renascence with mythoclasm and postmodern style; Crews responded with the unheard-of perspective of a poor-white southerner who refused the role of a Snopes or an Erskine Caldwell caricature. Their influence shaped the vision of many writers who followed them, through the gothic naturalism they passed on to Larry Brown, Barry Hannah, and other younger writers and through the opportunities opened by the lower-class perspective—a vantage point that has enriched the region's literature with such accounts of southern experience as Dorothy Allison's *Bastard Out of Carolina* and Kaye Gibbons's *Ellen Foster*. To the extent that the contemporary scene's own postmodern moment in literary history will allow for coherence, a significant portion of it may be attributed to the influence of McCarthy and Crews.

Yet I quote Rubin with a sense of irony. His outline of a second Renascence, however prescient in its prediction that the literature to follow the 1950s would be in some sense a counter-Renascence, a reaction against the conventions erected by the southern modernists, must be read as a caveat to the postmodern critic. In responding to it one feels the perennial proclivity toward narrative asserting itself: one feels an ingrained desire to fashion a story—either complementary or contrapuntal to Rubin's—from the variegated materials of contemporary literary culture. But to so engage the linear technique of tradition veers perilously close to an extension of the established paradigm. Any theory that purports to delineate a "recognizably new and different phase of the Southern Literary Renascence" is, after all, predicated on deference to the models of the past. To do so, even with revisionist intentions, would inadvertently validate Michael Kreyling's observation that "the consensus in southern literature is slow to change, especially in response to a movement that threatens its core. Better to try to fold the new into the established" (*Inventing* 155). The challenge of writing postmodern literary history lies in negotiating a delicate balance with the limitations of critical discourse—a discourse that by its generic recourse to categories threatens to annul the iconoclasm of contemporary writing.

Jean-François Lyotard's comments on postmodernity bear particular relevance to this conundrum in southern criticism. The postmodern artist or writer, Lyotard observes, "is in the position of a philosopher: the text he writes, the work he produces are not in principle governed by preestablished rules, and they cannot be judged according to a determining judgment, by applying familiar categories to the text or to the work. Those rules and categories are what the work of art itself is looking for. The artist and the writer, then, are working without rules in order to formulate the rules of what *will have been done*" (81). The truly lubricious nature of postmodernism emerges in the appraisal of the critic determined to resist the solace of these rules and categories. For even behind the deployment of naturalism as a reinvigorated term indicative of culturally disruptive narrative practices, behind the neologism and dissent of mythoclasm, lies the influence of the "preestablished." In light of the innovations made by contemporary southern authors, such terminology seems almost rudimentary, an intermediate step toward a critical lexicon appropriate to a decisive break from the models of the past. An image emerges of the critic following, at the usual distance abaft, the progression of the artist. Such is an aptly postmodern portrait of critic and author in pursuit not of history but of the inchoate future— what *will have been done*.

It seems only prudent in concluding, then, to proffer a suggestive postscript rather than to attempt a definitive summation—to point toward the future instead of the past. This future is evident in the way mythoclasm and naturalism have been absorbed—and more important, modified—in some of the most notable southern fiction of late. The perspective of the blue-collar white is more prominent than ever—to name but a few examples, in Dale Ray Phillips's *My People's Waltz* (1999), William Gay's *The Long Home* (1999), and especially Tom Franklin's *Poachers* (1999), which adopts a self-consciously "redneck" approach to southern community. The disparate prose styles of these authors indicate that Bobbie Ann Mason's signature spare realism is but one approach toward capturing the South's working-class milieu in fiction. Through a more urbane lens, the work of Josephine Humphreys continues to view Renascence conceptions of place and the past with skepticism. Perhaps the most highly praised recent southern novel, Charles Frazier's *Cold Mountain* (1997), uses the familiar topic of the Civil War as the vehicle of a revisionist approach to southern literary mythology, following the lead of proletarian writers in creating a yeoman protagonist who suggests that at least some measure of the region's genius lies with the people passed over by its mythology. The novel adopts a critical stance toward the antebellum system quite outside its dominant ideology—so much so that Inman's perception of the medieval disparity of his culture echoes that of Toni Morrison's Sethe in *Beloved*. Like Sethe, Inman is able to see the "fire and brimstone" hidden beneath the "lacy groves" of an Arcadian setting divided into "fiefdoms" (Frazier 205), aware that the "shameless beauty" of the plantation manor "never looked as terrible as it was" (Morrison 6). Frazier's protagonist is a new kind of Confederate hero, a symbol of valor minus its chivalric accoutrements, a simple man who seeks a separate peace in a place—to cite Noel Polk's phrase—outside the southern myth.

Naturalism, too, continues to flourish in the McCarthy-influenced Appalachian gothic of Pinckney Benedict's *Dogs of God* (1994) and throughout a host of working-class fiction evincing a naturalistic ethos that, like Larry Brown's, declines to sublimate form to philosophy, style to thesis. Cynthia Shearer's first novel, *The Wonder Book of the Air* (1996), is a resounding affirmation that naturalist prose may well receive its most eloquent expression in southern writers of the present. One of the central motifs of *The Wonder Book of the Air*, announced in its opening pages, is "We ain't lost, we is exploring." As the novel unfolds, however—as layers of the ignoble past are revealed, and as the daunting legacy of the small-town characters comes to seem inescapable—the motto is reversed. The catalyst of these disastrous events is not (as literary convention would have it) the senescence of a stable old order but a society that was always already dysfunctional, given to lying about—and to—itself. More than fifty years before Shearer's novel, another southerner skeptical of the region's mythology began his own debut with the declaration, "O lost." From the other side of the Renascence, Shearer validates Thomas Wolfe's assessment of the southern community, confirming—contrary to the intervening modernist mythology—that it was ever thus.

These authors demonstrate the artistic autonomy of those who have followed the great Renascence. Their work, and the critical acclaim it has generated, indicates that post-Renascence writers have achieved their own vision on their own terms, abdicating the custodial role of epigones for something more vital and, in the truest sense of the word, contemporary. The tendencies toward mythoclasm and naturalism are finally not destructive but quickening: they allow southern fiction to make the necessary break from the past that may ensure the future southern writer a position higher than that of the hierophantic interpreter of past glories. The South that Renascence authors inherited is gone, but as the vitality of the contemporary scene demonstrates, this fact is no cause for despondency. For the writers of the contemporary South to cling to the methods of their forebears would only result in southern fiction's being relegated to a collateral, and subsidiary, position in a dynamic American literature. The challenge faced by the southern writer is no longer how to present the region to the larger world but how to bring that larger world into the demesne of southern letters.

No longer can southern critics expect to encounter the familiar rhythms of a fiction that is primarily regional, romantic, or modernist. Crews, Allison, Brown, Mason, and Gibbons have henceforth problematized the mode of local color with their emergent class consciousness; McCarthy, Ford, Kenan, and Hannah have likewise demonstrated that a vital southern fiction of the present day will not adhere to the modernist and racialized structures of the past. The current interregnum might best be exemplified by the contrast between these writers' backgrounds and that of one of the last great regionalists. Fred Chappell, in "A Pact with Faustus," has described his first encounter with high modernism in the terms one might use to recount Allen Tate's or Robert Penn Warren's journey toward Nashville. Chappell and a friend found themselves drawn to Thomas Mann's Doctor Faustus and its picture of a wider world than the one known by two "young men of ordinary mountain background, with distinctly limited opportunities at High Culture, who have decided to pursue artistic careers" (480). Doctor Faustus, Chappell explains, "made it clear that as artists Fuzz and I were never going to catch up with the twentieth century; we knew already that we were starting from too far behind" (481). The days of such accounts are numbered. In their place we may expect more stories such as Dennis Covington's, who "came of age reading the great Southern fiction" of the Renascence but did not find in it a world he knew firsthand from his life in the city. Covington's first fiction, however, initially had "rural settings": as he explains in Salvation on Sand Mountain, "I was drawing my material out of a rich Southern literature, the texture of which I had never experienced myself. In time, the settings and people of my fiction began to resemble more and more those of the world I knew most intimately, the City" (xvi).

I cite these shorthand bildungsromane as evidence of the powerful transformations of the southern literary consciousness in the latter half of the twentieth century and also to pose the question of which narrative might serve as a parable for contemporary southern criticism. The twentieth century that seemed to have bypassed Chappell in rural North Carolina is emphatically present in contemporary southern prose, whether through the new perspectives of poor-white authors or through the postmodern poetics that southern critics have largely met with silence. Consequently, contemporary southern criticism finds itself in a position strangely analogous to the young Chappell's—almost an anachronism in the wake of a rapidly evolving and tumultuous moment in literary history, almost too far behind to catch up. The current era is a crucible for southern criticism, a thorough test of its adaptability, its resourcefulness, and its continued relevance; this time it is not so much the artist as the *critic* who is poised at a crossing of the ways, momentarily caught in the reverie of the backward glance. As Covington has sagely observed, "Knowing where you come from is one thing, but it's suicide to stay there" (236). The South's brightest authors have acceded to that maxim and in doing so avoided a static vision in a dynamic era. One hopes that the South's criticism will soon match their pace—that the southern critic will meet the new writing on its own terms, choosing to embrace, rather than deny, an evolving tradition as it claims its place in American literary history.

NOTES

INTRODUCTION

1. This split has been described succinctly by Kreyling in "Old Lights, New Lights"; in Frega, "Questioning History and Revision"; and in Hobson, "Of Canons and Cultural Wars," in Humphries and Lowe, 72–86.

2. Such a view of Hurston and Wright is not intended as appropriation—I do not mean to subsume them to cultural values with which they were profoundly at odds. On the contrary, my goal is to stress how white writers have adopted their methods to challenge the dominant aesthetic of southern literature. The case of Wright in particular is illustrative on this point. Michael Fabre has asked whether Wright's authoritative appropriation of naturalist technique "necessitate[s] a reassessment of what is commonly held for American literary naturalism" (38). The writers considered here answer emphatically in Wright's favor, demonstrating that his influence on contemporary naturalistic prose is at least as profound as that of its canonical (white) practitioners.

3. For evidence of Crews's influence on younger writers, see the tributes by Larry Brown and Tim McLaurin in the special issue of the *Southern Quarterly* devoted to Crews (37.1 [fall 1998]).

4. Some notable examples in Welty criticism are Donaldson, "Recovering Otherness in *The Golden Apples*," and Yaeger, "Beyond the Hummingbird." Noel Polk addresses similar issues in Faulkner in *Children of the Dark House*.

ARCADY REVISITED: THE POOR SOUTH OF HARRY CREWS AND DOROTHY ALLISON

1. This perspective is aptly illustrated in Crews's ironically titled *Esquire* article, "Pages from the Life of a Georgia Innocent." Crews describes the pastoral notion of the "poor but God knows honest" farm family as an "immoral and dangerous . . . fantasy" (30). The product of a life lived close to the land, he notes, is not character-building hard work but painful deprivation—something "pretty low and pretty common" (36).

2. In "The Athlete's Hand Filling Up," Donald Johnson describes another recurrent character type in Crews's fiction: the athlete. Johnson stresses that the athlete "epitomizes the duality of mind and body which is at the heart of the human condition" and of Crews's work in general (100–11). Yet the grit émigré characters augment this general duality with an important cultural one—the stress between the agricultural and the urban.

3. See, for example, the *Tobacco Road* motifs in Mirst's mistreatment of the new automobile in *The Gospel Singer* (61, 102).

THE NEW NATURALISM OF LARRY BROWN

1. Peter Applebome, "Larry Brown's Long and Rough Road to Becoming a Writer," *New York Times*, 5 March 1990, sec. C.

MEDIATION, INTERPOLATION: BOBBIE ANN MASON AND KAYE GIBBONS

1. See also Carol S. Manning's introduction to *The Female Tradition in Southern Literature*.

2. It bears noting here Mason's speculation on the catalyst of southern writing: "A repressive culture produces this energy of breaking out" (Mason, "Interview," Hill 106).

ATAVISM AND THE EXPLODED METANARRATIVE: CORMAC MCCARTHY'S JOURNEY TO MYTHOCLASM

1. Robert L. Jarrett has provided a thorough assessment of McCarthy's relation to the twentieth-century southern canon but without stressing the author's break from the past in the rather militant terms I use here. Jarrett sees McCarthy's work as pointing out an "ironic disjunction . . . between past and present" (11). I interpret McCarthy's mythoclastic temperament as a more aggressive reaction to literary tradition.

2. I am indebted to Brian McHale's *Postmodernist Fiction* for this critical framework. McHale sees the shift from epistemological to ontological modes as a widespread pattern of artistic development through which novelists such as Pynchon, Nabokov, and Coover have moved from early modernist novels to later, postmodern works.

3. For a discussion of religious parody in the novel, see Spencer, "Cormac McCarthy's Unholy Trinity."

4. Edwin T. Arnold reads this epiphany in more positive terms than I do. Regardless of our differences, however, Arnold does focus on the importance of Suttree's position in the tangible world, not on any teleological explanation for his survival. As he notes of the novel's concluding scene, "Where [Suttree] goes is unimportant. The fact that the hound of the hunter Death comes to sniff his tracks is simply another indication that he is still alive" (59).

INTO THE SUBURBS: RICHARD FORD'S SPORTSWRITER AS POSTSOUTHERN EXPATRIATE

1. See Michaud, "Richard Ford," for a discussion of these similarities.

2. Ford supports this definition in his comments in a 1996 *Paris Review* interview. Ford notes that he had been attracted to fiction in the style of such postmodernists as Barthelme, Coover, and Gass but found himself at odds with their "narrative practices and conceits." Eventually, he "quit writing that way [and] sort of reverted to the traditional, realistic fiction that suited what I could do" ("Art of Fiction" 51).

3. Ford seems well aware of the parallels to Babbitt—and especially to his vocation. Frank croons that "most Americans will eventually transact at least some portion of their important lives in the presence of realtors or as a result of something a realtor has done or said" (46). His literary antecedent heartily affirms that sentiment: "Jever stop to consider . . . that before a town can have buildings or prosperity or any of those things, some realtor has got to sell 'em the land? All civilization starts with him" (Lewis 134).

BARRY HANNAH AND THE "OPEN FIELD" OF SOUTHERN HISTORY

1. See Brinkmeyer, "Finding One's History," and Gilman, *Vietnam and the Southern Imagination*.

2. Hannah has in fact praised McCarthy's "relentless" and "atavistic" vision as "very rough—almost fascistic, as nature is" ("Interview" 25).

BIBLIOGRAPHY

Allison, Dorothy. *Bastard Out of Carolina*. New York: Dutton, 1992.

———. *Cavedweller*. New York: Dutton, 1998.

———. "Moving Toward Truth: An Interview with Dorothy Allison" (Carolyn E. Megan). *Kenyon Review* 16.4 (fall 1994): 71–83.

———. *Skin: Talking about Sex, Class, and Literature*. Ithaca, N.Y.: Firebrand Books, 1994.

———. *Trash*. Ithaca, N.Y.: Firebrand Books, 1988.

———. *Two or Three Things I Know for Sure*. New York: Plume, 1996.

Arnold, Edwin T. "Naming, Knowing and Nothingness: McCarthy's Moral Parables." In *Perspectives on Cormac McCarthy*, ed. Edwin T. Arnold and Dianne C. Luce. Jackson: UP of Mississippi, 1993. 43–67.

Baker, Houston A., Jr. *Long Black Song: Essays in Black American Literature and Culture*. 2nd ed. Charlottesville: UP of Virginia, 1990.

Baldwin, James. *Go Tell It on the Mountain*. New York: Alfred A. Knopf, 1953. Reprint, New York: Dell, 1980.

———. *Notes of a Native Son*. Boston: Beacon Press, 1955.

Barth, John. *The Friday Book*. New York: G. P. Putnam's Sons, 1984.

Baym, Nina. *Feminism and American Literary History*. New Brunswick, N.J.: Rutgers UP, 1992.

Bell, Vereen M. *The Achievement of Cormac McCarthy*. Baton Rouge: Louisiana State UP, 1988.

Berry, Wendell. *Sex, Economy, Freedom and Community*. New York: Pantheon Books, 1993.

Betts, Doris. "Randall Garrett Kenan: Myth and Reality in Tims Creek." In *Southern Writers at Century's End*, ed. Jeffrey J. Folks and James A. Perkins. Lexington: UP of Kentucky, 1997. 9–20.

Bragg, Rick. *All Over But the Shoutin'*. New York: Pantheon Books, 1997.

Brinkmeyer, Robert H., Jr. "Finding One's History: Bobbie Ann Mason and Contemporary Southern Literature." *Southern Literary Journal* 19.2 (spring 1987): 20–33.

Brooks, Cleanth. "An Affair of Honor: Larry Brown's *Joe*." Chapel Hill, N.C.: Algonquin Books, 1991.

————. *William Faulkner: The Yoknapatawpha Country*. Baton Rouge: Louisiana State UP, 1990.

Brown, Larry. *Dirty Work*. Chapel Hill, N.C.: Algonquin Books, 1989.

————. *Facing the Music*. Chapel Hill, N.C.: Algonquin Books, 1988.

————. *Father and Son*. Chapel Hill, N.C.: Algonquin Books, 1996.

————. *Joe*. Chapel Hill, N.C.: Algonquin Books, 1991.

————. "A Late Start." Chapel Hill, N.C.: Algonquin Books, 1989.

Bryant, J. A., Jr. *Twentieth Century Southern Literature*. Lexington: UP of Kentucky, 1997.

Buford, Bill. "Editorial" ("Dirty Realism"). *Granta* 8 (1983): 4–5.

Cash, W. J. *The Mind of the South*. New York: Alfred A. Knopf, 1941. Reprint, New York: Vintage, 1991.

Chappell, Fred. *The Fred Chappell Reader*. New York: St. Martin's Press, 1987.

Core, George, ed. *Southern Fiction Today: Renascence and Beyond*. Athens: U of Georgia P, 1969.

Couch, W. T. "The Agrarian Romance." *South Atlantic Quarterly* 36.4 (October 1937): 419–30.

Covington, Dennis. *Salvation on Sand Mountain*. New York: Addison Wesley, 1994.

Crane, Stephen. *The Portable Stephen Crane*. Ed. Joseph Katz. New York: Penguin, 1969.

Crews, Harry. "Arguments Over an Open Wound: An Interview with Harry Crews." *Prairie Schooner* 48.1 (spring 1974): 62–74.

————. *Body*. New York: Poseidon Press, 1990.

————. *A Childhood: The Biography of a Place*. New York: Harper & Row, 1978.

————. *The Gospel Singer*. New York: William Morrow, 1968.

————. *The Gypsy's Curse*. New York: Alfred A. Knopf, 1974.

————. *The Hawk Is Dying*. New York: Alfred A. Knopf, 1973.

————. *The Knockout Artist*. New York: Harper & Row, 1988.

————. "Pages from the Life of a Georgia Innocent." *Esquire*, July 1976, 30, 36.

————. *Scarlover*. New York: Poseidon Press, 1992.

————. "Some of Us Do It Anyway: An Interview with Harry Crews." *Georgia Review* 48.3 (fall 1994): 537–53.

————. "Television's Junkyard Dog." *Esquire*, October 1976, 95–97, 126, 128–30, 132.

————. *This Thing Don't Lead to Heaven*. New York: William Morrow, 1970.

Davidson, Donald. *The Long Street*. Nashville: Vanderbilt UP, 1961.

————. *Still Rebels, Still Yankees*. Baton Rouge: Louisiana State UP, 1957.

DeLillo, Don. *White Noise*. New York: Viking, 1985.

Donaldson, Susan V. "Gender, Race, and Allen Tate's Profession of Letters in the South." In *Haunted Bodies: Gender and Southern Texts*, ed. Anne Goodwyn Jones and Susan V. Donaldson. Charlottesville: UP of Virginia, 1997. 492–518.

————. "Recovering Otherness in *The Golden Apples*." *American Literature* 63.3 (summer 1991): 489–506.

Du Bois, W. E. B. *The Souls of Black Folk*. Chicago: A. C. McClurg, 1903. Reprint, New York: Dover, 1994.

Eliot, T. S. *Selected Prose of T. S. Eliot*. Ed. Frank Kermode. San Diego: Harcourt Brace, 1975.

Fabre, Michael. "Beyond Naturalism?" In *Richard Wright*, ed. Harold Bloom. New York: Chelsea House, 1987.

Faulkner, William. *Go Down, Moses.* New York: Vintage-Random House, 1942.

Faust, Drew Gilpin. *Mothers of Invention: Women of the Slaveholding South in the American Civil War.* Chapel Hill: U of North Carolina P, 1996. Reprint, NewYork: Vintage, 1997.

Fekete, John. *The Critical Twilight: Explorations in the Ideology of Anglo-American Literary Theory from Eliot to McLuhan.* London: Routledge & Kegan Paul, 1977.

Fiedler, Leslie A. *The Collected Essays of Leslie Fiedler.* Vol. 2. New York: Stein and Day, 1971.

Foote, Shelby. *The Civil War: A Narrative. Fort Sumter to Perryville.* New York: Random House, 1958.

Ford, Richard. "The Art of Fiction CXLVII" (Interview with Bonnie Lyons). *Paris Review* 140 (fall 1996): 42–77.

———. "A Conversation with Richard Ford" (Interview with Huey Guagliardo). *Southern Review* 34.3 (summer 1998): 609–20.

———. *Independence Day.* New York: Alfred A. Knopf, 1995.

———. "An Interview with Richard Ford." (Kay Bonetti). *Missouri Review* 10.2 (1987): 71–96.

———. *A Piece of My Heart.* New York: Harper & Row, 1976.

———. *The Sportswriter.* New York: Vintage Contemporaries, 1986.

Frazier, Charles. *Cold Mountain.* New York: Atlantic Monthly Press, 1997.

Frega, Donnalee. "Questioning History and Revision: Contemporary Southern Literature and the Canon." *Southern Quarterly* 34.2 (winter 1996): 9–21.

Gates, Henry Louis, Jr. *The Signifying Monkey: A Theory of African-American Literary Criticism.* Oxford: Oxford UP, 1988.

Gibbons, Kaye. *Charms for the Easy Life.* New York: G. P. Putnam's Sons, 1993.

———. *A Cure for Dreams.* Chapel Hill, N.C.: Algonquin Books, 1991.

———. *Ellen Foster.* Chapel Hill, N.C.: Algonquin Books, 1987.

———. *Frost and Flower: My Life with Manic Depression So Far.* Decatur, Ga.: Wisteria Press, 1995.

———. *On the Occasion of My Last Afternoon.* New York: G. P. Putnam's Sons, 1998.

———. *Sights Unseen.* New York: G. P. Putnam's Sons, 1995.

———. *A Virtuous Woman.* Chapel Hill, N.C.: Algonquin Books, 1989.

Gilman, Owen. *Vietnam and the Southern Imagination.* Jackson: UP of Mississippi, 1992.

Grammer, John. "A Thing Against Which Time Will Not Prevail: Pastoral and History in Cormac McCarthy's South." In *Perspectives on Cormac McCarthy*, ed. Edwin T. Arnold and Dianne C. Luce. Jackson: UP of Mississippi, 1993. 27–42.

Gray, Richard. *Writing the South: Ideas of an American Region.* Cambridge: Cambridge UP, 1986. Reprint, Baton Rouge: Louisiana State UP, 1997.

Gretlund, Jan Nordby. *Frames of Southern Mind: Reflections on the Stoic, Bi-Racial, and Existential South.* Odense, Denmark: Odense UP, 1998.

Grimsley, Jim. *Dream Boy.* Chapel Hill, N.C.: Algonquin Books, 1995.

Gwin, Minrose. "Nonfelicitous Space and Survivor Discourse: Reading the Incest Story in Southern Women's Fiction." In *Haunted Bodies: Gender and Southern Texts*, ed. Anne Goodwyn Jones and Susan V. Donaldson. Charlottesville: UP of Virginia, 1997. 416–40.

Hall, Wade, and Rick Wallach, eds. *Sacred Violence: A Reader's Companion to Cormac McCarthy*. El Paso: Texas Western Press, 1995.

Hannah, Barry. *Airships*. New York: Alfred A. Knopf, 1978.

————. *Bats Out of Hell*. Boston: Houghton Mifflin, 1993.

————. *Boomerang*. Boston: Houghton Mifflin, 1989.

————. *Geronimo Rex*. New York: Viking, 1972.

————. "An Interview with Barry Hannah" (James D. Lilley and Brian Oberkirch). *Mississippi Review* 25.3 (1997): 19–43.

————. *Ray*. New York: Alfred A. Knopf, 1980.

————. "The Spirits Will Win Through: An Interview with Barry Hannah." *Southern Review* 19.2 (spring 1983): 317–41.

Hassan, Ihab. "Toward a Concept of Postmodernism." In *Postmodernism: A Reader*, ed. Thomas Docherty. New York: Columbia UP, 1993. 146–56.

Hobson, Fred. *The Southern Writer in the Postmodern World*. Athens: U of Georgia P, 1991.

Holman, C. Hugh. *Windows on the World: Essays on American Social Fiction*. Knoxville: U of Tennessee P, 1979.

Howard, June. *Form and History in American Literary Naturalism*. Chapel Hill: U of North Carolina P, 1985.

Humphries, Jefferson, ed. *Southern Literature and Literary Theory*. Athens: U of Georgia P, 1990.

Humphries, Jefferson, and John Lowe, eds. *The Future of Southern Letters*. Oxford: Oxford UP, 1996.

Hurston, Zora Neale. "Characteristics of Negro Expression." In *Negro: An Anthology*, ed. Nancy Cunard. Revised edition, ed. Hugh Ford. New York: F. Ungar, 1970. 24–46.

Irigaray, Luce. "The Sex Which Is Not One" (trans. Claudia Reeder). In *New French Feminisms*, ed. Elaine Marks and Isabelle de Courtivron. New York: Schoken, 1981. 99–106.

Jameson, Fredric. *Postmodernism, or the Cultural Logic of Late Capitalism*. Durham, N.C.: Duke UP, 1991.

Jarrett, Robert L. *Cormac McCarthy*. New York: Twayne, 1997.

Johnson, Donald. "The Athlete's Hand Filling Up: Harry Crews and Sports." In *A Grit's Triumph: Essays on the Works of Harry Crews*, ed. David K. Jeffrey. Port Washington, N.Y.: Associated Faculty Press, 1983. 100–11.

Kartiganer, Donald M. "William Faulkner." *Columbia Literary History of the United States*, ed. Emory Elliott et al. New York: Columbia UP, 1988. 887–909.

Kenan, Randall. *James Baldwin*. New York: Chelsea House, 1994.

————. *Let the Dead Bury Their Dead*. San Diego: Harcourt Brace, 1992.

————. "Spies Like Us" (Interview with Dorothy Allison). *Village Voice Literary Supplement* 188 (September 1993): 26–27.

————. *A Visitation of Spirits*. New York: Grove Press, 1989.

————. *Walking on Water.* New York: Alfred A. Knopf, 1999.

Ketchin, Susan. *The Christ-Haunted Landscape: Faith and Doubt in Southern Fiction.* Jackson: UP of Mississippi, 1994.

Kreyling, Michael. *Inventing Southern Literature.* Jackson: UP of Mississippi, 1998.

————. "Old Lights, New Lights." *Mississippi Quarterly* 50.1 (winter 1996–97): 151–57.

Lawson, Lewis A. *Another Generation: Southern Fiction Since World War II.* Jackson: UP of Mississippi, 1984.

Lawson, Lewis A., and Victor A. Kramer, eds. *Conversations with Walker Percy.* Jackson: UP of Mississippi, 1985.

Lee, Don. "About Richard Ford." *Ploughshares* 22.2–3 (fall 1996): 226–35.

Levenson, J. C. "*The Red Badge of Courage* and *McTeague*: Passage to Modernity." In *Cambridge Companion to American Realism and Naturalism: Howells to London*, ed. Donald Pizer. Cambridge: Cambridge UP, 1995. 154–77.

Lewis, Sinclair. *Babbitt.* New York: Signet, 1991.

Lincoln, C. Eric, and Lawrence H. Mamiya. *The Black Church in the African American Experience.* Durham, N.C.: Duke UP, 1990.

Lyotard, Jean-François. *The Postmodern Condition: A Report on Knowledge.* Minneapolis: U of Minnesota P, 1984.

Lytle, Andrew. *A Wake for the Living.* New York: Crown, 1975.

MacKethan, Lucinda Hardwick. *The Dream of Arcady: Place and Time in Southern Literature.* Baton Rouge: Louisiana State UP, 1980.

Manning, Carol S., ed. *The Female Tradition in Southern Literature.* Urbana and Chicago: U of Illinois P, 1993.

Mason, Bobbie Ann. *Clear Springs: A Memoir.* New York: Random House, 1999.

————. *Feather Crowns.* New York: HarperCollins, 1993.

————. *In Country.* New York: Harper & Row, 1985.

————. "An Interview with Bobbie Ann Mason." Conducted by Albert E. Wilhelm. *Southern Quarterly* 26.2 (winter 1988): 27–38.

————. "An Interview with Bobbie Ann Mason." Conducted by Bonnie Lyons and Bill Oliver. *Contemporary Literature* 32.4 (winter 1991): 449–70.

————. "An Interview with Bobbie Ann Mason." Conducted by Dorothy Combs Hill. *Southern Quarterly* 31.1 (fall 1992): 85–118.

————. *Shiloh and Other Stories.* New York: Harper & Row, 1982.

————. *Spence + Lila.* New York: Harper & Row, 1988.

Matthews, John T. "The Sacrifice of History in the New Criticism of Cleanth Brooks." In *Rewriting the South: History and Fiction*, ed. Lothar Hönnighausen and Valeria Gennaro Lerda. Tübingen: Francke Verlag, 1993. 210–18.

McCarthy, Cormac. *Blood Meridian, or the Evening Redness in the West.* New York: Random House, 1985. Reprint, New York: Vintage, 1992.

————. *Child of God.* New York: Random House, 1973. Reprint, New York: Vintage, 1993.

————. *The Orchard Keeper.* New York: Random House, 1965. Reprint, New York: Vintage, 1993.

————. *Outer Dark*. New York: Random House, 1968. Reprint, New York: Vintage, 1993.

————. *Suttree*. New York: Random House, 1979. Reprint, New York: Vintage, 1992.

————. "Wake for Susan." *The Phoenix* (October 1959): 3–6.

McHale, Brian. *Postmodernist Fiction*. London: Routledge, 1987.

McHaney, Thomas L. "Brooks on Faulkner: The End of the Long View." *Review* 1 (1979): 29–45.

Michaud, Charles. "Richard Ford: What a Difference a Pulitzer Makes." *Firsts* 7.2 (February 1997): 50–55.

Mitchell, Lee Clark. *Determined Fictions: American Literary Naturalism*. New York: Columbia UP, 1989.

Modleski, Tania. *Loving with a Vengeance: Mass-Produced Fantasies for Women*. Hamden, Conn.: Archon Books, 1982.

Morrison, Toni. *Beloved*. New York: Alfred A. Knopf, 1987.

————. *Playing in the Dark: Whiteness and the Literary Imagination*. Cambridge: Harvard UP, 1992. Reprint, New York: Vintage, 1993.

Norris, Frank. *Norris: Novels and Essays*. Ed. Donald Pizer. New York: Library of America, 1986.

O'Connor, Flannery. *A Good Man Is Hard to Find*. San Diego: Harcourt, Brace, Jovanovich, 1983.

————. *Wise Blood*. New York: Farrar, Straus and Giroux, 1991.

Papashvily, Helen Waite. *All the Happy Endings*. New York: Harper & Brothers, 1956.

Percy, Walker. *The Last Gentleman*. New York: Farrar, Straus and Giroux, 1966.

Percy, William Alexander. *Lanterns on the Levee: Recollections of a Planter's Son*. Baton Rouge: Louisiana State UP, 1973.

Pilkington, John. "The Memory of the War." In *The History of Southern Literature*, ed. Louis D. Rubin Jr. et al. Baton Rouge: Louisiana State UP, 1985. 356–62.

Pizer, Donald. *Realism and Naturalism in Nineteenth-Century American Literature*. Revised edition. Carbondale: Southern Illinois State UP, 1984.

Polk, Noel. *Children of the Dark House*. Jackson: UP of Mississippi, 1996.

————. "Hey, Barry!" *Mississippi Review* 25.3 (1997): 7–18.

————. "The Southern Literary Pieties." In *Southern Literature in Transition: Heritage and Promise*, ed. Philip Castille and William Osborne. Memphis, Tenn.: Memphis State UP, 1983. 29–41.

Powell, Dannye Romine. *Parting the Curtains: Interviews with Southern Writers*. Winston-Salem, N.C.: John F. Blair, 1994.

Pratt, William, ed. *The Fugitive Poets: Modern Southern Poetry in Perspective*. Revised edition. Nashville, Tenn.: J. S. Sanders, 1991.

Pynchon, Thomas. *The Crying of Lot 49*. New York: Harper & Row, 1986.

Ransom, John Crowe. *Selected Poems*. New York: Alfred A. Knopf, 1991.

Ravenel, Shannon, ed. *New Stories from the South: The Year's Best, 1989*. Chapel Hill, N.C.: Algonquin Books, 1989.

Rubin, Louis D., Jr. *A Gallery of Southerners*. Baton Rouge: Louisiana State UP, 1982.

————. *The Wary Fugitives: Four Poets and the South*. Baton Rouge: Louisiana State UP, 1978.

————. *Writers of the Modern South: The Faraway Country.* Seattle: U of Washington P, 1963.

Sandell, Jillian. "Telling Stories of 'Queer White Trash': Race, Class, and Sexuality in the Work of Dorothy Allison." In *White Trash: Race and Class in America,* ed. Matt Wray and Annalee Newitz. New York: Routledge, 1997.

Sayers, Valerie. "Back Home in Dixie." *New York Times Book Review* (15 March 1998): 19.

Seib, Kenneth. " 'Sabers, Gentlemen, Sabers!': The J. E. B. Stuart Stories of Barry Hannah." *Mississippi Quarterly* 45.1 (winter 1991–92): 41–52.

Shearer, Cynthia. *The Wonder Book of the Air.* New York: Pantheon Books, 1996.

Shelton, Frank W. "The Poor Whites' Perspective: Harry Crews among Georgia Writers." *Journal of American Culture* 11.3 (1988): 47–50.

————. "A Way of Life and Place." *Southern Literary Journal* 11.2 (spring 1979): 97–102.

Showalter, Elaine. *A Literature of Their Own: British Women Novelists from Brontë to Lessing.* Princeton, N.J.: Princeton UP, 1977.

Simpson, Lewis P. *The Brazen Face of History: Studies in the Literary Consciousness in America.* Baton Rouge: Louisiana State UP, 1980.

————. *The Dispossessed Garden: Pastoral and History in Southern Literature.* Athens: U of Georgia P, 1975.

————. *The Fable of the Southern Writer.* Baton Rouge: Louisiana State UP, 1994.

Singal, Daniel Joseph. *The War Within: From Victorian to Modernist Thought in the South, 1919–1945.* Chapel Hill: U of North Carolina P, 1982.

Spencer, William C. "Cormac McCarthy's Unholy Trinity: Biblical Parody in *Outer Dark.*" In *Sacred Violence: A Reader's Companion to Cormac McCarthy,* ed. Wade Hall and Rick Wallach. El Paso: Texas Western P, 1995. 69–76.

Stengel, Marc K. "When Is Southern Literature Going to Get Real?" *Nashville Scene* (12 April 1990): 8–10.

Styron, William. *Darkness Visible: A Memoir of Madness.* New York: Random House, 1990.

Sullivan, Walter. *In Praise of Blood Sports and Other Essays.* Baton Rouge: Louisiana State UP, 1990.

————. *A Requiem for the Renascence: The State of Fiction in the Modern South.* Athens: U of Georgia P, 1976.

————. "Southern Novelists and the Civil War." In *Southern Renascence: The Literature of the Modern South,* ed. Louis D. Rubin Jr. and Robert D. Jacobs. Baltimore: Johns Hopkins UP, 1953. 112–25.

Sundquist, Eric J. *To Wake the Nations: Race in the Making of American Literature.* Cambridge: Harvard UP, 1993.

Tate, Allen. *Collected Poems, 1919–1976.* Baton Rouge: Louisiana State UP, 1989.

————. *Essays of Four Decades.* Denver, Colo.: Alan Swallow, 1959.

————. *The Fathers and Other Fiction.* Baton Rouge: Louisiana State UP, 1977.

————. *Memoirs and Opinions, 1926–1974.* Chicago: Swallow Press, 1975.

Tate, Linda. *A Southern Weave of Women: Fiction of the Contemporary South.* Athens: U of Georgia P, 1994.

Thoreau, Henry David. *Walden.* Ed. J. Lyndon Shanley. Princeton, N.J.: Princeton UP, 1989.

Twelve Southerners. *I'll Take My Stand: The South and the Agrarian Tradition.* Baton Rouge: Louisiana State UP, 1977.

Venturi, Robert et al. *Learning from Las Vegas.* Revised edition. Cambridge: MIT P, 1996.

Warren, Robert Penn. *All the King's Men.* New York: Harcourt, Brace, 1946. Reprint, New York: Harvest, 1982.

Weaver, Richard M. *Ideas Have Consequences.* Chicago: U of Chicago P, 1948.

Weston, Ruth D. *Barry Hannah: Postmodern Romantic.* Baton Rouge: Louisiana State UP, 1998.

Winchell, Mark Royden, ed. *The Vanderbilt Tradition: Essays in Honor of Thomas Daniel Young.* Baton Rouge: Louisiana State UP, 1991.

Wright, Richard. *Richard Wright: Early Works.* Ed. Arnold Rampersad. New York: Library of America, 1991.

———. *Richard Wright: Later Works.* Ed. Arnold Rampersad. New York: Library of America, 1991.

Yaeger, Patricia. "Beyond the Hummingbird: Southern Women Writers and the Southern Gargantua." In *Haunted Bodies: Gender and Southern Texts,* ed. Anne Goodwyn Jones and Susan V. Donaldson. Charlottesville: UP of Virginia, 1997. 287–318.

Young, Thomas Daniel. "The Fugitives: Ransom, Davidson, Tate." In *The History of Southern Literature,* ed. Louis D. Rubin Jr. et al. Baton Rouge: Louisiana State UP, 1985. 319–32.

———. *Tennessee Writers.* Knoxville: U of Tennessee P, 1981.

Index